THE CARIBBEAN FAMILY
Legitimacy in Martinique

MARIAM K. SLATER

THE CARIBBEAN FAMILY
Legitimacy in Martinique

ST. MARTIN'S PRESS
New York

ACKNOWLEDGMENTS

The preliminary plans for this book, which served as my doctoral dissertation in 1958, were developed during the course of a Columbia University seminar organized by Dr. Vera Rubin and Professor Charles Wagley. As an outgrowth of the seminar, I began field work in Martinique, an island of the French West Indies, in June 1956 as a Fellow of Dr. Rubin's Research and Training Program for the Study of Man in the Tropics (now known as The Research Institute for the Study of Man, or RISM). For the first ten weeks of my five-month field trip I was a member of a group of five people working under the leadership of Professor John V. Murra.

I wish to express my gratitude to the above people and institutions for the opportunity to prepare and carry out the work upon which this project is based. Professor Murra was particularly helpful in assisting me to orient myself to a French culture. I am indebted also to Professors Conrad M. Arensberg, Marvin Harris, Charles Wagley, and Morton Fried for their guidance in writing up the results.

To the many people of Martinique who gave so generously of their time and friendship, I wish to express my appreciation, particularly to M. Eugène Goyheneche, chief government archivist; Mlle. Rachelle Barfleur; M. and Mme. Alfred Lebielle; and all the members of *la famille* Edjam.

I also would like to thank my editor, Anita S. Morse, for her patience, skill, and understanding in preparing this book.

CONTENTS

Acknowledgments   v

Introduction   1

PART ONE: THE PROBLEM: THE AREA   25
1 Approaches to the Caribbean   27
2 The Island   42

PART TWO: THE COMMUNITY   71
3 The *Commune* of Capesterre   73
4 Association and Stratification   91
5 Economic Activities   106

PART THREE: THE FAMILY   123
6 Life History of the Household   125
7 Marriage and the Family   154
8 Historical Links and Chains   191
9 A Model of the Family Structure   204

Epilogue   224

References   252

Index   259

THE CARIBBEAN FAMILY
Legitimacy in Martinique

Introduction

Wherever they have gone, Africans in the New World—whether they be Caribbean cane cutters or tenants in the American South, Latin American peasants or street-corner urbanites—have lived in a distinctive family system.

Or have they?

Many believe that what some call an "ethnic" or "subcultural" pattern is only a mirage that disappears into a class phenomenon, a third world "adaptation," or simply into social pathology. Others see a certain kind of family structure built around females—often called matrifocality—as a precipitate of the "culture of poverty." But there is little agreement on whether matrifocality is an aspect of dominance, of a network of relations, or of cross-sex roles.

Answers depend on theory and semantics—and now sometimes on politics—as much as they do on facts. One extreme is that of Daniel P. Moynihan (erstwhile assistant secretary of labor). When he outlined his notion of the distinctive features of "the Negro family" in what became known as "The Moynihan Report,"[1] he "reported" that some 40 percent of the 5 million Negro households in America were fatherless nests whose fledglings were too poorly socialized to be useful citizens. And, as his subtitle (*The Case for National Action*) indicates, he urged nest mending to help fight poverty.

Floyd McKissick, leader of the Congress of Racial Equality (CORE), launched a counterattack: "Moynihan thinks everyone

1

should have a family structure like his own."[2] Moynihan's "case" was also attacked by fellow figure jugglers and other social scientists with different notions not only of causes but of cures. For example, Andrew Billingsley pointed out that there were only 1 million female-headed families among American blacks, but 4 million among whites.[3] Moreover, the majority of black families mirror the standard Western middle-class form. Ulf Hannerz gave some anthropological depth to ghetto studies with his participant observation in Washington, D.C. A quarter of the households are headed by women, he states, which is the same proportion as in the Labor Department's national sample;[4] however, he continues, this census category contains all women who live apart from a man for any reason whatever—the divorced, the separated, even the never married.

Clearly, the question of whether an Afro-American family type exists must go beyond the statistics of what might be called gynocentrism.

BLIND MEN AND LEVIATHAN

But even on qualitative grounds, the Afro-American label seems meaningless to the kind of theorists who emphasize matrifocal parallels elsewhere. Claims for matrifocality have been made for sectors of India, Peru, Java, London, Brazil, Africa.[5] Michael G. Smith, for example, notes a similarity between the Caribbean or Negro family and the urban South African Bantu, and also between the Caribbean family and the English family, in which a child's collateral maternal kin accept parental responsibility.[6]

Another influence that blurs the outlines of what a distinctive family system would be is the changing shape of the dominant Western family—serial monogamy; the postfamilial commune; the fact that 70 percent of divorced people remarry; "momism" in the stable conjugal home.

As we shall see, explanations that depend on these prior descriptive questions are also as various. From clinician to social anthropologist, at odds not only across disciplines but within them, the specialists of necessity work as blind men describing Leviathan, for we are examining pieces of a problem as big as society itself.

It is too early to say whether my own approach touches the foot, eye, or heart of the beast. But some vital part it must be. In presenting here, to a wide audience, something that began as a dissertation, I hope to provide enough descriptive material so that those who disagree with my ultimate abstractions can use the material in pursuit of other broad generalizations.[7] This book is a community study based on field work done in 1956 on the island of Martinique in the French West Indies. One advantage of the anthropological dedication to documenting the whole round of life in its wider setting, as in a community study, is that the net catches more fish than were expected.

Bones to Choke On

Some of the disagreements about the family are not so much about ethnicity as about whether to call certain phenomena "cultural" or "social." Oscar Lewis's phrase, "the culture of poverty," has acquired great political resonance in this aspect of the debate. It is excoriated by some on the grounds that to identify patterns as cultural is to deny· moral responsibility for them (compare with Leacock's collection).[8] It is only on the surface, then, that various proponents argue about whether certain groups lack a work ethic, for example, or whether they are hedonistic, childlike, or other such characterizations. The words sound as if the empirical presence or absence of easily operationalized claims about traits were the subject. One suspects that something else is at stake.

Lewis's antagonists are really criticizing his alleged notions of the causes and/or cures of social conditions. However, no necessary connections exist between his or anyone's concept of culture and of political policy, for the term "culture" takes on different connotations in conflicting intellectual traditions regardless of the writers' values. Some of these crosscurrents are so strong in Marvin Harris's review[9] of Charles Valentine's book[10] that a summary will illuminate several obscurities.

Harris says that Valentine makes the "false . . . assumption that social phenomena can be separated from cultural phenomena . . . [When culture is defined as] the rules which generate and guide [the behavior] called social . . . , [we choke on] that bone in our throats:

the poor cause poverty . . . [because they] get what they . . .
value."[11] Valentine is quoted as a man who finds violent revolution
impracticable, and the separation of social and cultural, says Harris,
"neutralizes his political sympathies . . . with the lower class."[12]

Thus, we have those who are the enemies of progress because
they talk of a culture at all, and others who are enemies because by
culture they mean values. But Harris's stance relates to more than
tactics of change or verbal convention. He characterizes himself as a
cultural materialist, a theoretical position he opposes to cultural
idealism.[13] As a materialist, he holds that such *core* institutions as
technology and economy—combined in an ecological matrix—are
causal; that is, the core determines values and other ideological
aspects of the *superstructure*. Cultural idealism, on the other hand, is
the fallacy of holding that ideas determine institutions. In the
framework of Harris's materialism, culture is not cut off as values
from social action.

Harris's broad definition of culture, he correctly states, is one
that "has always been true for most anthropologists in this country,
contrary to what Valentine learned at the University of
Pennsylvania."[14] What Harris and I both learned at Columbia (he
was a teacher of mine) is well documented in an examination of the
literature by Kroeber and Kluckhohn.[15] I shall come back to this. But
since we both absorbed this tradition in anthropology, something
new has been added by Harris that lodges a bone in my throat. In a
general text, he seems to identify some *tertium quid* that is neither
culture nor society, neither core nor superstructure, and this
phenomenon is called "adaptation." Patterns that are not acquired
via "enculturation" (i.e., during childhood by tradition) but that
crystallize without a past model apparently are ruled out of the
category of culture and are called "adaptive."[16]

Following Kroeber and Kluckhohn, I use the term "culture" to
point to a category of nature that contrasts with the built-in (genetic
or "instinctual"); the idiosyncratic (as distinct from shared or
patterned behaviors); and the pathological (neurologically
disturbed and hence deviant). As I use it, culture refers to learned,
shared behavior based on symbols. The only significant quibble
with this notion, I suggest, is the one that places the emergence of
culture in evolution back earlier in primate history, as indicated by

tool-using chimpanzees and baboons that learn different behaviors in different groups. But human adaptation is not the opposite of culture, only a kind of *cultural* response. David Bidney neatly pinpoints the levels where culture in this sense (having to do with symboling in general) is manifested. Culture appears as artifact, socifact, and mentifact.[17] It follows, then, that old and new economic and social features are every bit as cultural as values are. This is so, also, whether we choose to delineate such features as American "pattern" or British "structure." Causality is not decided by semantics.

The theoretical model I shall work out of the Caribbean or Afro-American family involves the following concept: all varieties share an absence of what Malinowski called "the rule of legitimacy."[18] This formulation is a diagnostic, not a causal theory. In short, this level of analysis does not commit me to a position on the seesaw as a mentalistic determinist. It is sociologically risky to create guilt by association in matters of lexical style, for each segment of a theory is relatively independent in today's fragmented practice of anthropology. Although authors who share a social philosophy or belong to a "school" of anthropology tend to use the same precise names for vague things, descriptive concepts are not eternally wedded to grand theory, and one person's stereotype is another person's typology. Bones in imaginary throats should not cause anyone to choke.

BEDFELLOWS

One more clarification on lexical conventions might be added here. Both Harris and Moynihan point to underlying socioeconomic bases of the matrifocal family (supposing for the moment that such a family exists). This agreement between strange bedfellows suggests that politics cannot be predicted from such convergence; nor can theory, for Moynihan alone believes the situation is pathological or deviant. All anthropologists, on the other hand, tend to see the same situation as variance. The real substantive rather than verbal differences in these opposed views will be elaborated in the epilogue. I simply wish to state at the outset that I do not find any family systems pathological, and if the word "deviance" occurs (I have tried to substitute "variance"), I merely refer to a statistical condition in the world, not to health or morality.

In my idiom, to state that a distinctive Afro-American family system exists is not to suppose that its traits are held as a monopoly. For example, the Navaho are no less matrilineal simply because the Trobrianders are also matrilineal. The specification of attributes of a type need not be exclusive, nor need it be reversible. No one said the Navaho and only the Navaho are matrilineal, and similarly, no one claims "Matrilineality, thy name is Navaho." Of course, unlike a question of lineal descent, the question of "focality" is not an all-or-nothing matter. One more caveat: an ethnic trait does not cease to exist because some members of the group, by another definition, have left the group or behave atypically.

My emphasis on matrifocality in the introduction does not mean that it will be a *sine qua non* of the model I plan to construct. The term, now widely used in animal ethology, was introduced to Caribbean studies by Raymond T. Smith in *The Negro Family in British Guiana* (1956). (Although this country is now Guyana, I will use its preindependence name because of Smith's reference.) My emphasis is undue because this term has become what some think the Caribbean family to be. Although you will frequently encounter this question in my community study, it will be helpful if I immediately update the literature that has appeared since then.

THE MATRIFOCAL FOCUS

Nancie Solien González suggests that the female dominance implied by "matrifocality" indicates that "women are somehow more important than the observer had expected . . . that the general status of women in the society is 'rather good.'"[19] Once such cultural relativity is recognized as important, I might add that women are bound to look good in any community where men look so bad, even if they have no more prestige than in the observer's own subculture. On the other hand, to the extent that women do not take part in the economic arena, their roles are often less shattered than those of men who have been subjected to drastic social change.

The term matrifocality seems vague for other reasons too. Virginia Heyer Young's careful analysis of a Georgia town with a population of 10,000 even reverses the matrifocal emphasis. "Mothering," she says, "is proper behavior for boys as well as girls and for fathers as well as mothers."[20] This tempts one to invert Edith Clarke's now well-known title, *My Mother Who Fathered Me* (a 1957 study in Jamaica) and talk of "my father who mothered me." This fact was part of the folklore in Martinique, where a Creole proverb states that as soon as you finish nursing your mother, you begin to nurse your father.

These variations might be signposts for readers to keep in mind as they venture into my community study. They will add interest, since one cannot help taking sides in some of the debates on this protean subject.

URBAN AMERICA AND A SEAFARING ISLAND

In Young's study of a lower-class urban setting, only three of her forty-one households were female-headed. "One cornerstone of the prevailing interpretation of the lower-class Negro family as female-headed," she states, "is a supposed advantage of Negro women over . . . men in wage earning . . ." But the facts she cites are otherwise.[21] Moreover, she shows that by some criteria the male role may be seen as dominant, and male self-esteem does not suffer. Role models for children are provided by men in a multiplicity of households, for in Afro-American communities the relationships are not "walled in." "At the same time," Young reports, "there are many illegitimate births, multiple sequential marriages, and frequent dissolution of marriage; practices the prevailing literature on the American Negro associates with family breakdown and the female-headed family."[22]

In resolving these "apparent inconsistencies," Young joins the long line of those who describe these patterns as *adaptive*, usually meaning variant rather than deviant or disorganized. The line includes Hortense Powdermaker (1939), Oscar Lewis (1961), Charles Valentine (1968), Nancy Solien González (1970), and myself (1958). "The potential for social dysfunction in the high illegitimacy rate and frequent marital dissolutions," says Young, "is compensated for by other parts of the system."[23] Although about half the women bore their children while living with their natal family, typically the child displays "a casual acceptance of" the situation.[24] And by their mid-twenties, most of these unwed mothers have a stable union.[25]

Hortense Powdermaker found that the psychological effects of an absent male on black families were not the same as those attributed to an absent male in middle-class Western white families. Among the Mississippi blacks she studied in the 1930s, the lone mother

> lacks time, opportunity and energy to lavish on her children the over-protection which leads to those emotional difficulties characteristic of certain fatherless white families . . . [and] most mothers . . . do not want for sexual outlet, and therefore are not impelled to seek from their children some substitute . . .[26]

It is out of such regularities, also encountered in Martinique, that I weave my hypothesis about the absence of the rule of legitimacy. I do so in an attempt to account for otherwise random data by identifying a structural principle, not by stating that rules generate behavior in some mystical fashion.

Matrifocality takes a curious twist in Ulf Hannerz's study, reported in 1969. Paradoxically, where women are most likely to dominate by default—where stable conjugality (legal or extralegal) is at a minimum—the male seems to be almost an archetype of authoritarianism or *machismo*.[27] Hannerz believes that it is the supermasculinity of the "street-corner" male that interferes with the achievement of "mainstream" domestic units of the kind Billingsley (see page 2) finds preponderant.

Earlier studies in a similar ghetto underscore similar themes. For example, participating with lower-class (as distinct from working-class) Chicago women, Esther Newton defined matrifocality as an aspect of antagonistic cross–sex role relations.[28] They result in unstable unions, she says, and involve submission of the woman.[29] She cites Rohrer and Edmonson's study of New Orleans, where there is the acceptance of love on men's terms. "Frankie and Johnnie," they say, is a drama of everyday life as the sexes exploit each other with mutual hostility.[30] Hannerz associates both the matrifocality and the sex antagonism with a male role set by a world of peers in street gangs or on street corners rather than by the family. This seems little different from Newton's statement that

"'Doin' right' is too near submission, loss of male dominance, and hence opening the floodgates to becoming a weakling and a sucker, which means in the end losing the woman one started out to please ..."[31] "Giving money ... signifies not control but lack of it ..."[32] "Furthermore, a woman's statement that a man is 'no good' is not a condemnation but is a normative statement about manliness."[33] These values, Newton concludes, are functional in the "culture of poverty" where "many lower-class values represent an attempt [primarily male] to circumvent ... [the] trap ... [of poor jobs] by getting 'outside' the 'respectable' frame of reference ..."[34]

But these roles do not accompany lower status and/or poverty among Afro-Americans in all places. How can the same constellation be present, whether adaptive or not, in the Chicago underworld, a cooperative Georgia town with "egalitarian spouses," and on various Caribbean islands or in their neighboring mainland subcultures? To take one of the more unusual of the Caribbean situations, let us turn to Michael G. Smith's study of Carriacou (off Grenada) as a final illustration of the complexity of discovering any common elements to form a type.[35]

In contrast with Raymond T. Smith, Michael G. Smith suggests that matrifocality is a chimera that appears when one concentrates mistakenly on the individual household instead of on the network of relations among households. In Carriacou, for example, a nonresident male is responsible for his offspring. Is the family, then, patrifocal on this seafaring island with a surplus of women? Two forms of mating are required: legal marriage with the expectation of female fidelity; and a nonresidential union between the married man and one of the surplus women. The usual consensual cohabitation of the Caribbean is entirely absent. It would be a mistake, I believe, to lop off this troublesome case by constructing too procrustean a model of the Caribbean family.

MALINOWSKI'S RULE OF LEGITIMACY

A common theme must allow for still undiscovered variations. The search for a common feature would be largely definitional rather than a scientific enterprise if we did not keep in mind basic theories of human behavior. It was in such interests that Malinowski hypothesized the rule of legitimacy as a human universal. As with the Nayar of India, the Afro-American case seems to create patterns bordering the limits of what seems possible or necessary in human adaptations. The Nayar have usually constituted a limiting case for the hypothesis that the nuclear family is a universal, for the Nayar give us insight into the phenomenon of marriage without sex. (This is not unique if one considers nonmodal marriages between women who give their offspring social anchorage in their natal clans, as in Dahomey.) Among the warrior castes of the Malabar coast, although a husband legitimates a child, it is fathered by a visiting husband.

It is always illuminating in explanations thus to observe the vanishing point of what seems to be panhuman. Had the Caribbean family not appeared on the empirical horizon, several basic principles of social structure, I believe, would have remained masked for a while longer. These principles are pinpointed by William J. Goode in response to statements I made about legitimacy in my dissertation.[36] Although Goode, as a sociologist, castigates anthropologists in general for their treatment of Caribbean material, I am singled out as the only anthropologist who elaborates the subject of legitimacy "norms"; others tend to mention the subject only in passing. Most ethnographies do not go beyond a functional analysis of households or networks related to the larger systems.

The significance of legitimacy, according to Goode, is this: Just as the family system is the keystone of any stratification system so is legitimacy the keystone of the family system. A study of variations in norms and practices related to legitimacy should therefore illuminate the operation of social systems."[37] He argues that if there were an absence of the rule of legitimacy, as I claim, "several notions in family theory would have to be discarded."[38] By all means, let us discard them, I suggest. But Goode concludes that the rule is present, for marriage remains the *norm*; it is just that most people have a "low commitment" to it. In view of this fact, however, he says that Malinowski's generalization must be reformulated. The function of marriage may now be seen as status placement, says Goode, instead of as the paternal protection that Malinowski thought it to be. Malinowski arrived at his formulation by coping with another limiting case that altered our views of human possibility. The matrilineal Trobriand islanders insist on marriage even though they believe that no man plays a procreative part in the reproductive process. (Some anthropologists argue that Malinowski was gullible to believe this.) The actors believe in spirit conception, and the husband thus must act solely as *pater* (sociological father) and not as *genitor*.

CONTINUITIES AND DISCONTINUITIES

Aside from the epilogue, where I shall continue this discussion of the rule of legitimacy, offering a rebuttal to Goode's argument, I have left the manuscript much as it was when it served as my dissertation in 1958. Those interested in the history of Caribbean studies will not be interrupted by anachronisms, and there are a few updated, parenthetical details. Recent reports show the situation to be largely unchanged, in that trends have not been reversed. The main work relevant to my interests is that of a demographer, which I shall briefly summarize here.

One might say that the population pressure today is the same as in 1956, when I did my field work, only more so. This is to be expected in lands such as Martinique where a number of "factors favor a rise in fertility," as Henri Leridon showed in 1970.[39] The successful use of contraceptives, he says, is still not widespread, but the "desire . . . is strong to limit the population in this manner." It is hard for me to imagine such an attitude at the rural level, since the men I knew there scorned condoms, the only type of contraception they knew, as an insult to women: one uses such devices with prostitutes. As for the women, when asked what they wanted in life or when they grew up, it was *"une poupée,"* a real doll. The male image of adult mates was that they were "mother hens" rather than lovers or companions. Leridon believes that the effects of artificial birth control "will depend partly upon the evolution of matrimonial custom . . . Already in the past half-century, the age at marriage has fallen, while the proportion of persons who have never married has decreased."[40]

The last census (1967) indicates that "age and matrimonial history . . . [influence] the number of live births . . ."[41] The three census categories of nonsingle women (married, visiting, and common-law) tend to have nearly the same number of children until about thirty years of age. After thirty-five a clear difference develops: women who have never married practically cease having children, while the married groups continue to bear ... for about five years ... The average unmarried woman gives birth to her last child when she is 34.5, while the average married woman ..., 36.5 ... [The fertility differentiation] is only indirectly the type of union; more directly it is the length of time spent in a union ... A married woman is continually exposed to risk ... [Women marry on the average by age 26; men by age 30.][42]

The population of Martinique grew from the time of my study, when it was 261,595 (1952 census) (see pages 47–48), to 320,000. The density is now 291 per square mile, still well below that of Barbados, which has the highest density of all the sugar isles.[43]

The political climate seems about the same as when I visited, judging from reports by Arvin Murch and Michael M. Horowitz. In 1967 Horowitz found no change from his 1959 dissertation, which he started when we were both in Martinique.[44] Independence from France has not become a big issue. There was only one proper French answer to a polite query concerning how "*touristes*" like me "found" the country. You found it "*jolie.*" Only once did irony break through the chauvinism when a man commented, "Oh, so you find poverty picturesque!" And a teacher told me how "*filles des couleurs*" chanted "*Nos ancêtres, les Gauloises, aux yeux bleus, aux cheveux blonds ...*" However, only we say "black" if something is not all "white," and most Martiniquans do have Gallic ancestors with blue eyes and blond hair as well as African ancestors.

Arvin Murch, a political scientist, shows that in 1971 the Antillean loyalty to France made it an anomaly in a nationalistic age when other Caribbean countries were opting for independence. He traces the difference to an acculturative situation in which French Enlightenment ideals were felt by Creoles to have been put into action. Given what Murch calls French metropolitan romanticism, he attributes the lack of interest in independence largely to the successful penetration of cosmopolitan patterns in the islands: "... the Antilles lack a strong, competing indigenous culture—a fact, incidentally, that sharply distinguishes France's successful Overseas Departments from Algeria."[45]

In Capesterre, the fictitious name for the community of my focus, more people have been driven off the land, as predicted. Jean

Griffin Goossen, while gathering data for her own dissertation on Guadeloupe,[46] was kind enough to revisit the scene of my statistical crimes and add to my perspective. The results of her observation appear in the epilogue along with other additions to and criticisms of my initial position on the family structure in this plantation area.

A NOTE ON METHODOLOGY

My basic procedure, described in chapter one, is the use of what Conrad M. Arensberg calls "the community study method."[47] This method permits presentation of data in a wide context for abstracting the model of family structure that is my main aim. Models of this kind are useful in comparative studies and in generating basic principles of social organization. Chapters two through five unfold the island-wide and community contexts, a necessary step in revealing crucial structural features. Here will be seen the social stratification and differential association patterns that maintain a separate subculture possessing what I claim is its own grammar of values.

In the next three chapters (six through eight) are the key aspects of family organization: household composition, mating patterns, duration of conjugal ties, relative strength of maternal versus paternal interaction in the family. An integral part of this section is an examination of variables involved in making systematic choices relating to marriage and the formation of domestic groups. The clue to my interpretation of family structure is that marriage is articulated with the domestic group and/or the family network differently from the standard Western pattern.

The model describes a structure peculiar in permitting the simultaneous existence of three sanctioned family types not usually found together in a single social system. Lévi-Strauss calls these types the conjugal, the subconjugal, and the supraconjugal.[48] To anticipate details given in chapters six and nine, the conjugal family consists of a mated pair and their children existing as a separate unit. Less than such a unit is a subconjugal family, that is, a unit consisting of a woman and her children alone. The supraconjugal family is one in which more than a mated pair (or truncated pair) and their offspring are considered integral to the unit, such as a matrilineal extended family, a joint family of brothers and their wives, and similar groupings. In Martinique the supraconjugal family involves a woman or a couple, one or more children belonging to the woman or couple, and the offspring of those children. There is no mated pair in the supraconjugal group, at least not in the second generation.

This model expresses the structural possibilities implicit in a value system lacking what Malinowski calls a "rule of legitimacy."[49] By a "rule of legitimacy" he refers to the allegedly universal cultural insistence that a girl be "married" before she gives birth to her children, and that illegitimate children be ascribed differential status (see page 154 for the full quotation). By "marriage" I mean what Lévi-Strauss observes, namely, a universal distinction between a "group-sanctioned bond between a man and a woman, and the type of permanent or temporary union resulting from ... consent alone."[50]

When I contend that there is no rule of legitimacy, I mean that there is no unequivocally preferred type of bond between parents. Among the many possible alternatives into which permitted relationships fall, no arrangement is favored as ideal. That there is no insistence on a group-sanctioned bond is shown by the fact that both subconjugal and supraconjugal families share equal status with both common-law and legally married households. Legitimate and illegitimate children (the latter being divided into recognized and unrecognized), all things being equal, share the same status.

The structuring of relationships about a *rule* is not found in Capesterre, but the society is not as a result disnomic or disintegrate. Certain areas of family organization that are usually structured simply fall into a zone of indifference, and the people show greater concern with other areas, for example, household management and care of children. Certain of the usual latent functions of marriage, such as admission to adulthood and validation of group membership, are in Capesterre associated with other culturally recognized events, as we shall see in chapters six and seven. In other words, I contend that the subculture in question has not institutionalized marriage in relation to the conditions under which children are produced or reared. Child-rearing units, child-producing units, and family in terms of economic or household solidarity do not necessarily coincide with one another, and certainly not with marriage, although child-rearing units tend to coincide with the economic household. An example of the noncongruence of the elements is that a woman might produce a child while living at home with her mother; the father, who lives elsewhere, might or might not contribute to his child's support; and the grandmother of the household might marry a *concubin* after her family has grown. Furthermore, this grandmother might have farmed out some of her own children to be raised elsewhere.[51]

In the standard Western family—whatever other institutions may have taken over in part or whole certain widespread functions of the family like education, recreation, economic production—reproduction still coincides with marriage, as revealed by the fact that 96 percent of births in America were in wedlock (1956).[52] However, according to a 1973 government report by Cecilia E. Sudia, illegitimacy increased in the United States between 1960 and 1972. This factor plus divorce increased single-parent families from 9.2 percent of all United States families in 1960 to 11.6 percent in 1972.[53]

An unexpected course for illegitimacy to take, if poverty is thought to be its necessary substratum, is shown by the behavior of white middle-class teenagers in the United States. Leslie Aldridge Westoff wrote in 1976 that

> Less than five years ago, when a single middle-class white teen-ager became pregnant, she had no choice. Her parents dragged themselves up out of the shock, shame and anger she had plunged them into, and covertly shipped her off . . . [to hide the whole accident]. Today this girl is no longer in disgrace, except perhaps in scattered areas . . . More than 200,000 teen-agers (85,000 whites and 121,000 blacks) gave birth to out-of-wedlock children in 1974. This accounts for more than half of all the illegitimacy in the country. And the numbers are rising even though the overall teen-age birth rate is dropping. Between 1971 and 1974, there was a 12 percent increase in illegitimate births to white girls aged 15 to 19 (with a corresponding increase of 5 percent among black teenagers). And in this same . . . period, illegitimate births to white girls under 15 increased by 32 percent (for blacks it was only 3 percent). If not for a number of quickie marriages . . . these figures would be even higher.[54]

The historical chain of events that produced an absence of the rule of legitimacy in Martinique is set forth in chapter eight.

Viewing the literature on the Caribbean family (chapter one),

one is struck first by the abnormally high degree of illegitimacy in recent decades: 56 percent of births in Trinidad,[55] 54 percent in Jamaica,[56] 67 percent in the Martinique community,[57] 53 percent in Guatemala.[58] Leyburn states that although no statistics are available, there is less marriage in Haiti than anywhere else in the world.[59]

Next, one is struck by reports in the literature of the dominance of the mother in the family, what we shall call matrifocality, which in its extreme form virtually excludes the male from any but a procreative role.

This study, too, reveals certain aspects of such features. Every region seems to produce its own variation on these two themes, and the forms display such diversity that one is tempted to seek some underlying process that would explain them. I discuss the relation of matrifocality to the family in Martinique in chapter six. Its relation to the model is left for the concluding chapter along with problems of "explanation" for the Caribbean family in general. The subjects of illegitimacy and marriage are discussed in chapter seven.

Community Choice   Together with a group of five other field workers, I spent the first five weeks of this field trip in Fort-de-France, the capital of Martinique. With the local high school (*lycée*) as a base, we traveled in small groups to different parts of the island, spending from one to three days in each place, with the aim of becoming acclimated, exploring the regional diversity, and choosing various representative communities for further study. We came together after each trip and pooled our experiences. At the same time, we were meeting the urban elite, forming friendships, interviewing officials, and making contacts (such as those with students from all over the island) that would aid us in deciding which communities to study. We traveled by bus and jeep, or we hitchhiked. Staying in local "hotels" in different villages, we met such people as the mayor and began to explore the hills, calling on families at random.

On three different occasions during this survey period I visited a community which I later decided would be my permanent base after the group split up to work individually. I shall call it by the fictitious name of Capesterre, which in the French Antilles means "east coast." Representative of one of several ecological regions of this island—which include areas of sugar, bananas, fishing, truck-garden cash crops—Capesterre has been dominated by large sugar plantations since the seventeenth century. Unlike settlers in the "peasant" areas of Martinique, most of the people in Capesterre work for wages as cane cutters. But unlike laborers in the largest sugar plains, some workers in Capesterre also own an acre or so in the hills behind the cane fields instead of living exclusively as landless town dwellers or people housed on the plantations.

A community shows the range of spatial and temporal dispersion and nucleation from nodal points of maximum communication.[60] From this view there are two ways of categorizing Capesterre, the name of both a village (*bourg*) and a larger political unit, the *commune*, of which the *bourg* is the nucleus. As a kind of county seat, the *bourg* is a line village with a main street on which are found houses, shops, the market, church, school, government offices, and recreational centers; here also is the large sugar refinery. The *bourg* includes agricultural activity as well as the services that a total population of 3,871 supports. Among the village personnel are farmers, fishermen, rich merchants, government officials and clerks, a resident priest, schoolteachers, and a few professionals; a large proportion is formed by landless agricultural wage earners living in slums—the rural proletariat.

Of the total population, nearly 75 percent live in dispersed settlements in the hills or on the plantations. The country districts are divided into neighborhoods called *quartiers*, one of which is so distant as to have its own school for the first few grades. Each district has its own shop.

In Capesterre live half a dozen of the white families of Martinique, who compose 1 percent of the total island population of some 261,595 (1952 census). Here, too, are a few representatives of the colored elite, those mulattoes who are completely acculturated to the standards of metropolitan France. (When I use the word "acculturated" throughout the text without qualifying it, it is this shade of its meaning to which I shall refer.) There is also in the *commune* a group of well-to-do people—the rural middle class—who are not acculturated to the values and manners of modern, urban France. They do not associate as equals with the elite of Martinique. I shall refer to such people along with the lower economic classes as "nonelite." The rural middle class includes both blacks (*noirs*) and mulattoes. And last, further duplicating the stratification picture of the island in general, there is in Capesterre a majority composed of lower-class wage earners (some of whom own a little land) who are chiefly black in phenotype, although among them are some mulattoes.

The Field Situation   To deal by myself with so large a population—about eight hundred households—within the limitations that time (five months) and my role in the society set for me required a blending of techniques. I picked up certain cues during the survey period when I could proceed by trial and error without having to live with my mistakes.

A white foreigner is free from many respectability expectations, but not all. With men of equal status I was free to come and go; with others I had to remain in public or be chaperoned. Unlike the native women, I could go to bars if escorted, but to go alone to a fair or a bar put me in a ridiculous position.

With lower-status families, the automatic superordination determined by my whiteness was not a barrier to intimacy if I participated at a maximum, which involved sharing the bed and board of a number of households.

My identification as an American was a liability among some country people incensed by their Communist newspaper's accounts of anti-Negro demonstrations in the United States. These people suspected me of some undefined malice, perhaps of trying to buy their land from them. They were afraid that America wanted to take over Martinique. However, it was difficult for all but the bitterest to conceive of any specific role that I might have in such a scheme. One way of overcoming hostility was to be introduced by their political leaders, in whom they had implicit trust. The best way to handle the situation was to get to know the people well, for friendship in every case dispelled most doubts.

In other neighborhoods the country people were not so politically conscious, and they expressed nothing but complete hospitality. Some were ignorant of the existence of the United States and assumed that I must be French despite my language difficulties, which shows a remarkable patience and tolerance. Other people found my ignorance of their culture an attraction. They wanted only to help me, to teach me, as one woman put it, like a little child. No one cultivated me for possible monetary gain. Unlike the poor of the British Caribbean islands, Martiniquans do not think in terms of leaving their country and gaining entrance to the United States.

I explained to everyone that I was a "*sociologue*" whose job and interest it was to learn everything about the way they think and live. That it was a woman rather than a man sent to do such work did not seem strange, for there are several patterns into which I was easily accommodated. There is a folktale, repeated in many frameworks, about a witch, old woman, or temptress to whom one refuses hospitality at one's peril; those who receive the creature with courtesy are enormously rewarded. I was told such stories on several occasions. They speak of Joan of Arc as a woman who did a man's job. Furthermore, not all positions of authority are primarily the province of men. There are the Legion women who do a form of social work, the nurse who questions mothers intimately, and the minor political leaders, not infrequently women, who were also concerned with many things in which I was interested. Many people equate any discussion of economics with the speeches of politicians, in whom they place their confidence. Discussion and debate appeal to most *Martiniquaises*.

Patterns of reticence in the culture did not impede my investigation of the family. Sex and paternity are not subjects which inhibit the people once they are past adolescence. There is seldom any motivation to hide real paternity, and if there is, cross-checking will reveal most irregularities, for although the people are discreet, most activities are general knowledge. However, because the people are opposed to what they think of as gossip, it was only in a professional role that I could learn some things. In obtaining the kind of information necessary for an analysis of family life, it was most helpful to work in a culture where everyone is accustomed to registering much personal information. Exaggeration and boasting are at a minimum. Earnings are carefully recorded, for the *allocations familiales*, or family allotments, are distributed on the basis of wages.

It was not difficult to determine what universal cultural lies exist, and the reasons for them, for close friends will let you know insofar as they are aware of them. It did not take long, for example, to learn that many cheat on taxes and lie about it. One method of evading taxes is to build a new house around an old one, for if one builds slowly, the new house can be considered as tax-free repairs. Fortunately, it was not necessary for me to discuss such details with many people.

In a large, nontribal society—especially one whose very structure involves unexpected alternatives—one must quantify certain data, and there are no subtle ways of doing it. I had to make house-to-house surveys with prepared questionnaires. At the same time, I had to be sure that the questions were the right ones and that they would be answered. It was necessary to maintain purely social relations with a sufficiently large and diversified group to learn answers to questions I had not thought of asking. In other words, I had to learn which questions to ask by using the technique of participant observation.

Data were most easily obtained when my relations with people were either intimate or official. Any relationship between friendship and the structured interview with open notetaking reveals the barriers created by pride, discretion, or ignorance of an anthropologist's aims. Casual social calls, therefore, were the least rewarding method when I wanted specific information rather than general impressions. Then, too, of course, one can see people frequently without learning intimate details, not because they begrudge information but because certain things are not naturally brought up in normal conversation. How often do we happen to know, even about old friends, what kind of marriage ceremony they had, how many maternal uncles produced children, or how their grandfathers made a living?

To solve these problems, I first established permanent head-quarters in the *bourg*, where I had a room to myself in a *pension*. When school was in session, teachers lived in the other rooms; road engineers and laborers also stayed there. Members of the *pension* owner's family would come to visit for a few weeks at a time, and travelers of all classes and races would stop over. We all ate at one table in a separate little house in the courtyard.

In the *bourg* I participated in all social activities open to me—

weddings, wakes, baptismal feasts, picnics, dances. I also made calls on people or invited them to the *pension*.

I took trips to the *quartiers*, sometimes returning the same day, sometimes spending weekends or staying a week. With me on these occasions was a companion, a local girl with exceptional mobility, a paid assistant whose very presence with me mitigated the strange impression that a lone white woman would have created and *did* create before I took my landlady's advice and acquired a companion. My assistant was most valuable in explaining my purposes to people with whom I did not have time to establish rapport, for example among a group of workers suddenly come upon in the cane fields. In house-to-house surveys she made possible a faster and less strained conversational pace than I alone would have been capable of maintaining. Above all, although this girl spoke no English, I needed her services as a French/Creole interpreter. I was also included in my assistant's social life, and her constant commentary clarified much that would otherwise have been incomprehensible.

I have singled out for deep focus the seventy-one households of the oldest *quartier*, the preemancipation Voltaire, and the eighty-one households that comprise the newest *quartier*, Fond d'Espoir. In Fond d'Espoir I used a prepared questionnaire in a house-to-house survey, concentrating in each household on the history of the *ménage*: economic activities, land tenure, conjugal status, kinship tables, and household composition. In Voltaire I also attempted life-history depth, but visited only some dozen houses, living for a while in one of them whose occupants gave me the information on the others. For the other *quartiers* I used single informants.

In those parts of the *bourg* and in those *quartiers* and plantations that I did not examine intensively, I checked with informants to see whether my samples contained or omitted significant deviations and to determine whether they lacked other regularities which one cannot usually detect without a larger number of cases. Even when initially derived from or illustrated by a survey involving numerical descriptions, my conclusions are largely qualitative in nature. I used the gathering of quantitative information as a springboard for the observation and discussion on a wide scale of certain facets of the life, some of which unfolded to me as I went along. At the same time, the survey served the auxiliary purpose of enabling me to choose willing and responsive informants of all ages and both sexes with whom I was later able to have deeper rapport.

I have, then, employed in this work participant observation, intensive interviewing, and survey techniques with and without a questionnaire. In addition, I made use of records kept by the manager of one of the plantations, various historical documents and texts, civil records from the town hall, and the parish books.

NOTES

[1] Daniel P. Moynihan, *The Negro Family: The Case for National Action* (Washington, D.C.: Government Printing Office, 1965).

[2] Thomas Meehan, "Moynihan of the Moynihan Report," *The New York Times Magazine*, July 31, 1966.

[3] Andrew Billingsley, *Black Families in White America* (Englewood Cliffs, N.J.: Prentice-Hall, 1968), p. 15.

[4] Ulf Hannerz, *Soulside: Inquiries into Ghetto Culture and Community* (New York: Columbia University Press, 1969), pp. 71, 214–215.

[5] For distribution, compare Nancie Solien González, "Toward a Definition of Matrifocality," in N. E. Whitten and J. F. Szwed, eds., *Afro-American Anthropology* (New York: Free Press, 1970).

[6] Michael G. Smith, *West Indian Family Structure* (A Monograph from the Research Institute for the Study of Man [Seattle: University of Washington Press, 1962]).

[7] My dissertation, "The Caribbean Family: A Case Study in Martinique," written under my maiden name, Mariam J. Kreiselman, appeared in 1958, Columbia University (Ann Arbor Microfilms, University of Michigan).

[8] Eleanor Burke Leacock, ed., *The Culture of Poverty: A Critique* (New York: Simon and Schuster, 1971).

[9] Marvin Harris, "Review of Culture and Poverty: Critique and Counter-Proposals," *American Anthropologist*, 73, No. 2 (1971), 330–331.

[10] Charles A. Valentine, *Culture and Poverty: Critique and Counter-Proposals* (Chicago: University of Chicago Press, 1968); see also a review of the book and Valentine's reply in *Current Anthropology*, 10, Nos. 2–3 (1969), 181–201.

[11] Harris, "Review of Culture and Poverty," p. 331.

[12] Ibid.

[13] Marvin Harris, *The Rise of Anthropological Theory* (New York: Crowell, 1968).

[14] Harris, "Review of Culture and Poverty," p. 331.

[15] Alfred L. Kroeber and Clyde Kluckhohn, *Culture: A Critical Review of Concepts and Definitions*, Harvard University Papers of the Peabody Museum, Vol. 47, No. 1 (Cambridge, Mass.: Peabody Museum, 1952).

[16] Marvin Harris, *Culture, Man and Nature: An Introduction to General Anthropology* (New York: Crowell, 1971), pp. 500–505.

[17] David Bidney, *Theoretical Anthropology* (New York: Columbia University Press, 1953).

[18] Bronislaw Malinowski, *Sex and Repression in Savage Society* (New York: Meridian, 1927; 1955 reprint).

[19] González, "Toward a Definition of Matrifocality," p. 231.

[20] Virginia Heyer Young, "Family and Childhood in a Southern Negro Community," *American Anthropologist*, 72, No. 2 (1970), 270.

[21] Ibid., p. 271.

[22] Ibid., p. 272.

[23] Ibid., p. 273.

[24] Ibid.

[25] Ibid., p. 272.

[26] Hortense Powdermaker, *After Freedom* (New York: Viking, 1939), p. 197.

[27] Hannerz, *Soulside*, p. 104.

[28] Esther Newton, "Men, Women and Status in the Negro Family" (Master's thesis, University of Chicago, 1964), p. 9.

[29] Ibid., p. 52.

[30] John H. Rohrer, Munro S. Edmonson, Harold Lief, Daniel Thompson, and William Thompson, *The Eighth Generation: Cultures and Personalities of New Orleans Negroes* (New York: Harper & Row, 1960).

[31] Newton, "Men, Women and Status," p. 47.

[32] Ibid., pp. 48–61.

[33] Ibid., p. 38.

[34] Ibid., pp. 57–59.

[35] Michael G. Smith, *West Indian Family Structure*.

[36] Professor Goode, who sat in as the visiting examiner on my dissertation defense, referred to my work under my maiden name, Mariam J. Kreiselman (1958), in his paper "Illegitimacy in the Caribbean Social Structure," *American Sociological Review*, 25, No. 1 (February 1960). As Mariam K. Slater, I later read an unpublished paper before the American Anthropological Association at Minneapolis in 1960 called "The Meaning of Illegitimacy in the Caribbean Family"; in it I addressed his criticism. This debate was published as "The Rule of Legitimacy and the Caribbean: A Case in Martinique," *Ethnic Groups*, 1 (1976).

[37] Goode, "Illegitimacy in the Caribbean," p. 21.

[38] Ibid.

[39] Henri Leridon, "Fertility in Martinique," *Natural History*, 79, No. 1 (January 1970), 59.

[40] Ibid., p. 59.

[41] Ibid., p. 57.

[42] Ibid.

[43] Ibid.

[44] Michael M. Horowitz, *Morne-Paysan: Peasant Village in Martinique* (New York: Holt, Rinehart & Winston, 1967).

[45] Arvin Murch, *Black Frenchmen* (Cambridge, Mass.: Schenkman, 1971), p. 10.

[46] Jean Griffin Goossen, "Kin to Each Other: Integration in Guadeloupe" (Ph.D. dissertation, Columbia University, 1970).

[47] Conrad M. Arensberg, "The Community Study Method," *American Journal of Sociology*, 60, No. 2 (December 1955).

[48] Claude Lévi-Strauss, "The Family," in Harry L. Shapiro, ed., *Man, Culture and Society* (Oxford: Oxford University Press, 1956).

[49] Malinowski, *Sex and Repression*, p. 187.

[50] Lévi-Strauss, "The Family," p. 268.

[51] In the Andaman Islands it is rare for children to live with their parents. Nevertheless, child-producing units are strictly limited to married couples.

[52] Howard Becker and Reuben Hill, *Marriage and Parenthood* (Boston: D. C. Heath, 1955), p. 781.

[53] Cecilia E. Sudia, "An Updating and Comment on the United States Scene," *Family Coordinator*, 22, No. 3 (July 1973), 309–311.

[54] Leslie Aldridge Westoff, "Kids with Kids," *The New York Times Magazine*, February 22, 1976, p. 14.

[55] T. S. Simey, *Welfare and Planning in the West Indies* (Oxford: Clarendon Press, 1946), p. 11.

[56] Fernando Henriques, *Family and Colour in Jamaica* (London: Eyre & Spottiswoode, 1953), p. 18.

[57] See chapter seven, pp. 159–160. See also Michel Leiris, *Contacts des Civilisations en Martinique et en Guadeloupe* (Paris: UNESCO, 1955), p. 160; he estimates 50 percent for Martinique from census data.

[58] Dom Basil Matthews, *The Crisis in the West Indian Family* (Jamaica: University College of the West Indies, 1953), p. 13.

[59] James G. Leyburn, *The Haitian People* (New Haven: Yale University Press, 1941), p. 187.

[60] Arensberg, "The Community Study Method."

Part One

THE PROBLEM: THE AREA

ONE

Approaches to
the Caribbean Family

THE FAMILY IN THE LITERATURE

Not many studies of the Caribbean are congruent to one another or to mine. The literature is a record of the unfolding and development of widely differing methods and interests, ranging from African survival research[1] to British functional-structuralism;[2] from economic welfare analysis[3] to ecological investigations;[4] from religious concern[5] to historical description;[6] from American[7] and British[8] sociology to culture-personality studies.[9]

A central feature of the family organization in all areas covered is, as I have said, the dominance of the mother, or matrifocality. Although variously described and expressed in each society, the Herskovitses' characterization, except for their reference to Africa, is a good summation: in the New World the man has the "institutionally remote, humanly somewhat secondary role that in Africa was his as the parent shared with the children of other mothers than one's own."[10] When the many nonfamilial roles of African tribal life were stripped away from the uprooted man during slavery, all that remained of Africa, in the Herskovitses' view, were the intimate characteristics, not the form, of family life; that is, the women were the transmitters of culture, although polygyny had disappeared.

Such institutional remoteness of the male is sometimes produced in many Caribbean areas by the fact that men are émigrés for long periods when they are forced to leave their respective communities to find work; or, as in Haiti, by the fact that the peasant father is a part-time member in several households simultaneously so that he has little interaction with any one domestic grouping. This system in which a man has a woman and children to work on several pieces of property is called *plaçage*.

The first to attempt a typology of family groupings or households in the Caribbean was Simey, who based it on a survey made by Louis Davidson in Jamaica: [11]

> *Christian family*, based on marriage and a patriarchal order approximating that of Christian families in other parts of the world
>
> *Faithful concubinage*, again based on a patriarchal order, possessing no legal status, but well established and enduring for at least three years
>
> *Companionate family*, in which the members live together for pleasure and convenience, and for less than three years
>
> *Disintegrate family*, consisting of women and children only, in which men merely visit the women from time to time, no pattern of conduct being established

Of a total of 270 families, 20 percent were Christian; 29 percent faithful concubinage; and 51 percent companionate and disintegrate.

> These figures must not, of course, be taken too seriously, since the samples were small in size and cannot be regarded as truly "random" from the statistical point of view. On the other hand, there is some justification for regarding them as a good general indication . . . of the frequency of the distribution of the various types of family.[12]

The figures coincide fairly well with the census data.

> Such evidence as there is, therefore, goes to show that in the majority of cases the relationships between the sexes which lead to the procreation of children are temporary, and the institution of marriage is unstable. . . . Promiscuous sex relations are regarded in the West Indies as normal behaviour.[13]

Of Davidson's 270 families, not a single one consisted only of parents and their children, for there is the institution of adoption. Children are valued as a kind of old-age insurance, and a relative or godparent ("goddy") will take in any number of charges.

Henriques[14] presents a similar typology of the domestic group in Jamaica:

Christian family
Faithful concubinage
Maternal or grandmother family
Keeper family

The grandmother family—consisting of a woman, her daughter or daughters, and their children—is also described among southern Negroes in the United States by Frazier,[15] who found the highest incidence of female household heads among urban families (31.1 percent). They were more prevalent among the southern, rural, nonfarming population (22.5 percent) than among farmers (11.7 percent). Frazier traces the female household to "Granny: the Guardian of the Generations," whose influence was established under slavery. The situation did not change, he says, until economically favored classes emerged or until communities grew up with a strong church which was always dominated by males. In tightly knit rural communities, a stable conjugality without marriage often appeared.

The consensus so far is that the family seems to become the usual patrifocal Western unit when property or a favorable economic organization makes it functional. "The presence of the maternal family may be largely accounted for on economic grounds," says Simey.[16] Frazier's analysis involves more than economy, as we have indicated, for he analyzes the domestic group in relation to the type of community it is in.

Raymond T. Smith rejects the validity of a family typology based on the mixed criteria of nature and duration of the conjugal bond and household composition illustrated by Henriques and Simey. In British Guiana, he finds that what appear to be separate household types are in reality stages in the developmental cycle of one kind of household, which is conjugal. Only at the beginning or end of the child-rearing cycle are females found without resident mates. Children are born to young women still living in their family of orientation, but the norm is for the mother shortly to leave that household to form a conjugal household with the father of her children. At the end of the cycle, when the children are grown, men are often absent from the household because women outlive them or because, for a complicated series of reasons, men are considered expendable at this juncture. Smith suggests that depth studies in other areas would show similar principles. He further differs from his predecessors in believing that ". . . economic and occupational factors do not operate as variables in correlation with varying types of family structure within the groups we are studying."[17]

The concept of matrifocality in family life is retained in Smith's analysis in several ways to be discussed in chapters six and nine. I shall say here only that the father-husband role is marginal in that its importance diminishes over time as the children grow and the wife becomes more and more independent of her spouse.

EXPLANATION

The disagreements discussed above can be classified in many ways. The majority seek an explanation for a social form in some aspect of historical antecedents. Others, represented by Raymond Smith, seek correlations among parts of the social structure in terms of a functional ongoing system. The latter analysis, of course, can be applied to a past epoch as well as to the present if enough data are available. But the point is that in any era the functional school (in different ways, to be sure) seeks correlations on a horizontal plane instead of pointing vertically through time to antecedents that are not necessarily functionally related to any aspects of an ongoing system.

Several people in the historical school seek more than mere antecedents,[18] but they worked in a tradition, whether anthropological or sociological, that lacks the details of the latest analysis. Raymond Smith finds the cultural-historical approach particularly "unscientific."[19] I, however, find its purest advocate, M. J. Herskovits, the most "scientific" in that he is the only one who seeks an explanation on the basis of a general theory—not of "culture," as Raymond Smith would have it, but of *cultural focus*. That the theory of focus has been invalidated (to my satisfaction) by Michael G. Smith[20] does not mean that it is not "scientific." A discarded scientific theory is nonetheless scientific, for discarding is part of the business of science. What makes a theory scientific (before or after attempts at verification) is, among other things, its attempt to generalize. As Leslie A. White says, "science is sciencing," not truth.[21]

M. J. Herskovits, in *Trinidad Village*,[22] sees extralegal mating in the New World as well as matrifocal attitudes as problems of acculturation in terms of selective borrowing. The alternatives to such a view, according to him, are hypotheses of stages, the group mind, a folk-urban continuum, or studies of how material elements change faster than values. Before his approach, he believes, students ignored the forces that maintain balance in society. Borrowing, he continues, is determined by the prior concerns of a borrowing culture. "This brings us to the concept of cultural focus: those aspects of the life of a people which hold greatest interest for them."[23] It is here that one finds, in the contact situation, the greatest resistance to change; or if resistance is futile, reinterpretation occurs (as opposed to survival, retention, or syncretism). The reinterpreted family focus is revealed in the fact that ". . . the women [are] the principal exponents of the culture,"[24] as they were in the polygynous households of West Africa where each wife had her separate house for herself and her children.

In rejecting this theory, Michael G. Smith[25] points out that the reality of the interdependence among parts of a culture precludes separating a focal aspect. He suggests instead the idea of foci in the contact situation itself rather than in the original cultures. These foci are pressures that vary in time and place. "Purity of form in survival might simply indicate marginality within the acculturative situation rather than any central significance of the elements retained in the original culture . . ." and vice versa.[26]

Frazier rejects Herskovits's explanation on the ground that no attitudes from Africa could possibly have survived slavery, which made a *tabula rasa* of its human material, at least in the American South. Matthews[27] shows how the rarity of polygyny for the mass of West Africans, even in tribes where it existed among the upper classes, renders its influence negligible.

Most members of the historical school find that the type of family in question can be sufficiently explained as a response to the conditions of slavery, that if American plantation life alone can produce the deviant phenomena, it is impossible to prove the African provenance of forms or attitudes.[28] Some authors also include other past determinants along with slavery: the colonial family, postemancipation developments, and the like.

One must distinguish between techniques for gathering data and modes of explanation. Henriques, whose work is not based on a specific field study, is transitional between the historical and functional approaches. He subscribes to the slavery theory as a mode of explanation, but adds to his description an analysis of the relation of the "lower-class" family to the elite forms. As Raymond Smith says, Henriques approached "a view of West Indian society which [for the first time] takes cognizance of the functioning system which . . . exists." [29] However, Raymond Smith seeks also a description of those structural relations which would permit a comparative study at a higher level of abstraction, contending that to relate the family to "other structures in the society . . . is [the] way of asking why the family takes that particular form." [30]

Smith hypothesizes the following structural constellation for the lower-class Negro family in the New World and finds indications of the same form among the Moche of Peru[31] and a lower-class group in Scotland.[32] Matrifocality, or the domestic marginality of the father-husband, is the result of the peripheral social position of the subsystem (the nonelite) in the total society, thus giving the male no status-defining functions. An essential part of this hypothesis is that the social subsystem, in which authority accrues to the woman solely because of her role as a mother, must be internally undifferentiated from the view of social status; that is, by virtue of being Negro, no person has opportunities for achieving any higher rank than any other person. The male, then, cannot define a family's prestige, since no role can elevate him.

Although his work was not based on a specific field study, Michael G. Smith had already, before Raymond Smith's work, written a critique of the "slavery" as well as the "African" schools, showing that slavery is neither necessary nor sufficient to explain the occurrence of the Caribbean family. He cites examples not only of slave societies with nondeviant families,[33] but also "'deviant, disorganized' family patterns strikingly similar to those found among New World Negroes" where there has been neither slavery nor West African influence.[34]

Another functional approach to the family is exemplified in the "ecological" studies made in Puerto Rico.[35] The thesis is that family organization and values differ from one community to another depending on the productive techniques and land tenure involved in raising different crops.

Among a landless group of laborers in a sugar-producing community, the family is conjugal, but only the woman is the stable member vis-à-vis the children. "Common-law marriage is just as prevalent among this group as it has always been. There are no new considerations of property, status, or religious orthodoxy to induce civil or religious marriage."[36] The same conditions prevail in a government-run, profit-sharing plantation; the nature of the crop, it is maintained, has a greater effect than nominal ownership.

In the mountains, the study reports, where sugar cannot be grown, there is the prospect of upward social mobility through land ownership, and a difference in family patterns is discernible. Coffee does not require great land concentration. Even among the landless workers in this region, the family is "strongly patrilineal, with the father controlling the family labor. . . ."[37] Ownership of land is important, and the man "determines inheritance and the disposal of any land, and dictates the social relationships of his wife and children. Marriage in this community is usually ritual [religious], even among the landless, and may thus reflect the importance of property as well as of the traditional religion [Catholicism]."[38]

With tobacco, still smaller holdings are productive. No machinery is required, the season is only four months long, and quick cash is earned for family labor. Authority is generally paternal, but not so strongly as among the coffee producers. Marriage is consensual (common-law) only where property is not important.

HISTORY

To an extent I share the aims of both historical and functional research in a manner that will be set forth in the concluding chapter. At no time, however, do I deal with the entire idiographic chain of history. Instead, I isolate links in that chain here and there to clarify aspects of my problem that other modes cannot illuminate. Even if it eventually proves to mean no more in social science, a knowledge of history is an aid to posing the proper functional questions. As Kluckhohn points out in discussing the Ghost Dance of the Sioux, if one asks why symbolic activities are directed toward the west, it is helpful to know that the founder of the cult came from that direction before one seeks a nomothetic (generalizing) reason.[39]

On another level, Homans and Schneider say of history:

> We believe present association betrays ultimate origin; the history of some institutions is repeated every generation; to some unknown degree the energies that maintain a system are the ones that created it, and to this degree Radcliffe-Browne is wrong in holding that the history of primitive institutions is forever lost to us.[40]

STRUCTURE

On the whole, the British school of anthropology (and particularly Raymond Smith) identifies science with the functional view and sociological analysis, while history is identified with the humanistic view and cultural analysis. I do not agree that the choice is such a simple, two-horned matter, but I do think that the techniques developed largely by the British school should be used today in any detailed investigation of social relations, whatever the general orientation of the investigator. Such techniques involve a concept of social "structure." Judgments as to which aspects of behavior should be included as parts of social structure have varied not only as people have approached different problems but as they have worked in different types of societies.[41]

Whatever the decision, there is the question of what the best general methods are for obtaining such data. In a small homogeneous kin-based society, an impressionistic technique may be self-correcting. Living *in situ*, one soon knows which informants are representative of the whole. Whether this theory of sampling is true or not, Herskovits followed such a plan in Trinidad and Haiti. Unlike him, the sociologists in the Caribbean gathered superficial statistics on their area in general, but not in the context of a single well-known community.

I believe that neither technique alone can adequately plumb Caribbean societies, for each community is an internally heterogeneous part-culture. Therefore, I used both methods. In print, as of 1958, only Raymond Smith had employed both participant observation within a community and the survey technique, adding to the latter the essential dimension of time depth. Using Fortes's definition of social structure, "an arrangement of parts brought about by the operation, through a period of time, of principles of social organization which have general validity in a particular society,"[42] Smith introduces the survey because he equates principles with norms.[43] The norms, he believes, must be established "by a numerically defined mode."[44] And the modal behavior within the subsystem he is examining is considered to be not only a deviation from the ideal of the dominant society in British Guiana, but also to represent a "differential ideal" of the lower-class Negro subsystem.[45]

ORGANIZATION

As we see, a structural study leads us immediately to the associated concepts of organization, norms, and values. Firth calls social organization the content of the relations composing the structure, which maintains the structure and serves its ends or functions.[46] He further links it with values by calling organization "directional activity that involves systematic choice," for the attitudes channeling choice can be called values. Firth illustrates organizational principles in operation by describing dilemmas that are, as he says, resolved by choosing variable ways of maintaining both rules and customs. In Sumatra, for example, the rule is that one cannot marry without a guardian; the custom is that one must marry. What does one do when one has no guardian? In this case, the person might find a substitute guardian. Whatever the resolution, in such conflicts we see, as Firth says, "action planned in conformity with selected ends." And we see what conflicts arise within the social structure and how their resolutions tend to modify that structure. As Redfield says in a discussion of Firth,

> We must consider social structure not only as a system of relationships, of existing kinds of ties between people and doings done by kinds of people, but also as a system of norms and expectancies. . . . So conceived, social structure is an important part . . . of that conception which we shall . . . call "ethos," or value system. . . . Related to and yet separable from this system of moral norms are the expectations of the people as to the realization of these norms. . . . It is well to include in social structure . . . the ideal, the desired, the expected, and the realized.[47]

It seems that Raymond Smith, by identifying principles of organization exclusively with the ideal expressed by realized *modal* behavior, leaves out many structurally *expected* patterns, the results of dilemmas and alternate choices which the structure creates and which reveal the very principles that in my analysis characterize Caribbean society. I include as structural elements not only modal deviations from the ideal of the dominant social segment, but also special kinds of deviations (the *deviant* or *variant modal pattern*) from the *differential ideal* of the nonelite subsystem. I do not include, in Redfield's terminology, all *realized* behaviors as structural. I exclude those that represent failures to achieve the desired or expected because of idiosyncratic transgressions or inadequacies. But I include those realized behaviors that may be statistically rare but are expected consequences under special conditions or circumstances and have the same positively sanctioned status in the ethos as modal patterns.

For example, Raymond Smith states, without evaluating the structural status of the phenomenon, that sometimes a woman inherits her mother's house and becomes a mother herself without ever entering a conjugal union,[48] that is, without attaining the norm. Again, he mentions that when women own their own houses in this manner, their unions with men are rare and unstable.[49] I found a similar phenomenon in Martinique, but consider it to be the result of regular organizational principles that reveal as important an aspect of structure as the modal conjugal union.

I maintain that sometimes even one occurrence in a small sample will indicate a pattern that is just as significant as the modal pattern, even though rare. For example, as we shall see, one *maison paternelle* in a *quartier* (an inherited house occupied by a female head) revealed the *structured* nature of the values attached to it. It is such considerations that show why despite my using a survey technique my interpretations for a qualitative analysis are not purely statistical.

In delineating structure, then, I contend that frequency is sometimes important, sometimes not, but a wide sample with its time depth is necessary for documenting certain kinds of conclusions. Much undocumented Caribbean description has recently been called into question. For example, Raymond Smith's results have made him doubt whether Henriques's material really indicates a "grandmother family" as an independent type rather than as a temporary appearance in life cycles that did or will include a father-husband.

My interpretation of structure leads me to differ with Smith about the place of marriage among the nonelite. Smith calls common-law marriage the differential norm of the subsystem, saying that the "real significance [of legal marriage] is an act of conformity to the 'respectable' values" of the dominant society.[50] In another context, he says, "The conversion of a common-law marriage into a legal marriage often serves to validate ... [the] new power distribution [between spouses]";[51] that is, it emphasizes the superior position of the woman, since it occurs late in the cycle of the household. Because legal marriage is statistically less frequent (not a norm), Smith implies that it is outside the subsystemic structure and calls it an act of conformity to another set of values. By considering only the statistical meaning of "norm," he does not explore the articulation of legal marriage with the family as part of the subsystemic structure, nor does he tell what values and conditions influence some couples to conform to an "outside" standard.

I shall demonstrate for Martinique that the subsystem contains multiple standards, that the structure provides or includes values that have a grammar of their own. In studying the choices involving marriage—not only mating partners, but the decision whether to marry and when—one touches values that reflect the past activities that gave rise to them and point to changes in social patterns emerging today. And these values repeated in varying contexts—themes—reveal certain functional relations (mutual dependencies) among economics, religion, acculturation to elite standards, and folk-urban factors on the one hand, and the principles of family organization on the other.

Values and Institutions

Implicit in this study is the place of values in relation to behavior as expressed by Conrad M. Arensberg in *Trade and Market in the Early Empires.* Anthropology, he says, sees institutions as "specific inventions" that diffuse, converge, evolve. It is in the social arrangements which crystallize into institutions that one finds the frame of reference for actions and motives.

> Social arrangements make their own values in the process of becoming culture patterns, or "instituted." The evolution of a culture pattern is just such an emergence of summary and symbolizing values, meaning, vocabulary and concept about a new pattern of action, making it ready for recognition, sanction, and transmission. Action comes first in anthropology's view of culture, whether it be the wheel, or divine monarchy, or parallel cousin marriage, and values come second.[52]

One discovers processes, he continues, by comparing common denominator social arrangements: the closest we can come to origins is to document these factors.

It is while tracing all organizational principles to their precipitating social arrangements that further use is made of history. I believe that in the Caribbean, with its short time depth, a family culture pattern can be seen as it becomes instituted. However, not only modal realizations, but the meaning, vocabulary, and concept of nonmodal regularities must be explored as well. For future studies, an interesting problem would be to see how much the "social arrangements" can vary from region to region and still give rise to similar values. The study of "family values" could also help us assess the stage of development of this distinctive institution of the Caribbean: How noncontradictory are the values? Perhaps, too, this could give an index of the stability of the form and point to the direction in which the subculture is likely to move.

COMMUNITY CHOICE

My approach to the community, as I said, is derived from Conrad M. Arensberg's "The Community Study Method."[53] The significance of viewing the family in its community is that less than this spatial and temporal range would not allow us to examine the mutual dependence of the elements of culture, "the topography of their interconnections." More than the community would be unnecessary and unmanageable, for in it exists a minimal duplication of the basic cultural and structural whole. This does not mean that every element of the entire culture is there in all its forms, but that the community is the unit of cultural transmission in which a generation can live through its life cycle with a model for all the roles the culture offers them. The community, as Arensberg uses the term, is not Murdock's maximum range of face-to-face contact.[54] People interact with others from outside their community, and they may not interact with all the personnel present. The community study method has no one purpose, not even that of knowing the whole culture, but seeks to provide the minimal and maximal contexts of an *in vivo* study.

SUMMARY

My method, then, in delineating family structure considers non-modal behaviors insofar as they are regular. In addition, my approach involves not only a structural-functional analysis, but also includes history: the organizational principles of the structure lead to an examination of values, which in turn form a culture pattern that is interpreted as resulting from what Arensberg has called a "specific invention."[56] That other histories can converge in similar structures throughout the world is evident; I restrict my search in history to Capesterre.

Although one of my tasks is to derive a model of the family structure in Capesterre, I believe that the model will in addition incorporate the various discrepancies shown in the literature from area to area, whether the discrepancies are objective features of the series or whether they reflect a different use of the tools of observation.

The framework, as I have indicated, will be the community study method.

NOTES

[1] M. J. Herskovits, "The Negro in the New World," *American Anthropologist*, 32, No. 1 (1930), reprinted in Frances S. Herskovits, ed., *The New World Negro* (Bloomington, Ind.: Indiana University Press, 1966); M. J. Herskovits, *The Myth of the Negro Past* (New York: Harper & Bros., 1941); and M. J. Herskovits and F. S. Herskovits, *Trinidad Village* (New York: Knopf, 1947). See also George F. Simpson, "Haiti's Social Structure," *American Sociological Review*, 6, No. 5 (1941); "Sexual and

Familial Institutions in Northern Haiti," *American Anthropologist*, 44, No. 4 (1942); and "Discussion," in Sol Tax, ed., *Acculturation in the Americas* (Chicago: University of Chicago Press, 1952).

[2] Raymond T. Smith, *The Negro Family in British Guiana* (London: Routledge & Kegan Paul, 1956).

[3] T. S. Simey, *Welfare and Planning in the West Indies* (Oxford: Clarendon Press, 1946).

[4] Robert A. Manners and Julian H. Steward, "The Cultural Study of Contemporary Societies: Puerto Rico," *American Journal of Sociology*, 59, No. 2 (September 1953).

[5] Dom Basil Matthews, *The Crisis in the West Indian Family* (Jamaica: University College of the West Indies, 1953).

[6] James G. Leyburn, *The Haitian People* (New Haven: Yale University Press, 1941).

[7] E. Franklin Frazier, *The Negro Family in the United States* (New York: Dryden Press, 1948).

[8] Fernando Henriques, *Family and Colour in Jamaica* (London: Eyre & Spottiswoode, 1953).

[9] Rhoda Métraux, "Some Aspects of Hierarchical Structure in Haiti," in Sol Tax, ed., *Acculturation in the Americas* (Chicago: University of Chicago Press, 1952); Yehudi Cohen, "The Social Organization of a Selected Community in Jamaica," *Social and Economic Studies*, 2, No. 4 (1954). For a good bibliography, see Michael G. Smith, *A Framework for Caribbean Studies* (Jamaica: University College of the West Indies, n.d.).

[10] M. J. Herskovits and F. S. Herskovits, *Trinidad Village*, p. 16.

[11] Simey, *Welfare and Planning*.

[12] Ibid., p. 83.

[13] Ibid.

[14] Henriques, *Family and Colour in Jamaica*.

[15] Frazier, *Negro Family in the United States*.

[16] Simey, *Welfare and Planning*, p. 87.

[17] Raymond T. Smith, *Negro Family in British Guiana*, p. 46.

[18] See Frazier, *Negro Family in the United States*.

[19] Raymond T. Smith, *Negro Family in British Guiana*, pp. 231, 238.

[20] Michael G. Smith, *Framework for Caribbean Studies*.

[21] Leslie A. White, *The Science of Culture* (New York: Farrar, Straus, 1949), p. 3.

[22] M. J. Herskovits and F. S. Herskovits, *Trinidad Village*.

[23] Ibid., p. 6.

[24] Ibid., p. 8.

[25] Michael G. Smith, *Framework for Caribbean Studies*.

[26] Ibid., pp. 15–16.

[27] Matthews, *Crisis*, p. 364.

[28] Some conditions of slavery that were conducive to the breakdown of family life were the following: On some plantations, children were taken away from their mothers and entrusted to an estate nurse. Often the slave master undermined the authority of the family even by forbidding parents to punish their children. Many people mention the fact that male slaves were sometimes used as studs, parents being sold separately.

[29] Raymond T. Smith, *Negro Family in British Guiana*, p. 238.

[30] Ibid., p. 146.

[31] John Philip Gillin, *Moche, a Peruvian Coastal Community* (Washington, D.C.: Government Printing Office, 1947).

[32] C. S. Wilson, unpublished dissertation (Cambridge University, 1953).

[33] Michael G. Smith, *Framework for Caribbean Studies*; for example, the Muslim Fulani and Hausa of Nigeria.

[34] Ibid.; for example, the urban South African Bantu, p. 19.

[35] Manners and Steward, "Cultural Study of . . . Puerto Rico."

[36] Ibid., pp. 125-126.

[37] Ibid., p. 128.

[38] Ibid.

[39] Clyde Kluckhohn, *Mirror for Man* (New York: McGraw-Hill, 1949), pp. 65-66.

[40] George C. Homans and David M. Schneider, *Marriage, Authority, and Final Causes* (Glencoe, Ill.: Free Press, 1955), p. 39.

[41] Cf. Robert Redfield, *The Little Community* (Chicago: University of Chicago Press, 1955), chap. 3.

[42] Raymond T. Smith, *Negro Family in British Guiana*, p. 107.

[43] Ibid., p. 96.

[44] Ibid., p. 149.

[45] Ibid.

[46] Raymond Firth, *Elements of Social Organization* (New York: Philosophical Library, 1951), pp. 35-37.

[47] Redfield, *The Little Community*, pp. 45-46.

[48] Raymond T. Smith, *Negro Family in British Guiana*, p. 121.

[49] Ibid., p. 113.

[50] Ibid., p. 179.

[51] Ibid., p. 148.

[52] Karl Polanyi, Conrad M. Arensberg, and Harry W. Pearson, eds., *Trade and Market in the Early Empires* (Glencoe, Ill.: Free Press, 1957), pp. 104-105.

[53] Conrad M. Arensberg, "The Community Study Method," *American Journal of Sociology*, 60, No. 2 (December 1955).

[54] George P. Murdock, *Social Structure* (New York: Macmillan, 1949), p. 79.

TWO

The Island

THE CARIBBEAN AREA

The underdeveloped Caribbean islands and parts of their neighboring continents are the heritage of mercantile Europe's once highly prosperous plantation empires and entrepôts. Here, in the beginning, when land was plentiful, the only labor that could be induced to work the plantations instead of being independent farmers were captives from Africa. Throughout the Caribbean area, slaves were not only the chief source of labor, but also one of the most lucrative trade commodities until land pressure made it more economical to free the slaves and pay wages. With good free land completely occupied, it was no longer difficult to induce people to work for others.

As during the period of mercantilism, most of these areas still import a large proportion of their manufactured goods and food. They still export raw materials, but these have largely ceased to be profitable in the world market, and most of the islands and underdeveloped continental lands are liabilities to their mother countries.

Whatever their diverse economic adaptations and aspirations, most of these Caribbean regions share certain broad ecological and social features.[1] Each is an underdeveloped, multiracial, highly stratified society with a large economically marginal base. A continually expanding population intensifies these features, and the depressed group becomes a larger and larger numerical majority.

Politically, Martinique enjoys the same status as any other *département* of France. Yet, like most of the other islands, she continues to have, as Eric Williams puts it, "a government of sugar, for sugar, [and] by sugar."[2] In typical monocrop fashion, sugar has led to the concentration of land in large estates owned by the few who can afford a heavy capital investment. A large, unskilled labor force is housed on the plantations or on parcels of land which, even when owned by the worker, are too small in most cases even for subsistence. Efficient cultivation of sugar confines the majority to only seasonal employment. The result is a living standard no higher than that of slavery for 70 percent of Martinique's inhabitants.[3]

Beyond the broad similarities of the Caribbean area are many specific local differences. For example, although multiracial stratification prevails, in Haiti there are no longer any native whites, their position having been taken by a mulatto elite; in Jamaica it is possible for people of Negro ancestry to pass into white society; and in Martinique a Caucasoid plantocracy is a closed group into which no one passes, and there are no "poor whites."

Regarding religion, there are such extremes as the largely African Vodun of Haiti and Candomble of Brazil, the multiplicity of revivalist Protestant cults in the British islands, the spiritualism of Puerto Rico, and the nearly exclusive Catholicism of Martinique.

Other important differences arise from geographical features. The flat topography of Barbados, permitting almost total exploitation in sugar, allows for no solidary, clearly demarcated "little communities,"[4] the capital city being the hub of all settlements. The tropical forests and mountainous terrain of Martinique, on the other hand, are useless as plantation land, and a proliferation of small villages has taken shape, each the nucleus for several rural neighborhoods. But such terrain is relatively limited, the island is small, and communications have been good for the last few generations. As a result, there is not the kind of isolation that developed in Haiti, where it permits the persistence of African traits.

Because these differences occur within a fundamentally unitary historical framework, the Caribbean is an exceptionally good social science laboratory. From island to island one variable after another can be held constant. And converging on this "American Mediterranean" are also elements, like the plantation system, which can lead research to other culture areas and back again. The particular problem I have chosen for this study is local, areal, and also capable of broader generalization. However, I shall start by taking the next largest unit after the Caribbean area just briefly described. Let us look at the entire island of Martinique as a bas-relief against which the community of Capesterre will be explored in the next chapter.

MARTINIQUE

The 385 square miles of fertile volcanic soil that is Martinique have been, since emancipation in 1848, the stage for a gradual shift in the distribution of power, wealth, authority, and knowledge which were once the exclusive possessions of the whites. The history of this changing social stratification will be sketched in this chapter.

We shall see that although the plantation still dominates the economy, the people have new opportunities for mobility and political participation. For example, as a *département* of France since 1948, Martinique sends "men of color" (as it is put locally) to Paris as its representatives, and its upper middle class is largely mulatto. But as long as the island remains an underdeveloped area, little further change can be predicted in the stratification that currently exists, for with a growing population and without changes in production, there is no way of accommodating an appreciably larger middle class.

Moreover, in the absence of fundamental changes in social arrangements, little change is likely to take place in the values of family organization. What those values are can be better understood in the context of the island-wide conditions through time set forth here.

THE PEOPLING OF MARTINIQUE

Aside from a few temporary British occupations and an initial short-lived treasure hunt by Spain in 1552, Martinique has been exclusively French since its European settlement in 1635. The aboriginal Caribs, who had replaced the Arawaks, were quickly destroyed, leaving only a heritage of a few items of vocabulary and some basketry techniques. Only 160 Caribs remained in 1692.

According to the historian Peytard, "the first French sallies into the Caribbean were as much for converting the heathen as for trade."[5] Interested in neither slaves nor sugar, the Compagnie des Îles d'Amérique established a military outpost in Martinique, bringing with them about one hundred small tobacco farmers who had been on the island of Dominica, which on a clear day is visible from Martinique.

Unlike the Iberian countries, France had had no tradition of Old World slavery, and indentured Frenchmen were imported to be the labor force on Martinique; within five years one thousand of these *engagés* had arrived. But as long as available land remained, even forced indentured laborers could not successfully be induced to work for others. Consequently, by 1686 there were as many slaves as *engagés*. Since the Indians had been killed off, African slaves became the producers. In 1698 there was only one indentured French worker under contract for every twenty slaves; and by 1774 not a single *engagé* could be found.

The growth of the Negro population parallels the emergence and flowering of the plantation system. As in Barbados, the impetus for this transformation came from the Dutch who, to promote the slave trade, introduced better techniques of sugar production in 1654. It was not long before the planters insisted on a cheaper source of labor, and in 1670, under Louis XIV, France entered the slave trade.

At about this time a trend that has continued to the present becomes detectable: Negroes began to have numerical ascendancy over whites. Revert's interpretation of the first census (1664) shows 2,694 whites and 2,710 blacks.[6] By the end of the seventeenth century whites numbered not quite 7,000, while there were 13,292 slaves.

What Revert calls "the colonial fever of the Regency," starting with Louis XV, boosted the white population to its apogee of 16,071 in 1742. As a result of natural catastrophes, wars, and economic crises, it has steadily declined ever since. So poor were health conditions throughout the seventeenth and most of the eighteenth centuries that neither whites nor Negroes could maintain their numbers without immigration. On the eve of the French Revolution, in 1788, the distribution was:[7]

Whites	10,603
Slaves	83,414
Free colored	2,326

For the whole of the French Antilles at this date, slaves numbered 683,121, or 90 percent of the population. For this to be possible, estimates Peytard, 3 million must have been imported from Africa, for half the adult slaves died each year.[8] Replacements continued to arrive until the slave treaty ended after 1830, not long before emancipation.

The Revolutionary Republic of France granted freedom to all those in slavery in 1794; but it was brief and illusory. Seeking release from the new French laws, the local government in Martinique invited the British to occupy the island. The Negroes remained enslaved; but after the Haitian rebellion of 1804 they became increasingly restive, the largest uprisings occurring in 1822 and 1824. From 1831 on, the planters had to make constant concessions. But the aristocracy fought bitterly, so bitterly that officials sent from the homeland had to submit to local pressure or resign. One man was deported for inviting mulattoes to dinner.[9]

The prosperity of Martinique had begun to collapse before the slaves were finally freed. The French islands had long ceased to be the substantial foundation for trade and industry that they had been when France ceded Canada, the Ohio and Mississippi valleys, and Grenada to the British in 1763 in exchange for Martinique and Guadeloupe. Not only had the sugar market become unfavorably competitive, but France itself had begun to grow beet sugar. Then, too, land pressure had appeared in Martinique, and under such conditions wage labor was cheaper than slaves. Financial setbacks finally placed the planters at the mercy of middlemen. It was prohibitive under the circumstances for France to pay an army of 3,000 soldiers to control 72,859 slaves for the benefit of 9,000 whites. Emancipation came and the indemnity paid to the planters (6 million francs) was less expensive than quelling the slightest revolt.[10]

The slaves then made a mass exodus from the plantations. Large numbers of them had to return immediately, however, and some never left; but a labor shortage remained. To remedy it, 25,000 East Indians, 10,000 Africans, 1,000 Chinese, and 500 Annamites were imported between 1852 and 1894 as indentured workers.

Today, the Chinese and Annamites are so few as not to form a significant separate group. As for the Africans, there are people today whose African surnames, such as Mbela, attest to their arrival during this period, and a few *quartiers* still bear names indicating settlement by such people. Although they were at first looked down upon as *les Congos*, the present generation has been completely absorbed into the lower class.

Of the East Indians, only 5,077 remained in 1895. There were three times as many deaths as births among them, and nearly 11,000 were repatriated after the expiration of their contracts. Those who remain today are Roman Catholic, and they have permeated every class, their social organization largely corresponding to that of the group into which they have become assimilated. Some are among the mulatto elite, some among the rural middle class. In neither case have they become identified with particular occupations. The majority are poor workers housed on the plantations of the northeast coast under conditions that have permitted some ceremonial retentions in addition to their Catholic practices. The priests look upon these as entertainments, even the temples with their idols holding cane-cutters' cutlasses.

When the Indians first arrived, villagers laughingly tell, they were incorporated into the social hierarchy in the following order: whites, mulattoes, Negroes, dogs, and Indians. The derogatory term "coolie" which was attached to them is disappearing. A local legend has it that the term is derived from the fact that the Indians arrived at the bottom of the boat, like packages (*colis*). Although their prestige among the rural blacks is likely to be low, intermarriage is frequent. Some have become so completely accepted as to be the *quimboiseurs*, the practitioners of magical traditions stemming from Africa and the French folk. The middle-class Indian is completely accepted. Most Indians themselves feel superior to the *noirs* by virtue of their characteristically straight hair and Caucasoid features, although their skin is either dark brown or a light copper.

It is difficult to say how many of each racial group exist today, for the census does not make racial distinctions. We know that of a total of 261,595 persons (1952 census), 2,072 are "metropolitans," people born in France.[11] Leiris estimates that 1 percent of the total population is white (3,500 to 3,800).[12] According to the 1952 census, ⅓ of the population are 14 years of age or younger (87,205); fewer than $\frac{1}{25}$ are 60 or over. Within the last one hundred years, the population has doubled, with an excess of births over deaths in 1946 numbering 5,276; between 1922 and 1946 the annual excess was only 2,000.[13] The natural increase was 600 a year between 1853 and 1877; after 1877, the year that fraud for election and financial purposes began to augment the official figures, the growth seems to have been about 1,000 annually.[14] At least 10,000 people of Martinique live elsewhere, says Revert,[15] the richer people rather than the lower class being the migrants.

The sex distribution shows a relatively equal division up to the age of 20, then a 1 percent to 2 percent preponderance of women. The average age at death between 1931 and 1946 was $36\frac{1}{2}$ for men and $41\frac{3}{4}$ for women—$39\frac{1}{2}$ for both; during the same period in France the average was 56 for males, $59\frac{1}{2}$ for females. Infant mortality in 1948 was 20 percent.[16] The recent population growth is largely attributable to improved infant care and a law confining childbirth to hospitals. (For latest figures, see pages 11–12.)

MISCEGENATION AND ITS SLAVERY BASE

An important feature of stratification and population composition in Martinique has always been the proportion of mulattoes. Because mulattoes in the beginning of the colony were often freed, we can get an index of their quantity in the old records by looking at the census category called "free colored": 16 in 1664; 2,326 in 1788; 11,400 in 1808; and 30,000 at emancipation. Today it is impossible to say how many people have some degree of Caucasoid admixture, but there is an elite class of several thousand mulattoes; however, there are also many light-skinned mulattoes who do not belong to this class.

Before 1685 manumission was achieved in three ways: (1) a slave's freedom could be bought; (2) a master could liberate a concubine; or (3) the children of such a union could take the status of the free father, a boy receiving his liberty at the age of twenty and a girl at fifteen, when the father paid the church 1,000 *livres*. Not all the free colored were mulatto, but a large portion was, for most of those who were manumitted were progeny of miscegenous unions.

In Martinique such mixed breedings always took one form, the union of a European man and an African woman, for (unlike the American South) a "poor white" (*Béké goyave*) class from whose ranks white women mixed with slaves quickly disappeared. After 1764 no *engagés* remained, and before that date as well as after there was a scarcity of white women. Because women were, as Lévi-Strauss calls them, a "scarce commodity," they were preempted by the white men.

Mixed-union relationships were influenced by the French upper-class institution of concubinage. Marriage meant increasing one's fortune, strengthening one's social position and connections, establishing one's children. As Leyburn points out,[17] romance was as irrelevant to all this as to choosing a business partner. It would not occur to a man to marry a woman of inferior social position; instead, he could openly keep her as his mistress. This institution did not lower a woman's status even among whites.

Concubinage stimulated the growth and power of the mulattoes to the point where the *petits blancs* considered them an economic threat. These whites, therefore, demanded a set of rules designed to halt as many manumissions as possible.

At the founding of the colony there were no rules for the treatment of slaves, who belonged to the companies that settled the islands until 1674, when they became part of the king's domain. Ten years earlier Martinique had become the *chef-lieu* (head) of the French Antilles with a *conseil* (governing body) that included a governor and officers appointed by the Compagnie des Indes. The colony, therefore, was accustomed to relative autonomy, and when the slaves fell under the king's jurisdiction, local ordinances continued to go counter to his desires. The interests of the French government and those of the planters were often at variance, and they remain so today.

At the instigation of the *petits blancs*, a royal questionnaire resulted in a body of laws called the Code Noir of 1685. The French government was convinced that to allow concubines and their mulatto children liberty would be the destruction of slavery. The code ruled, therefore, that thereafter the children of mixed slave-free unions were to remain the same status as the mother, whose freedom could no longer be bought.

Until the Code Noir, slavery had not been legally defined in France. The slave did not have any specified statutory position. With the introduction of the code, it was explicitly stated that slaves were chattels (*immeubles*), but at the same time slaves attained their first legal rights. As we shall see, the laws dictated the care that must be given slaves, and a victim could report a master who did not obey them. In actual practice, however, there was no more dignity in the life of a French slave than of a British slave, who was given no legal rights.

Although the Code Noir—influenced by canon and Roman law as well as by the Bible—placed the slave outside the province of metropolitan law, the Catholic slave was a part of the Church. However, this feature of Catholicism, automatic membership, was more an obligation than a privilege, and the demand extended beyond the slave population. No non-Catholic could become an overseer of slaves. All who attempted to prevent the practice of Catholicism, "even among slaves," were punished. Baptism became one of the few lures to accepting religion, for instead of burial in a holy cemetery, unbaptized slaves were, according to the code, "interred during the night in some neighboring field."

All religious practitioners except Catholics were forbidden to marry. Marriage itself was governed by the planters rather than the priests, who were forbidden to perform marriages involving slaves without the master's permission. Masters, however, could not force slaves to marry against their will, nor could a mother be separated from her small children. It was permissible for a white man or a freedman to marry a slave and thus secure her liberty; but a white master who had children by slaves without marriage, and the owner who permitted such unions would be fined 2,000 pounds of sugar; in addition, the master would lose the slave mothers and their children, who would be sold for the benefit of charity.

The greatest change brought about by the new code was the rule that in all cases children were now given the status of their mother; no longer could they claim the status of their free father if the mother were a slave. In the American South, a free mother's children by a slave had to spend a number of years as servants, but in Martinique the free mother was never Caucasoid, and the laws were designed to prevent the increase of mulattoes and manumis-

sions. Under the French law, a free mother's children by a slave
were free; regarding the children of two slaves, Article 12 states:

> Children who are born of marriages between slaves will be slaves and
> will belong to the masters of the slave women and not to those of their
> husbands, if husband and wife have different masters.

Laws regarding property allowed slaves to sell vegetables with
their master's permission, but not sugar cane. At death, however,
slaves could not bequeath their earnings. Two officers present in
every market were enjoined to confiscate goods found with slaves
not supervised by their masters.

Masters were forbidden (Article 24) to grant subsistence plots
to slaves. Instead, each slave was guaranteed a weekly ration of $2\frac{1}{2}$
pots of manioc flour or three cassavas weighing $2\frac{1}{2}$ pounds each,
and either 2 pounds of salted beef or 3 pounds of fish. Each child
under ten received half this amount. In addition, each slave was
given two outfits of clothing a year. The planters also had to care for
the sick and old, but no law prevented a master from allowing a
slave to die instead of paying for medicine. Not until the end of the
eighteenth century, says Peytard, were slaves considered "men like
us." [18]

Article 16 was designed to control rebellions:

> It is . . . forbidden for slaves belonging to different masters to gather in
> crowds by day or night under the pretext of weddings or otherwise, be
> it on the property of one of the masters or elsewhere.

It had a profound effect on association patterns. Masters who
permitted slaves other than their own on their property were
condemned. Slaves were also forbidden to use alcohol or to bear
arms.

For theft (even among freedmen), for striking a master, and for
a third attempt to escape, the penalty was death. Other offenses
were punished by flogging and mutilation.

Thus, we see the slave as a *thing*, an *instrumentum vocale*. But
reducing slaves to this status never prevented interbreeding in a
plantation society, nor did it do so in Martinique. As we have seen,
the code permitted a white man to marry a slave, but not to
interbreed under other circumstances. However, it was not within

such a frame that interbreeding continued, for custom was strongly opposed to marriage between partners who were not social equals. Père Labat, an able early chronicler, knew of only two cases of white-mulatto marriage and of none between whites and slaves.[19] Nevertheless, marriage as well as concubinage were explicitly forbidden in 1778. Permission to marry a slave was probably included in the original code as an empty copy of Leviticus, in which a master is enjoined to marry a slave with whom he has had sexual intercourse. Such a tradition was foreign to the medieval *droit de seigneur* that came to prevail in Martinique.

The increasing harshness of the ordinances of the eighteenth century shows how ineffective the code must have been in curbing the growth and power of mulattoes. So frequent was miscegenation that in 1714 noblemen were threatened with loss of their titles if they contracted mixed unions. Either this ordinance was ignored or secrecy prevented detection. Today, mixed unions are still surrounded by secrecy partially because the inheritance laws are such that an illegitimate child can inherit if paternity is proved.[20]

In the latter part of the eighteenth century the *petits blancs* aimed blows at the dignity as well as the prosperity of the growing mulatto class. In 1773 *mulâtres* were forbidden to have the usual French surnames, freedmen were not permitted to wear the same clothes as others, and they could no longer travel abroad. All occupations were closed to them except farming, crafts, and commerce. Moreau de Saint-Méry shows the folkloric reflection of this situation: the *blanc* is the child of God; the *noir* the child of the devil; and the *mulâtre* has no father. As to the origin of the Negro, it was said that the devil created a man equal to the white man, but the devil's impertinence in imitating God so angered God that He turned the devil's handiwork black to prevent confusion. In shame, the black man then fell on his face, suffering a flat nose and swollen lips.

The social ladder at the time of the Revolution reflected such images. There was also ranking among the slaves: *Nègres à talents* (skilled workers, usually household servants); *Nègres à culture* (fieldhands); and at the bottom, *Nègres pièce d'Inde* (recent arrivals from Africa). Even as late as 1880, as we can see from the following data, few people of color were given a share in the government:

Of 9 justices of the peace, all were white
Of 10 police commissioners, 8 were white
Of 18 in the Department of the Interior, 14 were white
Of 42 in the Department of Justice, 36 were white
Of 23 in the Department of Taxation, 20 were white
Of 37 bursars, 25 were white (27 were women, 21 white and 6 women
    of color)

Today, nearly every public office is held by a man or woman of color. Of the thirty-four political *communes* (administrative territories into which the island is divided) only two elected white mayors. In Capesterre not one of the twenty-three political offices is held by a white person. Mulattoes dominate professional positions, and some have entered big business. Part of such a change can be linked to education policies. The primary schools of 1837 held 3,000 children; 7,000 children of the same ages never attended school at all.[21] By way of contrast, in 1878 education was not only free to all but compulsory. In 1951–1952, 42,000 pupils attended elementary school.[22]

Settlement Pattern

The same social changes that have just been described can be seen in another manifestation of the historical and ecological forces that have shaped the island—the settlement pattern. The communal forms that have emerged in Martinique are crucial in maintaining distinctive subcultural patterns.

Politically, Martinique is divided into 34 *communes*, 21 of which are coastal. The average *commune*, double the area of its administrative counterpart in France, consists of 1,457 hectares, the unit of measurement in general use. (A hectare is 2.471 acres.) Each *commune* has a *chef-lieu*, usually a small *bourg* or town, which serves as the hub of rural activities.

The location of the *bourgs* is determined by geography and land use, the chief characteristic of which is that wherever there is flat terrain it is exploited in sugar. This condition, added to the fact that three massifs ridge the island, has limited settlement in such a manner that 90 percent of the population occupy one quarter of the 385-square-mile surface.

The highest points are the central Pitons du Carbet with peaks of 3,960 feet. Then there is Vauclin in the southeast, rising to 1,160 feet. The whole north end of the island is dominated by the famous Mont Pelée, an active volcano whose last great, and tragic, eruption was in 1902. Pouring lava down its 4,200-foot slopes into St. Pierre, Pelée destroyed the city that was considered the Paris of the New World. Although they had been warned to evacuate, the people had remained to settle an election that was taking place. (Political life is one of the main indigenous amusements.)

The extreme south has lower mountains, but much of it is dry, rocky thorn forest. The temperate grassland starts at 2,500 feet where there is more rain than elsewhere. The mean annual temperature at Fort-de-France is 79.2 degrees, with a seasonal range of only 5 degrees, and the average humidity is 80. Generally, the weather from the middle of January to the middle of July is dry. From then until October 15 there are hot storms, after which there is a relatively cool rainy season until January.

Although the Caribs lived at an altitude of 2,600 feet,[23] occupation today is limited to an average of 500 to 800 feet. The drier west coast and the south allow more scope, but modern settlements are rarely found above approximately 1,100 feet. Below these points, erosion makes the deep ravines and lower mountain slopes useless.

The plains, exploited for sugar, are chiefly located in the south central region of Lamentin and along the east coast.[24] The mountains rise too precipitously from the western littoral for plantations. The leeward (west) coast is, as a result, largely the location of most of the fishing villages. The scant food crops of Martinique are raised in scattered localities in a fringe between 500 and 1,100 feet in soil that lacks nitrogen. The following data gathered in 1936 are still representative of the division of cultivable land:[25]

Size of holding (hectares)	Number of farms	Area (hectares)
From part to 3	4,697	5,876
3 to 10	1,019	5,924
10 to 40	456	8,993
40 to 100	157	10,669

Size of holding (hectares)	Number of farms	Area (hectares)
100 to 200	126	17,381
200 to 500	71	21,099
500 and more	11	10,412

Properties above 100 hectares occupy 61 percent of the cultivated land. If those from 40 to 100 hectares are added, 74 percent of the land is divided among 365 *domaines*—not far, Revert points out, from the 437 of 1770. Properties of 3 hectares or under correspond to those parts of the island where the escaped slaves and illegitimate mulatto children of planters lived during the early colonial days: Rivière Salée, St. Esprit, Vauclin, Morne-des-Esses, Lorrain, and others. The *communes* where the properties from 3 to 10 hectares are found are located either where the soil is poor or in those recent agglomerations, such as Morne-Vert, where truck farmers supply Fort-de-France, the capital.

With three quarters of the cultivable land devoted to large estates, it is clear why 60 percent of the population live in the eleven largest centers, 20 percent of them (66,000) in the capital. The overall density is 679 per square mile, with a range from 50 to 1,000. The largest concentration of people is south of a line drawn from Trinité to Fort-de-France. Here from 80 to 120 houses are built per square kilometer, as opposed to 40 to 80 in the northeast, the region of Capesterre.

The semiurban character of most of the population is a recent phenomenon. Before 1848, from 60 percent to 70 percent of the population lived on the estates, of which there were just under 500 between the end of the eighteenth century and emancipation. But not all of the estates were large, self-sufficient, paternalistic organizations, for both big and small properties have existed in every period. In addition to the large sugar estates mentioned earlier, in the eighteenth century there were 948 plantations devoted to coffee, 101 to cacao, and 233 to cotton, averaging 6, 11, and 7 hectares each, respectively. Those who did not live on the estates, except for the city populations, were chiefly the free colored who settled the mountain communities.

After emancipation, the recently freed slaves managed to acquire land in several ways. Some took poor land in public forests. There were many precarious government cedings of unoccupied terrain that were later disputed when the planters wanted land for grazing or other purposes. Other ex-slaves were given usufruct or plots bordering the plantations, and their descendants received title.

Another method of obtaining land is evidenced after economic slumps, when the government receives land to pay off debts or the planter is forced to sell directly to the *Nègres*. For example, in 1900 six plantations in this manner yielded 692 lots of from 4 to 5 hectares each. Another prevalent method of acquiring land, a method still operant, is through squatters' rights. Particularly in the south are little oases of small plots in the very middle of good sugar land. Right after emancipation such land was wrested from the planters as much by insurrection as by squatters' rights. In the north there are few of these oases, and the *petit cultivateur* lives almost exclusively on mountainous land that was never suitable for sugar.

Technological changes have also caused the whites to relinquish some of their land. Before 1860 each estate had its own plant (*sucrerie*) for extracting sugar from the cane. When the individual *sucreries* were replaced by a few central factories (*usines*) transportation problems rendered some distant plantations useless, and the small *cultivateur* was able to acquire some of this land.

Any trend toward division of *Béké* land is countered each time the market rises, when the whites accumulate cash again and band together to keep the property from falling into "impure" hands.[26] Auctioneers often take a loss rather than sell to someone of color, although some of this group have managed to become big planters. But over the generations the mulatto estates become smaller and smaller. There are entire *quartiers* today inhabited by the descendants of a single *mulâtre* planter, each now possessing only an acre or two. The reason is that under the Napoleonic laws of equal inheritance, nothing is left unless, as among the whites, family lands are kept intact by inbreeding.

By 1914 the people of color, aware of their hopeless plight in most cases, began to direct their children's efforts away from the land. To avoid joining the landless proletariat, they turned to commerce. New *bourgs* grew up as a product of the roads—*bourgs* with rum shops, provision stores, restaurants.

The first road in the colony was only coastal. Soon a road between Trinité and Fort-de-France (then Fort Royal) opened the interior, a military necessity. La Trace, the road plowing through the tropical forest between the north and the capital, was not opened until 1850, but in 1732 travelers could reach Sainte Marie from St. Pierre via Morne Rouge. By 1902 Trinité was the leading business center. The main thoroughfares were never dependent on the location of the plantations, for shipping was done by boat, and they were joined very late by private roads. Today there are 1,100 kilometers of roads—the bad ones called *"Maman, prend deuil"* (Mother, put on mourning)—but there are still rainy days when automobiles cannot move.

The network of commerce, once the domain of the hardy *porteuses* who could walk 50 kilometers with as many pounds on their heads, is now maintained by the *autobus* or *voiture*, which made its debut in 1903. By 1936 there were 1,500 of these *garennes lapins* (crazy rabbits), which have become essential for communication as well for carrying produce and passengers.

COLOR AND STRATIFICATION TODAY

Michael G. Smith, in *A Framework for Caribbean Studies*,[27] offers an economic scheme for analyzing race and culture. In those areas where color plays a part in stratification but is not the only determinant as it is in "caste" societies, the situation must be analyzed in several dimensions. Five referents for the term "color" are: (1) phenotypic, (2) genealogical or genotypic, (3) associational, (4) cultural or behavioral, and (5) structural.[28]

The phenotypic color of a man is his appearance; the genealogical or genotypic his racial ancestry. In Martinique, where it is impossible to hide ancestry, if a man is phenotypically Caucasoid and yet has one or more Negroes in his ancestry, he would always be called a *mulâtre*, not a *blanc*. A phenotypically black individual who is known to have partly Caucasoid heredity may, if his achieved status is high, be called a *mulâtre brun*, but more often he is simply referred to as a *noir*.

Associational color is determined by the status of the people with whom a person interacts, and the observer must carefully evaluate the occasions. If someone is genotypically *noir*, but is educated and urbanized to the point where his social contacts are completely *mulâtre*, his associational color is *mulâtre*.

Behavioral or cultural color refers to people's values, attitudes, expectations, manners, speech, visible status symbols—in short, their style of life. The norms differ hierarchically from group to group. Behavioral color is largely determined by associational status. But total status in Martinique is not, in turn, summed up by behavioral color, for in the Caribbean color differences are not ignored, no matter how similar the cultural behavior of the two groups may be. (In sharp contrast, despite slavery, the Hausa and Fulani of Muslim Zaria create no differentiation on the basis of phenotype.)[29]

Michael G. Smith discusses these dimensions further:

> It is methodologically useful as well as revealing to assume initially that there is a complete correspondence of cultural (behavioural) with associational colour, and of both with the biological dimension . . . ; and then to proceed to empirical examination of this assumed correspondence, to determine the extent to which it in fact obtains . . .
>
> The structural dimension is an abstract analytic category reflecting the distributions and types of power, authority, knowledge, and wealth, which together define and constitute the social framework. When we speak of structural colour, we employ an allocation of these variables among colour-differentiated groups which obtains presently and reflects historical conditions.[30]

In this sense a rich *noir* would be structurally white; an educated black would be structurally white; a poor, uneducated mulatto would be structurally black.

In addition to Smith's suggestions for analysis, I shall mention the terms used in the culture to describe discrepancies between genealogical and structural color. For example, under what conditions is a structurally mulatto Negro called a *mulâtre*? I also find that in Martinique it is fruitful to consider color in terms of a rural-urban and folk-elite continuum.

THE "BÉKÉS"

Setting aside metropolitans, there is a phenotypically and genotypically Caucasoid group in Martinique that has been classified as a distinctive group for many generations. Most of them are related, and 89 percent are considered to be descendants of early colonials. They form only 1 percent of the population, some 3,500 people, all of whom are members of about a dozen families. They are usually referred to as the *Békés*, although this term can be used for any Caucasoid. Whatever their role or economic condition they are *blancs*, set apart from all people with any Negroid ancestry whatever. Unlike the pattern in Brazil, no one with a nonwhite genotype of any degree, even though possessing the characteristics historically associated with the *Békés*, is called or considered one of them.

Mixed marriage means the expulsion of the *Béké* from his group. Mixed breeding without marriage, on the other hand, does not impair his status. In either case, his children are considered *mulâtres* if their mother's status justifies the classification; if her status does not, then the children are behaviorally and associationally black. If they are phenotypically light, they are referred to as *chabins* or *chabines*, or as *capres* or *capresses* when they have reddish coloring; but these terms are descriptive like our words "brunette" or "blond." The father never openly acknowledges his mulatto offspring, but he can assure them mulatto structural status by secretly seeing that they receive money, education, or high positions.

The *Béké* class, in the economic sphere, owns about 75 percent of the land and all thirteen of the central factories in which the sugar of the island is processed. The *Békés* control almost 85 percent of exports (1938 figures), which are chiefly rum and sugar. The only other export of any importance is bananas, cultivation of which was started after the market crash of 1929. The banana export was originally in the control of small farmers, and some 5,000 still grow them. But the plantations have taken over this crop with such success that there is no longer hope that the few small farmers will develop into a large, prosperous peasant class.

Some of the central factories belong to families, others to anonymous companies, but all originated with old native capital. In the crisis of the 1880s, when the planters of Guadeloupe were forced to leave, the planters of Martinique were able to survive as an indigenous class because they were financed by the bank (Crédit Foncier Colonial). Revert estimates that about 100 *Békés* are millionaires (in francs), a few many times over, but most are no longer as rich as they were in the eighteenth century. Nevertheless, most

Békés fall into that prosperous class which in 1949 consisted of some 1,000 families with an annual revenue of 200,000 francs, while from 150,000 to 170,000 families earned less than 10,000 (most of them below 5,000) francs a year.[31]

Although the scale is different, the *Békés* of Martinique have never lost their dominance. Every *Béké* has an ascribed status above all others regardless of his or her role; as a consequence, nearly every *Béké's* role is one with prestige. Indigent whites (*Békés goyaves*) never cease to be ranked as aristocrats, and associationally they remain with the gentry.

THE "MULÂTRES"

Although every *Béké* has prestige status, not everyone whose role carries prestige is a *Béké*. Among those in the upper-middle-class income bracket who earn from 50,000 to 200,000 francs a year (1949 standards)[32]—about 1,000 families—not all are white. The group is preponderantly nonwhite, and for the historical reasons we have outlined the majority is *mulâtre*. In this group with French education and elite styles of life, there is what Michael G. Smith calls a "chromatic status scale,"[33] illustrating what Henriques[34] calls the "white bias." The more Caucasoid a person's physical appearance— "good" hair, thin lips, light skin, narrow nose—the greater his or her prestige.

The chromatic color scale is particularly noticeable within the group that has achieved high occupational positions or relative wealth. Not every phenotypic mulatto is a member of this elite. Regardless of appearance, if a man is behaviorally black he is not a member of the *mulâtre* group, although he can be called a *mulâtre* in a descriptive sense. The term can also be used disparagingly by the lower class to describe persons of their own group whom they consider snobs. There is no associational equality between the "poor *mulâtre*" and the darker members of the elite class.

Although the *Béké* and the *mulâtre* are associationally separate groups, they overlap in certain areas, for Martinique is not a "caste" society in the sense that people can be equal but entirely separate.[35] One index of the "noncaste" character of the society is that the *Békés*, unlike whites in the United States, do not fill all the necessary higher occupational roles; but the subcultures of *Béké* and *mulâtre* are not as a result homogeneous. Ironically, the prestige of the *mulâtre* is derived specifically from those behavioral attributes that differentiate him from the *Béké*. There is, indeed, a "white" and a "native" culture in Martinique, but paradoxically the respective carriers of these two subcultures are reversed when the *Béké* and the *mulâtre* are considered: the *mulâtres* are behaviorally white, but not the white of the island; the *Békés'* style is found only in Martinique and can, therefore, be called "native."

The *mulâtres* display behavior learned to a great extent either directly in France or from people who were enculturated there. Some marry metropolitans who have come to Martinique and are acculturated also within the local family to middle-class European patterns. Braithwaite finds in Trinidad that the middle class of today is the upper class of yesterday in terms of values.[36] However, the *mulâtres* of Martinique reflect not the customs of the nineteenth-century aristocrat, but the contemporary values of their peers in France. There are, of course, some *Békés* who share these patterns, but most of them are educated only to maintain the values of a landed aristocracy: it is they who reflect upper-class attitudes of an earlier age.

The "Noirs"

The lowest economic class of Martinique encompasses 70 percent of the population. These people can all be classified as culturally black. Most of them are phenotypically *noir*, but, as we have seen, the "poor *mulâtre*" also belongs to this group.

Most of these people live by agriculture, at least during the four months of the sugar cane harvest. In the dead season (called *chomage*), they either practice a trade or get a few days of agricultural work now and then. Some of the poorest can be included among the 12,000 small property owners, most of whom work on the plantations in addition to exploiting their own land. At the very bottom of the scale, behaviorally and economically, are the 5,000 *gens casés*, "people housed" on the plantations who are not free to work where they wish or to own land. Not far above them are some 4,000 fishermen whose archaic methods do not begin to supply the demand. As we shall see in chapter five, such classifications are not very useful, for a fisherman may also be a government employee who has invested his money in a boat; a cane cutter may sell rum or make dresses. Occupational specialization is not advanced.

Among those who are phenotypically and behaviorally *noirs* are also people who are structurally white in terms of education, wealth, or power. Here one finds shopkeepers, rural government officials, rural lawyers, and the like. Some are transitional in terms of social status. Most of their values are identical with those of the poor among whom they live, yet they are upwardly mobile. In this group are most of the lower middle class, who earn from 10,000 to 50,000 francs a year (1949 standards). Their actual number is impossible to determine, for they are lumped among the 2,000 families (including the mulatto elite and whites) that form the entire middle class. Although the *noirs* can never be considered elite, either by themselves or by the *mulâtres*, they are highly stratified internally, as we shall see in the next section on the community of Capesterre, most of whose inhabitants are culturally black.

A certain resemblance may be seen between the current stratification of Martinique and three of the "estates" formerly found in France: the *Békés* are analogous to the nobility; the *mulâtres* to the bourgeoisie; the *noirs* to the *canaille*.

RURAL-URBAN AND FOLK-ELITE

In assessing the extent to which *Békés*, *mulâtres*, and *noirs* associate with one another, rural life must be separated from urban life. Under no conditions is the *mulâtre* permitted to enter the intimate family circle of the *Béké* as an associational equal. He is not included among the guests at private parties where female *Békés* are present. Since interaction among both *Békés* and *mulâtres* is primarily familial outside the city, there is little contact between them in a rural or town context. Exceptions occur when the village has a white mayor, but this is rare. The priest is usually a metropolitan, not a native aristocrat, and in both cases his participation in the daily or ceremonial round is on a professional basis only. (There are very few nonwhite priests.) The only other whites regularly in the village are the metropolitan *gendarmes* who, when not totally isolated, are associationally black. The most characteristic rural mixing involving whites is in the sex life of the *Béké*.

When the *mulâtre* goes to the village or country *quartier* to visit his family of orientation he is associationally black. Rarely does a member of the *mulâtre* elite live outside the city. Notable exceptions are some of the schoolteachers, who form a large enough group in most *bourgs* to be somewhat of a class apart. Depending on their personal qualities and appearance, they may or may not be accepted by the urban elite. Many are associationally both black and *mulâtre*.

The urban environment provides many opportunities for *Béké* and *mulâtre* to interact as equals. At the *lycées* (the French equivalent of our senior high school and first year or so of college) in Fort-de-France the *Békés*, outnumbered by the others, are associationally *mulâtre* (although many *Békés* go to religious schools, which are for whites only). After being graduated, however, they sever these close relationships as they impinge on intimate family life. But even after the *lycée*, *Béké* men continue to join *mulâtre* families on outings, although only on the most public occasions—attending the theater or official government parties—will *Béké* women associate with *mulâtres*. Metropolitan white families, however, meet with *mulâtre* families at intimate gatherings, and intermarriage between them is frequent.

Békés and *mulâtres* meet freely in business and professional relations. In some offices the women as well as the men of the two groups interact, for there is no prejudice against a white woman's necessity or desire to work. In religious life, rural or urban, all groups mix, but only in the public manifestations of worship, not in the exclusive gatherings for *rites de passage*.

In Martinique as elsewhere, it is oversimple to identify the rural exclusively with folk characteristics and the urban with nonfolk traits. The city is more disorganized and individualized (but not more secularized) than the rural *commune*, as the classical hypothesis would predict; and although there are behavioral differences between the two, there is a squeezing of the rural-urban continuum itself. That is, although a range exists, the poles are not very far apart and the categories in between overlap considerably. Because the island is small and communications relatively good, the rural population often goes to the capital. By the same token, the urban inhabitants are exposed more to rural influences than they are in the typical complex Western society. The planter is both rural and urban, and the elite, as we have seen, have relatives in the *commune.* There are, of course, patterns of behavior which are exclusively rural, as we shall see in the analysis of Capesterre, but most subcultural differences between economically subordinate and superordinate groups cut across rural-urban divisions. It is relevant to consider a folk-elite continuum independently of whether the attributes are found in the city or the village, the large town or the mountain *quartier.*

As Sidney W. Mintz indicates in a critical article on Redfield,[37] a type of society exists that is not urban and yet is not adequately described by the epithet "folk." Mintz uses the phrase "rural proletarian community" to describe it. There may be other seminal factors that produce the rural-proletarian culture, as Mintz points out, such as the influence of the previous culture of the people forming the labor force, but here he speaks of it in terms that are pertinent to this study—as a distinctive type of culture brought about by the plantation.

> Many of the features of life generally associated with "urban," "Western," or "modern" society ... are introduced through plantation organization and seem to produce particular sociocultural effects. Yet the people are not affected in terms of an "urban" or "Western" complex, but rather in terms of the impact of specific innovations.[38]

Among the characteristics Mintz lists as folk traits,[39] the following are *absent* in Martinique: preliteracy; minimal division of labor (although the proliferation of specializations is not greatly developed in Martinique); simple technology with everyone a primary producer; social organization based on kinship; uncritical and traditional behavior; tendency to regard the nonhuman world personally; sacralization of traditional objects; pervasiveness of magic, religion, and ritual; absence of economic motives that conform to all other aspects of life.

The folk traits which are *present* in the rural *communes* of Martinique are these: a high degree of cultural and genetic homogeneity; small size of the community; a high degree of functional coherence among aspects of the culture; social organization, if not based exclusively on kinship, at least more family-centered; simple technology except for work on the plantations.

Thus, even though there are few specifically traditional folk elements in Martinique, there are many traits which I shall call "nonelite," for they are found in greatest concentration among those groups that have the lowest prestige and exhibit the greatest social distance from the elite. Such nonelite characteristics as special speech, dress, and ceremonials abound. Above all, there is a distinctive kind of family organization, and the social arrangements with their attendant values which maintain the family are different.

But, again showing a squeezed continuum, these elements affect the elite more directly than in the usual Western society. For example, the *mulâtre* judge can explain the African stories which the rural lower class tell at wakes. The doctor can play African drum rhythms. Planters are more comfortable when speaking Creole. Persons of all strata tend to believe equally in séances. From *Béké* to French-trained engineer, personal testimonies to some magician's clairvoyance are given. Each person has a wider knowledge of the whole culture than he or she would possess in a large and/or industrial country. All of this reflects greater contact among the entire range of social types. Such forces create a substratum of homogeneous culture traits which underlie the differences pointed up by the stratification—a substratum of homogeneous manners, mannerisms, and tastes in food, music, and many other things.

RACE RELATIONS

Although education in Martinique creates a people like the American mobile generations who "can't go home again," Martiniquans cannot escape home physically. The island community prevents class rigidity among those ranked below the *Békés*. Moreover, relations with the *Békés*, even though most of the people are held in economic subordination, display no organized racism. Nor are there nativistic cults; the closest approach to such a development is the literary expression of a small clique[40] and their intellectual Communist followers, who aim at totally different targets from those usually found in the industrialized West. For one thing, in Martinique there is neither the "Protestant ethic" nor the bourgeois spirit that Cohen[41] finds in Jamaica. The rebels of Martinique are not familiar with all those *bêtes noirs* that have aroused the shame and contempt of the critics of the American, British, and French scenes. There is no Dos Passos, John Osborne, or Louis-Ferdinand Céline[42] among them. The people of Martinique are striving toward what the continental critics are rebelling from—those things the latter call "materialism," "rootlessness," or the "cultural mediocrity" wrought by mass democracy and industrialization.

Here in Martinique, no black Sinclair Lewis could despise the street that is his only example of freedom from physical hunger and the beginning of a hunger for knowledge—the street where the schoolteacher is man and master, where the policeman closes his eyes to the fish he weighs for tax purposes, where the mayor continues his job as barber. There are no lace curtains for rebel poets to burn to light their way to freedom. Nor is the shopkeeper despised, for she is what the poor aspire to become.

Here is *demos*, where the *mulâtre* lady kisses her maid goodbye because she is a *parent* (kinswoman), where the boss on the construction job shares a room with his worker. There is no focus for hostility among the majority of the people. The village Communist wants more work for everyone, and he is not hostile to the capitalists who provide what little work there is. Most people cannot be characterized, however, as possessing the "Protestant ethic," because there are few channels for such desires. Perhaps it is this that leads the naive observer to call the people lazy; it is rather that they are hungry for work. Anyone with a steady job is given relatively high status.

We have discussed the absence of hostility in any organized form. Nevertheless, there are certain isolated *quartiers* where hostility to the *blanc* has been organized by political leaders. We will touch on this again in discussing economic activities. Among the *mulâtres*, for the most part, the *Békés* are not enemies. To think they might be is to assume a caste system. Insofar as *mulâtres* not only have a "white bias," but identify with whites, they lack a caste-system mentality. To be colored, that is, does not make *mulâtres* feel that they belong on one side of the fence. They are as much white as black and do not want their progenitors insulted by either kind of racism. In a country where *family* is such a source of pride among the upper class, the *mulâtres* are not only the descendants of slaves, but also the scions of French nobility. At the same time, some *mulâtres* feel that the uneducated *Békés* are like the near-slaves they associate with on the most informal occasions. Nor are the people so much in awe of the whites as they were before participating in both world wars, bringing home reports of downtrodden whites as well as Negroes in the world.

What is the criticism of this life by the intellectual Communists? Sartre[43] has described the poetry of the French Negro, and the word he uses to represent it is "*négritude*," minted from the verbal treasury of the mayor of Fort-de-France, surrealist Aimé Césaire (who has recently [1957] broken with the Communist party). *Négritude* to Sartre is a "tension of the soul . . . a way of going beyond the brutal givens of experience." He calls the patience of *négritude* "the active imitation of passivity . . ."[44] The Negro is doubly victimized, says Sartre, having the white proletarian's Marxist fight and also the desire for racial equality.[45] That is why the white worker is not a poet and why the black man is the one to fight everyone's battle for liberty. This doubly damned position of the Negro is what gives all of them throughout the world a common state called *négritude*.[46] There are, he continues, only three solutions: revolt, nativism, or interiorization in poetry.[47] Such poetry he calls Orphic[48] because the descent of the Negro into himself is like Orpheus seeking what he wants in Hell. What the white poet finds after looking within touches on everything, but this colonial poetry deals only with *négritude*, using the same symbols over and over: nature (growth), sex (strength), wrath (courage). And it all offers the same geographical mystique: an imaginary Africa, then dazzling isles, then colorless Europe. The poets in this book do, as Sartre says, make a Manichean division between black and white, for the colonial Negro belongs to neither culture. And he is anti-Christian because religion "wishes to make him partake of the responsibility for a crime of which he is the victim [original sin]."[49]

However, not many in Martinique are burning with so clear and gemlike a flame, and those who are have been influenced by their image in the mirror of another world, such as Sartre's. Most people do not carry their *négritude* with them as a priori judgments of the economic facts from a distance lead certain theorists to think. One reason is that the Negro of Martinique has full legal equality with every other citizen of France.

Despite legal equality, the Negroes of Martinique are a depressed group, since most of the wealth is in the control of a dozen families of another race. Nevertheless, the Negroes are not the *pejority*, to coin a term, that they are in the United States or in South Africa. The personality of the Martinique Negro shows none of the bitterness, resignation, or insecurity characteristic of some "colonial" Negroes.

Obviously, the difference is not explained by their numerical preponderance, for such is the case in South Africa as well. But within the framework of legal equality and other factors, there is a difference that sheer numbers make, both psychologically and structurally. It is possible to conduct a normal life for days without seeing a single white person. And it is quite different for people to live in a place wondering whether they will be waited on in a restaurant than to live where they own the only restaurants. People of color will serve the whites if they come; and if the whites dine out, it must be with them.

Part of the personality difference is also attributable to the situation described by one *mulâtre* when accused of being an antiwhite racist because he subscribes to Sartre's ideas: "We didn't push the whites aside; they withdrew." And the whites have withdrawn. It is not their world now that the overwhelming numbers of colored people are no longer restricted to slave quarters, the mountains, or shantytowns. The politicians, professionals, artists, civil servants—they are people of color, not a duplicate set catering only to fellow caste members or allowed in as a concession, but generally the only ones aside from metropolitans that exist. The landed aristocracy live a hidden life, traversing roads from one plantation to another.

The *Békés* are in two senses like Adam Smith's "invisible hand," that allegedly automatic regulator of free enterprise imagined by the eighteenth-century optimist.

NOTES

[1] John Y. and Dorothy L. Keur, *Windward Children: A Study in Human Ecology of the Three Dutch Windward Islands in the Caribbean* (Assen, Netherlands: Van Gorcum, 1960) shows the Dutch West Indies to be exceptional in many of these features.

[2] Eric Williams, *The Negro in the Caribbean* (Washington, D.C.: Association in Negro Folk Education, 1942), p. 99.

[3] Eugène Revert, *La Martinique, Étude Géographique* (Paris: Nouvelles Éditions Latines, 1949), pp. 457, 460.

[4] See chapter 1 of Robert Redfield, *The Little Community* (Chicago: University of Chicago Press, 1955).

[5] Lucien Peytard, *L'Esclavage aux Antilles Françaises Avant 1789* (Paris: Librairie Hachettes, 1897), p. 7.

[6] Revert, *Martinique*, p. 235.

[7] Ibid., pp. 239–240.

[8] Peytard, *L'Esclavage aux Antilles*, p. 140.

[9] Victor Schoelcher, *Esclavage et Colonisation* (Paris: Presses Universitaires de France, 1948), p. 56.

[10] Ibid., p. 133.

[11] Between 1954 and 1961 the population increased from 261,595 to 290,000; more than 42 percent are 14 or younger.

[12] Michel Leiris, *Contacts des Civilisations en Martinique et en Guadeloupe* (Paris: UNESCO, 1955).

[13] Revert, *Martinique*, p. 471.

[14] Ibid., p. 473.

[15] Ibid.

[16] Ibid., p. 274.

[17] James G. Leyburn, *The Haitian People* (New Haven: Yale University Press, 1941).

[18] Peytard, *L'Esclavage aux Antilles*, p. 153.

[19] Père Jean Baptiste Labat, *Nouveau Voyage aux Îles de l'Amérique*, 1722 (Paris edition: Duchartre, 1931), II, p. 190.

[20] See pp. 52, 160–161, and 90, note 11.

[21] Revert, *Martinique*, p. 474.

[22] Leiris, *Contacts des Civilisations*, p. 73.

[23] Revert, *Martinique*, p. 286.

[24] Leiris estimates that in 1950 there were 20,000 hectares planted in sugar in Martinique. *Contacts des Civilisations*, p. 46.

[25] Revert, *Martinique*, p. 268.

[26] Ibid., p. 263.

[27] Michael G. Smith, *A Framework for Caribbean Studies* (Jamaica: University College of the West Indies, n.d.).

[28] Ibid., pp. 151–157.

[29] Ibid., p. 52.

[30] Ibid., p. 56.

[31] Revert, *Martinique*, p. 456.

[32] Ibid.

[33] Michael G. Smith, *Framework for Caribbean Studies*, p. 53.

[34] Fernando Henriques, *Family and Colour in Jamaica* (London: Eyre & Spottiswoode, 1953).

[35] I use the word "caste" here only in the sense that it has been used to describe Negro-white relations in the United States. See Buell G. Gallagher, "American Caste and the Negro," in A. A. Locke and B. J. Stern, eds., *When Peoples Meet* (New York: Hinds, Hayden & Eldridge, 1946).

[36] Lloyd Braithwaite, "Social Stratification in Trinidad," *Social and Economic Studies*, 2, Nos. 2 and 3 (October 1953).

[37] Sidney W. Mintz, "The Folk-Elite Continuum and the Rural Proletarian Community," *American Journal of Sociology*, 59, No. 2 (September 1953).

[38] Ibid., p. 137.

[39] Ibid.

[40] Leopold S. Sengher, *Anthologie de la Nouvelle Poésie Nègre et Malagache de la Langue Française, Précédée de "Orphée Noir," Jean-Paul Sartre* (Paris: Presses Universitaires de France, 1948).

[41] Yehudi Cohen, "The Social Organization of a Selected Community in Jamaica," *Social and Economic Studies*, 2, No. 4 (1954).

[42] In one of his most striking works, Céline describes French life in terms of his title, *Death on the Installment Plan* (Boston: Little, Brown, 1938).

[43] Sengher, *Anthologie*, Introduction.

[44] Ibid., p. xxix.

[45] Ibid., p. 40

[46] Ibid., p. 14.

[47] Ibid., p. 15.

[48] Ibid., p. 17.

[49] Ibid.

Part Two

THE COMMUNITY

THREE

The *Commune* of Capesterre

Let us look at the minimal reproduction of the cultural and social features of Martinique revealed in the sugar community of Capesterre, a larger than average *commune* of 3,082 hectares. Capesterre borders the Atlantic, and its evolution—like that of the other *communes* on the island—is different from anything in France or in any other colony.[1]

All the preemancipation *bourgs* of the island were originally port or church centers. (Capesterre belongs to the latter type.) Because of their good harbors, the west coast villages were established first. Diamant, on the southern tip of the island, was settled in the second phase and Capesterre in the third phase of expansion, which was still in the seventeenth century. Not many inhabitants lived in the early *bourgs*. Only Marin and Trinité had larger populations than plantations, and the former as late as 1764 had only ninety houses. Even the biggest *bourgs* today, like Robert and Lamentin, have only some five hundred houses.[2]

Most *bourgs* came into being only with the growth of roads and the *autobus*. Old *bourgs* like Capesterre did not begin their growth until the postemancipation exodus from the plantations. The role of the village has increased in importance with land pressure and the rise of the lower middle class. At present there are additional stimuli to its growth, such as administrative policies[3] which necessitate more government functionaries. Moreover, even without political appointments increasing numbers of people have shown a desire to be near the road and the school. Even people with land are moving to the *bourgs*, traveling as much as 5 kilometers to cultivate their fields. Another factor, according to Revert, is that improved agricultural methods throw more and more cane cutters out of work.

The east coast was occupied in 1658 by people pushed out of the northwest by land pressure. Capesterre was established as a parish only five years later, and the *bourg* is in the same place today that it was then. But the boundaries of the rural sectors of the *commune* were once much more extensive than they are now. When we give early population figures for Capesterre, then, they are for the entire east coast whose hub was the present *bourg*.

The oldest records show a population of just above 200 whites and 202 blacks. Among the former were many soldiers, for the Caribs still presented a threat. It was a preponderantly adult male population (68 males to 28 females), and a youthful one, distributed on 53 properties. Some twenty of the owners had no slaves at all, but the majority had 2 or 3, and three masters had from 10 to 16 slaves; the largest plantation had 78.

A land survey made in 1671, listing the companies and their holdings, shows that on the average the concessions extended along the shore for 100 to 200 *pas*[4] and back toward the mountains for 1,000 to 1,500 *pas*. The largest plantation had 800 *pas* of coast and grew the only sugar in the parish, producing 50,000 pounds annually. Sugar had not yet come to dominate the economy; the first plantation on the island for its exclusive growth was leased in 1639 and yielded 40 to 50 tons per hectare.[5] Like the few others, and like the many that would soon spring into being, this plantation was an autonomous unit with its own *sucrerie, moulin à boeuf*, and also its own cacao and subsistence crops. About thirty *cases* (shacks) surrounded the master's house; the arrangement can still be seen among the *gens casés*. Revert estimates that the early sugar concessions, measuring 200 to 300 by 1,000 *pas*, were occupied by some 120 slaves, among whom there were on the average 7 sick, 10 old or incapacitated, and 25 children too young to work.

In this period, the only industrial cultivation was *pétun* (tobacco), which produced all the revenue of the region. The uplands had already begun to be exploited; 12 *étages* (concessions in the hills) were planted in indigo and ginger. The population at this period was 300 people.

During the next ten years (1639–1649) the population grew to 1,360, and it was a little more than doubled within the next century. Sugar had slowly begun to dominate. In the hills it was accompanied by cacao; then after 1721 by coffee (which continued until 1931). After 1736 the plantations ceased to grow enough subsistence crops to feed the workers.[6]

There is a descriptive record of the early history of Capesterre in the journals of Père Labat,[7] who visited the district in 1694. It was here, says Labat, that the Dominicans had one of their most important settlements. They produced 12,000 pounds of sugar and had built a large church measuring 60 feet by 24 feet. Surrounding the church were the *presbytère* (priest's house), pasturage, a garden, and fifteen or twenty houses occupied by merchants, workers, and publicans.

Père Labat mentions one Claude Cocquet, *conseilleur*, secretary to the king, and captain of the *quartier*. He was the "cock of the entire east coast, rich, well-placed," born in Paris of a merchant family, and brother of a chaplain of Notre Dame. He bought his plantation, which measured 1,200 by 3,000 *pas*, and established three *sucreries* with 200 slaves. The priest was particularly impressed by the hospitality given him by this man and his young wife with thirteen children. Labat emphasizes the extravagant feasts, the creole food, the magnificent furniture.

Labat also dined with a rich wine merchant who had arrived in Martinique as an *engagé* and then married a planter's daughter who brought with her as a dowry a *sucrerie* and a cacao plantation. Of the entire east coast *quartier* Labat said, "It is undoubtedly the most beautiful, the best and most established of the island."

In 1752 Capesterre was at the height of its prosperity, peopled by 3,000 inhabitants of whom 1,000 were white. It possessed 11 *sucreries*, 192,000 *pieds* of coffee, and 73,700 *pieds* of cacao.[8] After this period, hurricanes and market depressions plus the destruction brought about by the eruption of Pelée in 1902 have steadily diminished its riches.

Like the other parishes of Martinique, Capesterre was made a *commune* in 1837. At this juncture it comprised territory that is today divided into four *communes*. The amputations occurred in 1889 and 1945.

The first rural-urban population figures in the records are for the year 1847: 442 urban and 2,601 rural. The *Annuaire* of 1877 reports 873 urban and 4,454 rural; the population virtually doubled in the *bourg* and the rural populace grew nearly as much. In 1877 we also have a breakdown by sex: 2,830 men and 2,497 women. The total population today of the four *communes* represented in the old records (between 1847 and 1877) is 8,353 (1956 census) as opposed to the 1877 total of 5,327.

In the one area that retains the name Capesterre today, the unit to which we shall limit ourselves, the population is 3,871, divided into 1,010 in the *bourg* and 2,861 dispersed. The total population of the *commune* since 1931, when there were 3,272 people, has risen as follows: 1936, 3,365; 1946, 3,522; 1954, 3,871.

The last census analysis by *commune* (1946), when the population was only 349 fewer than today, shows that there were 856 houses with 916 *ménages*, 40 fewer than in 1936. Of the population of 3,522, only 576 were urban, which means that the village section has nearly doubled in ten years. The population by age and sex in 1946 was:

Age (years)	Population
1	69
1-5	538
6-14	401 male, 371 female
15-19	169 male, 167 female
20	31 male, 31 female
21-65	808 male, 819 female
Over 65	50 male, 65 female

My personal check on the number of children up to the age of five years showed 489. (These are the children brought regularly to be weighed by the nurse, a government service.)

The other important demographic changes reflected in the

current situation are the substantial Indian population, which settled chiefly in the north, and the diminution of *Békés*, of whom fewer than two dozen, including children, remain in Capesterre.

THE "BOURG"

Most of the *bourg* is built along both sides of the coastal road. On this main street are about forty houses, among them the P.T.T. (Post Office, Telephone, and Telegraph), in which the two managers live upstairs; the old religious dormitory used as the cinema; the church, *presbytère*, and cemetery; the town hall; the school buildings; a large bar; the market square with its police station and covered booths; and the tax office. Here, too, are the largest stores and a number of small bars or rum shops.

The south side of this street cannot expand, for the *habitations* (plantations) own the land, which is planted in sugar down to the sea. The planters who own the north end of town, however, made it possible three years ago for some citizens to buy land between the sea and the road for 100,000 francs ($285) an acre. This expanding part of the *bourg* is now occupied by six relatively prosperous houses and a soccer field.

Paralleling the main street for about one-eighth of its length is another prosperous residential street with a few stores. There are two more roads in town. One bisects the highway and leads to the large sugar factory of the *habitation* at its western end and to the "hotel" on the east. The hotel is really a restaurant, bar, and public shower; no guest rooms are available without displacing the family. Perpendicular to the main route, ending in a wooded section of the *habitation* on which stands the *usine* (sugar refinery) is the Rue des Bâtards, settled in 1902, where some twenty families occupy shacks. Bordering the Rue des Bâtards and continuing one hundred yards or so into the sea is the river, where the women launder while the children play.

The most densely populated portion of the *bourg* has not yet been mentioned. It sprawls over the area of a city block on a promontory along the beach to the east of the road and north of the bridge that spans the river. Most of this district, called Bottom, is a slum with no land except the space on which the shacks are built.

But there are a number of more substantial houses in this section, too.

In every part of the *bourg* there are little *boutiques*, some performing the functions of *épicerie*, *mercerie*, and *bazar* at the same time. Some are so small as to occupy the corner of a living room; others are the entire first story of a 30-foot-long house. A few sell chiefly cotton goods: one specializes in kitchen equipment; but most sell a bit of everything. There are only two large grocery stores.

The most ubiquitous activity in Martinique is that involved with the *débit de la régie*, a location licensed to sell rum. If the count for Guadeloupe holds for Martinique, there is one for every 85 persons.[9] In 1935, 3,174 liters of alcohol were consumed in Martinique.[10] The *débit de la régie* is sometimes part of a large general food store, but more often it is the sideline of a housewife. The hotel and large bar are also, of course, *débits de la régie*; at the larger ones men can sit and order a drink; at the others, bottles are bought to be taken out.

Most of the people of the *bourg* are agricultural workers—the rural proletariat. In addition, there are many small garden plots, and hardly a living room exists without a few chickens wandering in and out. The courtyards between the more crowded houses harbor a number of animals, and nearly every household has a pig.

The "Habitations" (Plantations)

Those of the six *habitations* that do not come down to the sea start on the west side of the road. All of them extend as far as the plains permit the raising of sugar, ending at about 200 meters (some 650 feet) from shore, where the *quartiers* begin.

Each plantation has at least the vestige of an old *manse* (mansion). Even those in which people live are hardly distinguishable from the outbuildings on the estates, for few of the colonial houses and their grounds are kept up. As social centers, most *habitations* have decayed.

Only one estate in Capesterre is occupied by its owners, a group of siblings and their families. Three others are managed by one local *Béké*, who is the son-in-law of the chief stockholder of one of them. The fifth is managed by a local *Béké* for a nobleman now in France, and the sixth is owned by nonresident but local people. These few whites are the only *Békés* living in Capesterre, except for one poor relative who runs a *boutique*. With the exception of this shopkeeper, none of the *Békés* live in the *bourg*, where they go only for church and occasionally for commercial services.

The large *habitation* where the local manager of the other two lives is the one where the big factory, the *usine*, is located. Surrounding the *usine* are a score of garages, offices, machine shops, and the like. Among them are the master's house and one of equal size for the East Indians who come from British Guiana during the cane season. (Local *chimistes*, as these sugar technicians are called, do not exist.) Here, too, is the local Indians' temple. There are some half a dozen other principal houses where the executive overseers, usually mulattoes, live. The grounds are muddy paths and fields of stubble crossed by the railroad track where the open carts wheel in the cane from the fields. They directly join the quarters of the *gens casés* who live in two long, one-story buildings with forty and twenty rooms, respectively. These rooms face an alley that separates them from the row of cook rooms.

On most of the other *habitations*, instead of living in these "slave rows," the landless laborers are differently housed. On one they have straw houses in the center of little plots of land far in the hills, where they live in a similar manner to those who dwell in the landowning *quartiers* well back in the *mornes* (low hills). On others they have small settlements of single houses placed in the middle of the plantation. Sometimes they have half-acre gardens and a few animals. From time to time they have been deprived of their tiny plots as a goad to make them work. Occasionally, *habitations* have several clusters of *gens casés* settlements. The material conditions of living vary from whole families living in a single room without a floor to two-room wooden dwellings. On one *habitation* the *gens casés* lived in some of the rooms of the old *manse*.

One of the *gens casés* settlements, far from the *bourg*, has its own *épicerie*, making the group a more solidary community. It is not a company store. This infamous institution, as well as the practice of paying salaries in coins good only in the *boutique*, were abolished by the Code du Travail of 1913. These *gens casés* even own their own minuscule plots through squatters' rights.

THE "QUARTIERS"

Although the French word "*quartier*" means any kind of village or city district or quarter—including residential parts of a city—in most Martinique *communes*, as in Capesterre, the *quartier* is synonymous with the neighborhood of rural landowners. Landowners are proud people, but their economic life in most instances is little different from that of *gens casés*. Despite their own crops, landowners are dependent on the plantation for what is nearly their only cash income. There is scarcely a family in Capesterre's *quartiers* that does not have men and women who either cut or tie cane during the short harvest season. The reason for this is that in most cases there is not enough land for a family to own more than one to five acres at present.

Under French law, legitimate and illegitimate children inherit virtually equal shares of all possessions, provided the latter are recognized.[11] A poor man's property is quickly dissipated even after one generation. Whether a man comes from a preemancipation *quartier* where his ancestors once owned forty acres, or whether he has come into possession of his land within the last ten years when a plantation was sold, he owns an equally small plot. It is customary for children not to quarrel over the inheritance, and when it becomes too small for use the land may be abandoned by all of them, or only one heir may remain. The decision as to who will be this one heir is not patterned in any definite way. It usually happens that the daughters are the ones to leave when they find a mate. Those who have good opportunities through education or learning a trade also leave willingly. Technically, any heir can claim his share of the produce or land at any time, but the people are pragmatic: zero divided by twelve is still zero.

As we have seen, the land affords no means of entering the upper class, and the one who abandons the land may or may not be less fortunate than the one who stays. On the other hand, land is considered a good capital investment by the richer residents of the *bourg*.

Occupying neither the extreme *fonds* (ravines) nor the humid mountaintops, the four *quartiers* of Capesterre extend in the low mountains as far up as 450 meters (about 1,450 feet). The tendency to maximum dispersal over large areas, which is typical of the south, is not found in the north of the island. "Not even an embryonic agglomeration can be found," says Revert, between Rivière Pilote and Vauclin,[12] but the topography in the north does not allow for this settlement pattern. In both places, however, the house is placed in the middle of the field. Delawarde[13] describes choices regarding such matters as a reaction to the crowded slave quarters—the *Martiniquaises* wish to be close enough to one another to hear a shout but far enough away for privacy. Revert points out that a desire for independence, even today, often prompts people to choose work at a distant *usine* rather than at the one bordering their *quartier*. At Petit Bourg, for example, there is a migratory population that moves in only for the season. On the other hand, one informant attributed such traveling simply to feelings of loyalty to a particular boss. In Capesterre, however, workers in the *usine* and its plantation are, with very few exceptions, residents of the *commune*.

The houses, about eighty per *quartier*, although located in the center of the fields rather than in rows along a road, resemble a suburban layout. One reason is that between the road and the ravine, between the road and the plantation or whatever boundary exists, there is usually no space for more than a single plot. Today people consider the parcels of land on the road the most desirable, and it is the squatters or sharecroppers who tend to inhabit the distant fields behind the roads. Only they enjoy the isolation considered a symbol of independence in early days.

We have already described in general the determinants of land tenure and settlement which operated in peopling the *quartiers*. In Capesterre we have examples of several methods. The oldest of the four *quartiers* dates back to the eighteenth century, a hundred years before emancipation. Many people there are the heirs of a famous man, and for that reason we shall give it the fictitious name of Voltaire. The second oldest *quartier* was peopled, like most on the island, at emancipation in 1848, and shall be called Morne Liberté. Hauteur Pelée, which I have named after the volcano that accounted for the circumstances of its origin, has only been occupied by the current families of landowners since 1902, the year of the eruption. The last *quartier* will be identified as Fond d'Espoir. Its inhabitants rented their land until 1947, when they won a long battle for the privilege of buying it. The origins of *quartiers* are often indicated in the choice of names—Fond Gens Libres, Fond Mulâtre, Morne d'Afrique—and in choosing fictitious names I have followed suit.

Voltaire   Around 1765, the *étages* of the northern *quartiers* were settled in one-acre plots by Europeans.[14] Not long afterward, and continuing into the nineteenth century, planters acting in groups bought much of this land for their illegitimate children. The settlements of freeborn mulattoes interbred with the colonists and with one another, establishing communities composed of persons who had never experienced slavery. Voltaire is the only such community in Capesterre that has survived, on the whole, as such. Although some families have entered over the years who remember slavery and who bought their land, most of the families cannot name the particular ancestor who bought the land. None of them can report any original *Béké* progenitors.

With such a past, there are differences between Voltaire and the more recently established *quartiers*. There is a larger proportion of light mulattoes among the residents, some of them phenotypically Caucasoid, who are described as "*plus aristocrats.*" Psychic tensions arise in these households that are not so often experienced by the people of the other *quartiers*; for example, a lone dark child in a family is rejected. Moreover, many of these people feel association-ally cut off from their less aristocratic neighbors. They do not attend the community functions, disdaining the blacks in their midst, even though they are usually no richer or better educated than the blacks. Both men and women of this kind are doomed to bachelorhood or spinsterhood because they can find no equals among potential mates. There are, in Voltaire, a greater number of relatively good old houses, whose owners are almost isolated; for many, there are no direct heirs.

Another difference between Voltaire and the other *quartiers* is that more of its residents are independent of the *habitation*—steadily employed artisans or owners of prosperous *débits de la régie*. But the majority are victims of the land fragmentation that occurs through the generations regardless of the more auspicious beginnings of the community, and the owners of the small plots, despite their higher expectations and ambitions, must work as cane cutters for the plantation.

Morne Liberté   Of the sixty houses in this emancipation *quartier*, most trace their ancestry back four generations to a white man who married a woman of color and left his six children with adequate little farms. Here, too, some people have achieved freedom from the plantation, but they are poorer on the whole than those of Voltaire. In contrast to the other *quartiers*, more people here are engaged in *colonage* (sharecropping). The form it tends to take in Capesterre attaches to the *habitation*, and at the same time the planter gets his forests cleared. (Once his land is cleared, however, the planter is likely to turn it to grazing.) In such arrangements, the tenant usually keeps two-thirds of the produce.

There are also some dozen parcels of land in Liberté on which no one lives. Some of these are worked for the colored owner by people on a sharecropping basis; most of these cultivators keep only half the yield, for certain provisions are given to them. Others hire people to work the land, which they own as an investment, for they either live in other *quartiers* or they have emigrated from the country. These parcels of land on which no owner lives result from decisions made by the heirs, who at times find it impossible to continue occupying the land without depriving certain claimants. Occasionally a man inherits land from his mother as well as from his father and can work only one plot, selling his share in the other to half-siblings. Ideally, a man remains on his father's property.

Hauteur Pelée   The largest and most distant *quartier* is Hauteur Pelée. So long is the walk to the *bourg* that it has its own school for the first few grades. Most of the people here are descended from one family who settled at the time of the eruption of the volcano in 1902. They are considered "*plus sauvages*" than the residents of the above two settlements, and they in turn feel superior to those of the *quartier* where the people have most recently acquired their land.

Hauteur Pelée is the most solidary of the *quartiers*. Its residents come into town infrequently, and they are more hostile to the *Békés* as a group than others. Their activities during strikes have earned them a reputation that inspires fear in most of the townspeople, some of whom say they would not walk alone in the district. A white manager was recently murdered in this *quartier*, but hostility is generally channeled into political participation in their Communist cell. Most of the people think the murder was committed by a hothead who did not express a widespread wish, and they regret its occurrence, particularly since they all say that the victim was a "good" man. The culprit was never arrested.

Hauteur Pelée is distinguished as the location of the *savane*, which is the pasturage for all cattle in the *commune*. Two of the five owners of this large tract of land are local residents. The remainder are prosperous villagers who hire local residents to tend to their interests or who visit on Sundays. Many *petits propriétaires* from other *quartiers* pay to keep a cow there, and they travel as often as necessary to take care of it.

Fond d'Espoir   Since Fond d'Espoir is the *quartier* I selected as a point of concentration, I shall describe the land tenure in greater detail. Most of the property that now constitutes the *quartier* belonged to one *habitation*, a sugar plantation of 31 hectares, 7 *ares*, and 80 *centiares* (317,080 *mètres carrés* or square meters). In 1902 the lava from Mont Pelée disturbed the water supply in such a way that the successful exploitation of sugar became impossible. The last heir began renting the property to the *gens casés* who had been there for generations. He operated through a sublessor whom I shall call M. Blanc, for he was the white ancestor of the most numerous family there today.

M. Blanc married a mulatto, and after his death the property was put up for sale by the original owner. At this juncture M. Blanc's mulatto wife tried to buy the *habitation*. She wanted to continue renting to the people. But the Communist mayor sided with the people who felt they should not have to pay rent on the land, thereby winning for his party their undying support. He managed to prevent the sale of the *habitation* to anyone who would continue the "exploitation," and saw to it that the people received title.

To the former *gens casés* the prospect of owning their own property was a great step forward. The residents were able through cooperative activity to make a down payment of 125,000 francs, each household head contributing what he or she could to this deposit. The total value was 1,860,000 francs ($5,314), and most of the people had two years in which to pay 45,000 francs (about $127). In 1958 the value of this land was four times that of 1947.

The modal holding is only 45 *ares* per household, almost half a hectare, or about 1 acre. Such lots were bought in 1947 for 6 francs a square meter. Even if able to afford it, no one was permitted to purchase more at the time, although some property has changed hands since, permitting a few to own several lots. In addition to the down payment of 5,000 francs, the person who bought a plot had to pay three times that amount for interest and a title to the property. The total cost of 45 *ares*, then, was 27,000 francs for the land and nearly half again as much for the title, *plan* (a formal blueprint or deed that assesses the property), interest, and the like (about $130 at current rates).

But not all of what is today the Quartier Fond d'Espoir belonged to the plantation. Parts of another plantation which border the property to the south were sold to various "good workers" as a reward for their loyalty. These plots were bought at different times, some about fifteen years ago. There are in addition some ten families who own through inheritance of long standing. The range of tenure is from squatter to the possession of 5 hectares. There are three large owners.

One widow has occupied her house on its present site for sixty years, originally having rented it from a plantation executive who had bought it from his *patron*. Then one of the present residents bought it and allows her to continue living there because she is so poor, an example of friends rather than kin who help people. There are also a few squatters on *habitation* property.

One man bought his land in 1930 from a mulatto relative who was the offspring of a woman whose white *concubin* had given her the property, still a frequent manner of acquiring land throughout Martinique.

RURAL HOUSE TYPES

There are four general types of housing: (1) concrete block, cement, or stucco for the most desirable; (2) wood or stone for the substantial; (3) straw or woven fronds bound by mud or dung for the poor; and (4) a *chaumière* of bamboo for the very poorest. There are few of the woven kind in the north. None of the houses uses glass, for shutters are considered sufficient; a kind of Venetian blind is used in the rich houses. Roofs on the simplest dwellings are made of straw, cane leaves, or corrugated iron (*tôle ondulée*) when the owner can afford it. Tile and slate are the best materials. Many houses are mixtures of several types, a common house being wood with a concrete base reaching up a few feet around the house. Floors vary from mud through wooden planks or cement to tile on the best.

With the exception of some very new buildings—the best houses, the schools, the *mairie* (town hall), the richest bars and stores—the buildings are unpainted, the wood has rotted, and the whole impression is one of a ghost town. Often the houses of the "*aisés*" (well-off) are also unpainted. The interiors are poorly slapped-up boards that separate rooms, although in some houses paneling is used. Even cement interiors are usually unpainted, and even when electricity is present, rarely is there anything but un-covered wiring and bare bulbs. Electricity does not extend beyond the *bourg*, and only a few there can afford it.

The "rich" have a miscellaneous collection of straight-back chairs placed against the wall or around an old table; a sideboard with a marble top and closed storage space; a large electric clock in a varnished wooden case; and an elaborate radio. If there is a refrigerator it is usually in this living-dining room. The wall decora-tions are religious pictures, calendars, snapshots, diplomas. The poor paper their walls with old newspapers. An iron or wooden bed with a homemade mattress is commonly found. No closet space is ever built into a house; the rafters are used for storage. Rare is the desire for display, and when it occurs, it is in the form of garish pictures, plaster dogs, metal animal sculptures, and embroidered satin squares. Upholstered furniture is hardly ever present.

From the poorest to the richest house there is a remarkable uniformity of taste in furniture arrangement and serving etiquette. A table in the center of the room surrounded by chairs is the rule. The floor plan ranges from a one-room *case* with a curtain partitioning off the parents' sleeping quarters to a central room with bedrooms in the back or upstairs. The kitchen is usually a separate building. In the simple houses the children sleep on the floor protected from the dampness by rags. The children eat standing, using metal dishes, and there is no regular mealtime for them. The man is usually served by the woman alone, who does not sit with him or with guests, although these customs vary with status, the family meal occurring only among those who are the most acculturated to elite patterns. Even then, the family will often not eat together at the table because it is easier for a woman to serve standing.

Although the straw house (*paillotte*) is comfortable and healthful, everyone's ambition is to own a more substantial one. The cost of even this simplest house is often so great that the young people remain at home. The widowed squatter mentioned earlier paid $52 for her house (18,500 francs), a feat which took years, adding an improvement here and there. The planks for flooring cost 400 francs each, and on this alone she spent 3,500 francs ($10). Her straw roof, which leaks on her good old creole clothes, cost 2,500 francs ($7). The carpenter charged 4,000 francs ($12).

The widow's house is unusually poor and small, consisting of one room with a curtain between the bed and the rest, a kitchen across the path. A better one is a two-room straw house belonging to a couple. Each room is about 10 feet square, and the house is not called a *paillotte*, but a *tôle*, because of the corrugated iron roof, whose overhang makes it unnecessary to put shutters on the one window. The plan is a living room and bedroom side by side, each with a door. The kitchen is some 10 yards from the house, but an attached storage and serving pantry of bamboo and a bamboo-covered patio stand at the front. This house, the walls of which are covered with newspapers for decoration as well as to prevent leakage, was built at a cost of 61,500 francs ($175), although its value is more because of the work done by the owners and friends. From three to six friends came each Sunday for several weeks, and they had to be supplied with rum. The carpenter was furnished with a dinner in addition to his 15,000 francs ($42) in wages. The table on page 88 is an estimate of expenses, not counting the informal aspects. They built a bamboo porch, kitchen, and pantry themselves, finding the materials in the forest.

This couple would like to build a cement house, which would cost 200,000 francs ($570). The method would be to build it in pieces over many months or even years, surrounding the existing structure, for then property taxes can be escaped. They are not paid if construction is considered merely a series of improvements on an existing home.

Amount paid (francs)°	Materials and services
9,000	Floors
10,000	Woodwork
7,500	*Paille* (75 packets at 100 francs a packet. They did own labor)
15,000	Carpenter
20,000	Tôle
61,500	

°The current (1958) rate of exchange was 350 francs to the dollar.

A wooden house with one cement wall at a slight distance to one side is a familiar sight. The cement house is much less comfortable, hotter than the neatly bundled straw, and the unpainted cement is aesthetically less pleasing to many people than natural straw. But many reasons are given for wanting a cement house. Protection from wind and fire is one, although there is little wind. Then there is the feeling that a straw house must be guarded from enemies who can easily break in or set fire to it, so that the occupant is not free to spend a night out. Also, with a straw house extensive repairs must be made each year, and people with cement houses will not help, because now they will not need help in return. Finally, a *paillotte* is not considered presentable for bringing friends home.

Straw versus cement, however, is not always an indication of rank, for often cement is only a product of age, to which no particular respect is due: it is later in life that certain people can sometimes afford the cement. Some relatively young people, on the other hand, have cement houses if they are "fortunate enough" to have many children; for it is children that have brought wealth since the introduction of the *allocation familiale*, which enables families to receive relatively large sums of money in one lump. People can also have a good house because they prefer to spend their money this way instead of on a marriage *fête*. Choice depends on many factors.

Some people keep their *paillotte*, even with a *tôle* roof, because it is not a taxable possession. The couple with the *tôle* described earlier pay only 2,500 francs a year (about $8) in taxes because of all their possessions, not because of their house. Another motive for building bit by bit around a house is that a *plan*, which costs 15,000 francs, is not necessary. It is not that this price is excessive, but that if it is not paid immediately the interest (18 percent a day) mounts until the *plan* costs more than the property. ("*La France est trop voleur* [*sic*]," meaning "France is too greedy.") Moreover if a *plan* exists, taxes are based on it, whereas if the building is considered a series of repairs there is no record of what taxes should be paid. As a result, owners declare the price paid for property to be less than half what it is before the notary, and they have a private agreement with the person with whom they do business. One can, of course, do such business only "*avec les gens sérieux.*"

When a cement house that costs 200,000 francs ($570) is discussed, it is the simple, small, two-room house in the *quartier* that is meant. The standard is quite different for cement houses of two stories with tile floors (in this *commune* they appear only in the *bourg*); the cost is 2,000,000 francs ($5,700) for a dwelling 6 meters by 4 meters. A stone house can be equally expensive, depending on whether stones are readily available in the area. Finally, a *paille* house with a tile roof can cost as much as 150,000 francs ($430), but as we have seen, there is greater prestige in owning a poor cement house than a good *paille*.

NOTES

[1] Eugène Revert, *La Martinique, Étude Géographique* (Paris: Nouvelles Éditions Latines, 1949), p. 271.

[2] Ibid., p. 300.

[3] Ibid., p. 297.

[4] One *pas* equals 50 centimeters.

[5] Revert, *Martinique*, p. 259.

[6] *Ibid.*, p. 317.

[7] Père Jean Baptiste Labat, *Nouveau Voyage aux Îles de l'Amérique*, 1722 (Paris edition: Duchartre, 1931), II.

[8] A *pied* is the amount of land occupied by one plant of any crop.

[9] Michel Leiris, *Contacts des Civilisations en Martinique et en Guadeloupe* (Paris: UNESCO, 1955), p. 38.

[10] R. P. Delawarde, *La Vie Paysanne à la Martinique* (Fort-de-France, Martinique, 1937), p. 18.

[11] Michael M. Horowitz states that recognized children "have fractional shares, the amount depending on the number of legitimate children." *Morne-Paysan: Peasant Village in Martinique* (New York: Holt, Rinehart & Winston, 1967), pp. 29–30.

[12] Revert, *Martinique*, p. 292.

[13] Delawarde, *La Vie Paysanne.*

[14] Ibid., p. 54.

FOUR

Association and Stratification

Let us now examine facets of the life that goes on within the setting just described. Social ranking, as I shall describe it for the *commune*, involves association patterns; the people's expressed, subjective stereotypes; attitudes of deference; and economic and occupational differences. To make this social stratification clearer, I shall first give an impressionistic description of the rhythms of life—individual, collective, daily, occasional, and annual. Throughout, I all but exclude the whites, for although a few live in Capesterre, none participates personally in the community except as the "invisible hand."

Rhythms of Life

It is five o'clock in the morning and still dark and cold. In the *bourg* the only people about are those who are involved with the *autobus*, the first one to leave. Some are traveling for a day of errands in the city four hours away. Some are sending garden vegetables to relatives. In the *quartier* the *petits cultivateurs* have been up for an hour if they have a cow to take to another pasture or a water barrel to repair before setting out on a two-hour walk to the *habitation*, cutlass in hand. Those without work are awake out of habit.

Between 5:30 and 6:00 A.M. it is light enough to read the notice on the door of the big house on the main street announcing the funeral of the assistant councilor. The street lights remain on. In the harvest season the *gens casés* have begun cutting the cane and binding it in bundles. They are soon joined by the workers who come from a distance, for no one wants to work in the heat of the day. The women bind their legs with rags to reduce the number of wounds suffered from the jagged cane stalks. The overseers walk their horses slowly through the fields.

Girls and maids who do not empty their slops at night are walking toward the open gutters or the river with pails on their heads. West Indian brooms (a bamboo stick shredded at one end) stir the dust in the *boutiques*, some of which, like the bars, begin to open. The church doors are ajar, but no one has come yet. The bread truck starts with its daily load for the country, and the road workers have been picked up in a truck to go to the adjacent *bourg*.

Cascading down the steep bluff by the sea is the fresh underground spring where the men have begun to shower. A few houses have a private outdoor *douche*. The men and boys walk down the hilly dirt road carrying towels and toothbrushes and stand naked on the rocky gray beach where the fishermen's canoes lie covered with palm fronds against the rain. The women will bathe before noon in their bathing suits. In the *quartier*, one must walk half an hour to the river to wash or else make do with the rain barrel. The policeman's stall in the market opens; he prepares the day's tax accounts. And two *marchandes* (market women) stride like ballet dancers across the sugar plain with 20-kilo baskets of *légumes* on their heads.[1] Shut tight against the night air are the shutters of the tropical sleepers. Night air brings sickness, and, as in Wales, there are things that go "bump" in the night.

Now everyone is awake. It is 6:30, and five people have emerged to attend the early weekday mass; such piety is rare. The dry goods stores are not yet open, and still there is the line of men and boys going to shower, some coming on bicycles. The crowd has gathered to launch the fishing canoes. A boy and a girl push through them with trays of dirty pots on their heads to wash in a little mud pool where they stand at the same time. They are followed by three little children eating their breakfast of large hunks of bread.

The roads are dotted with children going to school. Their mothers, the morning meal well over, are sweeping and scrubbing.

Older girls are making a game of the cleaning, skating along the slippery floors on wet rags. Hotter than the sun are the little bamboo kitchens where the *pâtisserie* women are baking their coconut *tartines*. The women of the *bourg* are gathered in the stores exchanging greetings, telling who beat whom during the night, who is still sick and must have a visit paid. The workless men are leaning against the wall of the cinema or sitting with their hats pushed over their faces.

Shopping done, everyone returns home to prepare the midday meal. Those without women go to the hotel to eat, or lacking the money, to drink away the afternoon. When the drinking money goes, they too join the loungers at the cinema or on the bridge, where they can watch the women spreading out the linens on the river stones and chasing away the children who in their fishing zeal might splash the clothes.

The whole village is at rest after a day's work, for life stops in the full sun and does not resume until evening, although around three o'clock the town hall gets busy again; for white-collar workers, work is never done. Many seamstresses are also active, and shops are open in case someone should enter. Around four, when the fishing boats unload, there is time for visiting again on the market square, at the beach. And the early bus has returned, depositing travelers and the mail. People can go to the P.T.T. for a bit of conversation. In the *quartiers*, mail will not be delivered until the following dawn, when the postmen arrive by bicycle or car.

The *gens casés* have left the bridge to play volleyball at the plantation. Gambling usually waits for darkness. Schoolboys go to the soccer field to prepare to meet visiting teams that occasionally come. None of them uses shoes. A young *instituteur* (teacher) whizzes by on his "*moto*," a motorbike that is the envy of all the small boys. Sometimes at this hour there will be a religious procession that passes by shops decked out in crepe paper. The women and children march behind the priest to a given point and back again.

A man really wakes up at six o'clock in the evening, when he meets his friends at the big bar or at the hotel. He talks until dinnertime, for several hours. When he returns home, his family has already eaten, and after a meal alone he goes to bed.

On special nights, if a person has prestige he or she will go to a ball, a dance to which invitations have been issued. It may take place in a larger nearby *bourg*. For most people, however, there will be no dancing until someone gives a marriage *fête* or unless it is the annual feast of the patron saint of the *commune* or the special *fête* given in each *quartier* once a year. And, of course, there is the great *Carnaval* with masked and costumed paraders at the Lenten season. On such nights as these, as when there is a *veillée* (wake) for the death of a *petit propriétaire* or one of the *gens casés*, the merriment sometimes goes on till dawn.

At the *fêtes* there is a merry-go-round propelled by little boys running in circles under the platform. Other attractions are drinking booths set up in the market square or along the *quartier* road, gambling games, races, and contests like climbing a greased pole for a bottle of champagne. All this is for the men. Proper girls often will not deign even to watch such "dull" events, and of course they can no more be seen in a drinking booth with a man than at a bar or walking out with a man to whom they are not engaged. But sometimes they will go on such occasions, properly chaperoned, to a restaurant where drinks are served, and these girls do go to the dances. Even at the *fêtes* there are balls where the invitations are exclusive and expensive—700 francs for men and 500 for women. The 300-franc dances, which anyone can attend, are too rowdy for any but *les poules* (chickens; i.e., fast women). A woman can go to an exclusive dance with members of her family, with respectable couples, or in a relatively large group of women. At the end of each dance the men go to one end of the room, the women elsewhere. Usually, a restaurant gives the dance for the purpose of making money. Tables are set up where people sit and drink, again in chaperoned or large groupings.

If a girl rebels against such propriety, she will be relegated to the dances for *les poules*; and if a respectable man ever courts her, he will be informed that "she is no better than she should be." After this, she might as well emigrate to Fort-de-France, for she will feel that there is no such thing in Martinique as friendship, that *les noirs* are jealous of her and have "long tongues." A girl like this may redeem herself if the fruit of her promiscuity is surprisingly light-skinned.

Some girls who disapprove of the regulations nevertheless adhere to them even more strongly, their only thought being to leave the *commune*, perhaps for a life in France; or to remain so above the crowd, especially if they are pretty and educated, that there is a chance for an urban marriage to free them. Very few girls are so hopeful. The women do not criticize them, but the men feel they are "*stupides*," with the pretensions of an aristocrat. Most are busy all day sewing, cleaning, working, and they are content to confine their outings to weddings and baptisms, church on Sunday, an occasional family picnic.

Even married men and women seldom go out in public together except to a dance, to pay family calls, to go to the city. In the rural setting, a couple does not often pay a social call together, even the people who are most acculturated to elite standards, unless it is a sick call or a condolence visit.

Men, however, call on one another frequently. In some houses the wife of the host neither serves the drinks nor even makes an appearance. If it is a one-room house, she will busy herself with some chore. If a woman pays a visit to another, no drinks are served except among the acculturated. This type of behavior decreases directly with higher status and varies somewhat with personality as well. When the women, for whatever reason, participate in the conversation, such as during my visits as a stranger, they do so as equals. But at one point when there was doubt about the wisdom of being friendly to an American in a Communist *quartier* at the time of a strike, women would not talk to me until their husbands (nonlegal as well as legal) returned.

One reason given by a schoolteacher for the fact that his wife never paid any visits is that he would not tolerate it: "*Les hommes n'aiment guère sortir les femmes*" (Men scarcely ever like their wives to go out). Women keep their friends for life, he believes, but do not have time to spend with them if they are good mothers and wives. Furthermore, the man is boss, and a jealous one. Moreover, he needs "*changements*." His visits are not criticized, even if an amorous nature is suspected, because the woman does not usually criticize such behavior. If the woman should object, and if the man is "hardhearted," he might leave her. Or he might make his sex life more discreet and more casual so that it will not be noticed.

At the *veillée* (wake) perhaps a hundred men, women, and children gather around a man who acts as mime and storyteller. For hours he recites, chants, gesticulates, with the rhythmic cries of the spectators punctuating the words. "Cric! Crac!" he intones, which is echoed by a chorus of similar cries. A few members of the audience answer his remarks like straight men; the rest respond with peals of laughter at every well-known punch line. The raconteur's voice is pitched at a shout; the content of his stories, acts, and songs resembles a burlesque show. He uses a stick as a penis which has orgasms and urinates, as a club for beating a fictitious victim who is not yet dead, as a baton to produce metamorphoses. The tales involve werewolves, witches, princesses, and manioc farmers along with the Compère Lapin (Br'er Rabbit) variety of characters. It is with impatience that many of the spectators pay their respects to the dead, who is laid out on the bed with a cup of water and a sprig to sprinkle him with on one side and a votary candle on the other.

The *veillée*, with its counterpoint of *contes* (stories) and *chants* blended with Christian hymns sung by the bereaved (who do not participate in the festive part of the occasion), is nearly the only vestige of African syncretism left in Martinique. A few Africanisms are found in occasional country dances and a ritualized fight between men at the *fêtes*, a fight to the beat of bongo drums. Birth takes place in the hospitals accompanied by no non-Western rituals, and funerals of the rural elite are purely Western.

The cinema is open two nights a week, but it is not very popular except among young boys, who go to talk and run around the benches. A few teachers, chaperoned girls, and single men sit in the balcony and try to hear over the constant chatter, the running about, and the whistling below where the children are loosed. Every few minutes a red "SILENCE" sign is flashed on the screen to little avail. The films are usually American, German, or Spanish of ripe antiquity with French voices dubbed in. Few know that it is not Frenchmen on the screen. Much of the audience have difficulty with anything but Creole and understand little of what they hear. It matters little, for the subjects of most of the films are far removed from any experience meaningful to the audience. The assumptions of *You Can't Take It With You*, for example, are pure gibberish to them. As for stories of orphans who long for and uphold the values of the Western family, or tales of the ravages of divorce—these are as meaningless as the "love stuff" in the period pieces of gallants singing under balconies. Most films find no counterpart whatsoever in the courtship or mating patterns of the rural people, and only the most educated or traveled make any sense of them at all.

Cowboy movies, on the other hand, engender real enthusiasm, and they live on in the play and dreams of young boys, as they do in the United States. Hardly ever will a film provoke any discussion at all except among the educated. But no matter what the film, everyone will say that it was "*joli*."

"Allocation Familiale"

Although Capesterre, the location of one of the thirteen sugar factories, is chiefly agricultural, a community where the rich *commerçants* try to invest their capital in as much land as they can buy, not a single family depends exclusively on its own land for all its income. But just as there is no peasant population, so too is there only a small exclusively proletarian population. The majority of people both own some land and work for the *habitation*. A larger proportion of people might be free of the plantation if it were not for the artificial economic factor of the *allocation familiale*, or family allotment. It is advantageous to work for wages even if it is not necessary, for the insurance system called the *allocation familiale* pays a family only if one of its members works for wages. Because of its influence on the occupational distribution and the social ranking as it cuts across occupational divisions, I shall discuss this insurance system at the outset.

The *allocation* is a method of furnishing family assistance on a double basis: the number of children in a family and the number of days that one member of the family has worked for wages. In France there is no income tax deduction for dependents; instead, they have had the *allocation* since 1932. The difference between the application of the law in Martinique and in the mother country is that in the latter agricultural workers do not benefit, presumably because rural children are an addition to the work force rather than a financial liability. The government's policy admittedly aims at promoting population growth in war-torn Europe. But although population growth is the last thing that needs stimulation in Martinique from any economic point of view, no political party on the island would agree. The Communists, for example, believe that what they need is industrialization sufficient to support their population, not a reduction in the numbers, any demand for which they consider a way of masking the real problems. And the "capitalists" think that the more people there are the greater the need for building schools, roads, hospitals, and the like. The poor *petits propriétaires* in the *quartiers* approve of the system as their only hope of getting lump sums of money. Furthermore, the reward for large numbers of children articulates with previous values of a similar nature.

Since 1944 France has legislated that the worker must contribute toward this insurance, but in Martinique such a rule does not apply. The family in Martinique is larger than in France, over three children per woman (5 in Capesterre) as opposed to two on the Continent, so government expense is greater. But it is an efficient way of tying workers to the plantation, for such labor is the best source of wages since money earned through self-employment is not counted toward insurance benefits (although some nonsalaried persons receive what is called *assistance à la famille*).

Under the provisions of the *allocation*, an adult collects 53 francs (about 15 cents) for each child considered his or hers for every day the adult has worked for wages, until the child is sixteen years old.

The *usine* worker is considered an agricultural laborer. Since no self-employed individual—professional, peasant, fisherman, seamstress—can benefit from the system, many people who could otherwise be independent find it expedient to cut cane, even though such menial work lowers their prestige.

The *locataire*, the individual who collects the money on the basis of his or her days of work, is not determined on the basis of any specific relationship to the children. Parent, distant relative, friend—anyone responsible for raising the child can collect; nor does legitimacy enter the question. An otherwise independent, self-employed person will, then, seek a wage-earner's job, and the plantation is where he or she will usually find it, for the degree of education is too low for many white-collar jobs. Nevertheless, there are more applicants than jobs.

OCCUPATIONAL AND
FINANCIAL DISTRIBUTION

Not only does almost every household within itself represent a diversity of occupations, but most individuals do several kinds of work. The daughter of the mayor may be a *couturière* and sell school supplies, his son an electrician and barber—all living in the same house. A woman may be a teacher, her husband an entrepreneur. The financial hierarchy, then, cannot be seen by dividing the households into occupational categories. Among the 800-odd households in the *commune*, the largest single unequivocal category is that of combination *propriétaire*-plantation worker, and some of these are as poor as the landless day laborer (*journalier*). Despite such cross-cutting and overlapping, the most meaningful tabulation of the *commune* can be made by dividing the households (in round numbers) into the following mixed categories:

> 5 rich (*bourg* and *quartier*)
> 60 *aisés* (*bourg, quartier,* and *habitation*)
> 300 *petits propriétaires*
> 50 fishermen (*bourg*)
> 250 *gens casés* (*habitation*)
> 150 *journaliers* (*bourg*)

Those who own land but combine their farming with large-scale commerce would be in the category of rich or *aisé* (well-off). Some members of about twenty-five families are successful *commerçants* or entrepreneurs, whether they own land or not, and these people are either rich or well off. I am not including among them the little shopkeepers who may sell a few dry goods or an occasional bottle of rum. An entrepreneur is a well-off, self-employed man who is occupied other than as shopkeeper or restaurateur. He may own an automobile or a busline, or he can be a building contractor or own a bakery. The *commerçant* owns a shop, a *débit*, a *pension*, a restaurant, or a hotel.

The vast majority of the *aisés* live in the *bourg*. Among them, in addition to *commerçants* and entrepreneurs, are the steadily employed plantation executives, full-time artisans, and *fonctionnaires*. The last include municipal employees such as teachers, policemen, nurses, and the white-collar personnel of the government offices (tax bureaus, town hall, P.T.T.). There are at present only two fully professional men resident in Capesterre.

Most of the *petits propriétaires* together with the luckier fishermen, poor artisans, and *commerçants* form a middle financial level between the two top categories and *les pauvres*. These poorest, the majority, are squatters, destitute old people, *gens casés*, or landless townspeople (*journaliers*) who might find an occasional day's work as servants or laborers for the plantation. The *journalier* may or may not have less in worldly goods and security than one of the *gens casés*.

The actual incomes and consumption patterns as well as the activities involved in these ways of life will be set forth in chapter five.

EXPRESSIONS OF STATUS DIFFERENCES

When trying to spell out the criteria of status equality or to correlate it with association patterns, several factors should be noted. First, there is little association of any kind in public between the sexes. Even conjugal pairs rarely visit anyone except relatives. Men can form cliques at the bar, but women have no occasions for contact with one another except the most casual interaction in the course of doing their daily chores. They meet at the river while doing laundry or they meet while shopping. Young women as a rule have few close friends unless some external factor, such as a mother's taking in a neighbor's daughter as an apprentice to learn dressmaking, pushes them together.

Outside the elite, urban life there are no formal clubs or lodges that are based on status. The church conducts no functions other than religious processions, and membership in a church organization simply involves taking Communion on prescribed days. Participation in patron-saint *fêtes* is based on territoriality alone, as are the *quartier fêtes*. Only at private parties is status a factor in group membership, but such groups are temporary and shifting.

The one local society, although open to all and therefore not a means of expressing status differences, does give its officers an avenue for leadership. This group—the Société Amicale—is a member of the Fédération Mutualiste de la Martinique, an institution for saving money for emergencies. It is a kind of sick-benefit and burial society. The entrance fee, payable upon reaching the age of fifteen, is 700 francs; monthly dues are 100 francs. Benefits can be received at any time after three months' membership unless payments have been four months in arrears. For sickness the benefits are 500 francs a week for six weeks. The society also pays half of the cost of medical prescriptions up to 5,000 francs, 600 francs for pregnancy, and 20,000 francs for funeral expenses.

The extent to which wealth creates status differences is not so great as other factors. The rich per se have not yet become the rural elite, although they are universally ranked above the poorest. In general, there are great differences in wealth and, at the polar extremes, conspicuous differences in living conditions. But there is little disparity in style of life between the *instituteur* (teacher) and the rich merchant. Each lives in a substantial, unpretentious wood or stucco house. They dress alike and accumulate the same amount of material possessions. There is no correlation between wealth on the one hand and education or urbanity on the other, with the exception of certain, not all, schoolteachers. Nor is there a necessary correspondence between education and urbanity and a desire to leave the rural district.

There is, in most cases, an adhesion between wealth and occupation, and of the two with overall rank, but not necessarily. Exceptions to this tendency are of two sorts. There are opportunities for group leadership that are open to persons with otherwise low status: a *cultivateur* can attain prestigious political posts. The church offers no such channels. Persons of high status can lower their prestige through moral misdemeanors. For example, a promiscuous woman clerical worker is snubbed by people who would ordinarily accept her as an equal. A bad marriage can produce the same results.

Conversely, there is little correlation between status and intimate associational groupings; that is, nonfamilial associations are usually between status equals, but status equals may not be friendly, for there are cleavages that are not based on status. With the exception of some schoolteachers or those whose jobs are dependent on the Communist mayor, the *aisés* tend not to be Communists, and a Communist is not likely to be friendly with the *aisés* non-

Communists. A reverse exception to rules of the association of status equals is that the *petit propriétaire* can, if he has *mulâtre* appearance and manners, be friendly with, for example, the school director.

In short, opportunities for the expression of status equality through association are limited. The greatest opportunity for its expression, marriage, will be taken up in chapter seven.

Typical poor villagers have the impression that they live in a classless society—except for the whites—but they are equally impressed with the number of what they call *égoïstes* who surround them. These *égoïstes*, they will say, never *se fréquentent* (associate with people). Upon examination the egoists, with few exceptions, turn out to be exactly those people who have superior status to poor villagers.

Like the *pauvres*, most of the egoists have not paid a visit to one another in years, nor is anyone invited to the house for any occasion except a life crisis. Moreover, some of the egoists call their status equals egoists. The *fonctionnaires* other than schoolteachers, when asked to describe the stratification of their *commune*, tend to make a division between *fonctionnaires* and the proletariat. When pressed, they include professionals like doctors and lawyers at the top of the highest group, their own. Similarly, the *instituteurs* spontaneously place themselves at the top. They are likely to think that people associate with others chiefly on the basis of having the same profession; but only they are a sufficiently large group to do so, and in many ways they form a group apart.

When asked about the rich merchants and entrepreneurs whose positions have been achieved without education, most *fonctionnaires* will say, "Yes, we are on the same rung," but they add: "We do not see much of one another because they are nice, but backward" (*Ils sont gentils, mais pas évolués*).

The top rank, then, is given to the people who are both educated and well-to-do. Next are the well educated. Beneath them are those who are *aisés*, but uneducated. Below them are relatively pretentious artisans, who in most cases outrank fishermen. Some place all others in the society in one bottom group, the proletariat. But others, particularly those involved, make a careful distinction between *gens casés* and *petits propriétaires*. Among the latter are at least as many different ranks as there are *quartiers*, as we have seen.

In other words, on each level we find lumpers and splitters, each group being most sensitive to distinctions among those most like themselves. To the *petit cultivateur* there is no difference between the teacher and the tax collector. To the teacher there is. "Family" also enters as a criterion, the hierarchy depending on the same criteria used in individual ranking.

The words "low class" are used on many occasions in Cape-sterre to indicate a consciousness of status difference that is felt more often than it has an opportunity to be expressed in overt behavior. Among the indices of low-class status is the giving of the *veillée* at a death rather than simply the conventional Western funeral. Although Creole is spoken even by the white aristocrats, the near inability to speak standard French is known as "lower class." Dress, gesture, and manners are also criteria of status.

In chapter seven we shall examine the hospitality complex. Here it need only be said that elaborate manners create an ease of interaction that masks feelings of class difference. All people upon greeting one another shake hands. If one walks into a room of twenty people seated at a baptismal dinner, one must shake hands with each and every guest. When meeting on the road or when taking leave on no matter how casual an occasion, the hand is offered. Each child in a family must be kissed by each visitor. Greetings are "Bonjour, Monsieur, Madame, Mademoiselle," never informal, unless close friends are addressing one another by name. To offer a drink to someone who enters the house is mandatory. When an artisan comes to do some work in a *fonctionnaire's* house, he is given a drink. The artisan, then, would never be made to feel himself a social inferior if it were not for private balls, when he would stand outside the door among the uninvited who look in at the dancers. And the lower-class individual is excluded not only from being a guest, but of course from being a participant in any upper-class affair. When a prospective suitor makes his intentions known, every subtlety of status difference is minutely examined, from the way he spells a word in a letter to his color, from his occupation to his grandmother's family.

Despite these differences, the higher-status groups usually feel concern, understanding, pity for the others. There is no class antagonism. Yet a dark child born into a light family can develop such feelings of inferiority that, as in one case I saw, he refuses to eat at the same table with the rest. There is also a feeling among all groups in the *commune* that the entire society has suddenly grown unfriendly, divided into separate islands. They all say that it was not like this in father's or grandfather's day, that hospitality has declined.

Some trace this change to what they call the Revolution of 1939, known elsewhere as World War II. This period of the Vichy government's occupation of Martinique under Admiral Robert was a time of fascist terror and famine. Rationing gave what meat there was to the whites, the blacks being given little more than the hide. Fishing was prohibited. Elected mayors were dictatorially replaced—often by white men who would keep order. A curfew was imposed. Customary behavior underwent a period of anarchy. People have saved the sugar sacks they wore as a reminder of the poverty. It was after this period that communism for the first time became a part of Martinique life. Many refer to the pre-Robert period as halcyon days, saying that now people have forgotten gracious manners, that neighbors are enemies, that children are rude, that the working man is no longer content simply with freedom.

New criteria for status differences have indeed entered the *commune*. But still the sharpest line is drawn according to a very old standard—that of dependence or independence vis-à-vis the plantation. The *gens casés* are universally ranked as socially lower than any others chiefly because their lack of initiative is deplored as reminiscent of slavery. A free *journalier* to whom no house is given by a white man may be poorer, but he has hope. And his credit is better. As a *fonctionnaire* described the contrast, talking first about the free landless poor in the *bourg*: "He is a man. He can buy a dress for his *concubine*. He pays for his room. He has more free will [*volonté*]. He can say, 'I am not the *Béké's* Nigger.' *Les bons Nègres* [Uncle Toms] get more food, but they sleep on the ground and don't have a *sou* for their own rum." These people on the plantations, however, are usually more pitied than despised. And sometimes they join the *sauvages* of the *quartiers*, those who have an adamant and open antiplantation stand that occasionally breaks out in violence.

Notes

[1] Lafcadio Hearn states that a woman could walk 50 miles carrying 120 to 150 pounds on her head. *Two Years in the French West Indies* (New York: Harper & Bros., 1890), p. 105.

FIVE

Economic Activities

"Commerçants" and Entrepreneurs

With the exception of the whites, all the rich at Capesterre are *commerçants* or entrepreneurs, including the professionals. Most started out in this generation with a small *boutique*, which was slowly and industriously (sometimes unscrupulously) enlarged. A few earned their initial investment from a steady job, such as that of plantation executive, and invested all their earnings in cattle and land, later adding a *boutique* to their activities. In a minority of cases a white parent was the springboard to success. A few made good marriages. Hardly a person started with inherited wealth, although a few Capesterre natives have in this way moved on to urban or continental society as professionals or big businessmen.

The general feeling is that a person can no longer make money by starting with the small *boutique*. Upwardly mobile young people, unless they are the heirs apparent of the larger commercial establishments, see their opportunity through education, and their material expectations are more modest. Few aspire to the highly paid professions. Most are attached to the locality. There are only three students from Capesterre currently preparing for a profession.

The owner of the busline will serve as an example of the prosperous entrepreneur. (Capesterre supports five such companies.) The fare from the *bourg* to Fort-de-France is 290 francs, about 85 cents, and a bus holds some forty persons crowded onto wooden

106

benches built from one side to the other. The bus chassis is imported from abroad at a cost of 2,300,000 francs ($6,570). The bodies are locally made in two styles: a wooden body that lasts three and a half years costs 500,000 francs (about $1,430); a metal "tropical" cabin involves double that amount and has a life expectancy of five years. The entrepreneur who is his own driver can make a yearly profit of 1,500,000 francs ($4,285) per bus.

The largest grocer (only one other competes with him) makes approximately 3,000,000 francs in profit, or about $10,000 a year. Such people with their land (usually no more than around 10 hectares in scattered holdings), their cows, setting up their children in business or sending them to France for an education, their investment in fishing equipment, their spouses working as *fonctionnaires*, could within thirty years become the millionaires the townspeople claim them to be—that is, the whole family collectively would represent such an income

Several, known as the *blanc noirs*, are said to be worth 50,000,000 francs (about $150,000). The richest resident of Fond d'Espoir is worth about $30,000 in land. All the entrepreneurs and *commerçants* work personally in their businesses, waiting on customers, slaughtering cattle, driving buses, mixing drinks, cooking, or whatever. It is usually the women who work in stores. None, however, works as a farmer on the land, but they must own land to be rich, for the consumption capacity is not enough to make such money with a store alone.

"Instituteurs"

Among the steadily employed with the highest wages, the largest single group is formed by the *instituteurs*, the teachers. There are some twenty permanent residents in Capesterre who are *instituteurs*, and another six are assigned to this region, living in a *pension* or with relatives during the season; openings in the home town are not always available. Teaching is an occupation open to both men and women, and both sexes are equally proud of the position.

The educational program in Martinique provides a nursery school for babies, who enter at the age of two or three so that working mothers will be relieved of responsibilities. Regular schooling begins in the *école première*, where a child enters at five and remains by law until the age of fourteen, whether promoted or not. If the child progresses at the normal rate, there are five primary grades, which is the extent of educational facilities in Capesterre. To continue schooling the child must go to a larger *bourg* or to one of the two *lycées* in the capital. Beyond the *lycée* (beyond the twelfth year of schooling, which is considered similar to the freshman year in an American college) a student must go abroad except for local training in law. If students continue for an extra year at Capesterre they receive the *Certificat d'Études*. If this optional year is ignored, the next grades are the sixth through the ninth, the completion of which is marked by a degree called the *Bachaut*, First Part. The young teachers who are *pensionnaires* at Capesterre have completed this stage. Those who wish to continue take the examination for the *Brevet Élémentaire*. They can then finish the twelfth grade, majoring in philosophy or mathematics, whereupon they receive the *Bachaut*, Second Part.

With the *Bachaut*, First Part, a teacher is qualified to instruct the first five grades. To teach through the ninth grade the advanced *Bachaut* is required. To instruct the tenth grade or beyond the *Licence* (three college years) was considered sufficient until 1951, when the *Agrégation* (four years further) became a prerequisite.

The first coeducational primary school was started in Capesterre by a religious order in 1850; it was replaced in 1882 by the lay schools, which now hold about 1,000 pupils, only 50 percent of whom are likely to receive as much as the *Certificat d'Études*. Compulsory attendance was not enforced until after departmentalization in 1948. Except during school hours, there is no law against child labor in Martinique.

A six-point scale regulates teachers' salaries. Beginning at the lowest grade (about $130 a month), in four years there is a promotion to a salary of $150 (54,000 francs). The next four-year period leads to 59,000 francs. Then, after several five-year periods, a teacher qualifies for the highest grade, earning 74,000 francs (about $210) a month. One member of a teaching couple is entitled to an additional allowance of $11 a month for room and board. The *pensionnaires* spent $40 a month for room and board. One couple in the village, both of whom are in the fourth ($170 a month) category, lived in one of the best houses in town, a large two-story cement dwelling with tile floors. They had a servant and owned an automobile. A couple in this position can own their own four-room house by getting credit after some fifteen years of renting for about $57 a month. No credit at all is extended to people without such a guaranteed job or the possession of valuable equipment. Another advantage of being a *fonctionnaire* is that every five years one is given a *congé*, a year in France.

"Petits Propriétaires"

Among *petits propriétaires*, whose holdings range from a fraction of an acre to 10 acres, the agricultural calendar is largely influenced by three factors: (1) climatic fluctuations; (2) the period of unemployment when there is no money to buy food; and (3) the natural season of the *fruit à pain*, the large, pulpy breadfruit tree which was imported from Tahiti in 1793. There is so little to be gained on small holdings by planning commercial crops and so small a market for vegetables that the agricultural methods are not designed for maximum productivity.

The only implements used are the hoe, the fork, and the machete. These tools are used by either sex, and by the age of eight both boys and girls have mastered them. For growing vegetables there is no sexual division of labor, the work being easily done by anyone in the family without any customary rule. If there is coffee, however, it is traditionally the woman's job to harvest it, whereas only men climb fruit trees and prepare the ground for bananas. Cutting the ripened bananas is once more woman's work.

It is difficult to estimate the amount of land necessary to grow enough vegetables for any given number of people, for soil fertility varies. Under the best conditions, the space for 5 *pieds* of *légumes* (garden vegetables) will feed ten people, but seldom are such conditions found. No land is scientifically rotated or allowed to lie fallow long enough, nor can these people afford fertilizer at 4,200 francs for 50 kilos. Most people try to keep chickens, sheep, and pigs for fertilizer, and the vegetables are interspersed to allow the larger to shade the smaller. There is no irrigation. Careful consideration is given to the problem of whether to leave plants in the ground or whether they must be harvested quickly before spoiling.

The work itself is done not only by family members but also by hired hands or by cooperative group labor called *atélage*. About five men compose such a group, the membership of which is frequently changed. Not based on kinship, the teams are formed spontaneously by the men while visiting along the road in the evening. Each man might put in a few dozen plants about a meter apart. Neither a time factor nor necessity is involved, the motive being only that it is more pleasant to work together than alone. The members of the group sing, but there are no planned entertainments or musical instruments except during house building.

Since the months of plantation employment are from January until some time in July, planting is geared to maximum maturation during the months of unemployment when there is no money to buy food. Part of the stress of this period is mitigated by the breadfruit season, which furnishes free nourishment for the picking on any property. Breadfruit is plentiful from July through October. November, therefore, is the month of direst need, and the planting is done accordingly.

In January there is not much work on the small plots; and if an owner has little land, absolutely none. *Choux* (cabbages) planted at this time would yield a superfluous harvest in June when the breadfruit is abundant. Those who buy all their food would prefer a breadfruit for 10 francs to a *chou* for 40. The food picked in January was planted in June. Furthermore, the earth should have some rest.

In February there is little planting for the same reasons, but people probably put in a few yams. March is a big month for working in the gardens, for it ensures food during the terrible months of November and December when not a single breadfruit is to be found.

April is a bad season climatically, and May is too hot and dry for everything except potatoes and manioc, neither of which is a large part of the diet. Manioc is not often made into cakes any longer, but is occasionally eaten as *farine* (flour) mashed with avocado and seasoned with *piment*, a very hot pepper. As a staple it has been completely replaced by bread.

The *commune* is supplied by two bakeries, one producing 500 loaves a night, and even this must be supplemented by a truckload from the largest neighboring *bourg*. A 2-foot loaf weighing 750 grams costs 58 francs; the 375-gram loaf is only 29 francs. Each adult, if he or she can afford it, consumes an average of two large loaves a week, eating bread at every meal and in between.

In June and July the *petit cultivateur* starts the serial planting of various *choux*. The busiest seasons are August and October, forming along with March the period of maximum work in the hills; but even at its peak not much labor is required in the *quartiers* of Capesterre. On a 3-acre plot, for example, there is never more than five days' work for two people each month, a day lasting from seven to eleven in the morning. Only if sugar cane is grown is hired labor necessary if people are healthy and live on their land.

One man with a family of two, devoting as much of his acreage to sugar as his vegetables would allow, which amounted to 200 *pieds* of cane, collected 18,000 francs for the harvest (about $50) for the year. Since cane must be shipped immediately after cutting, he hired four men at 756 francs each for a task they completed in one day. After paying, in addition, 6,000 francs for the privately owned truck for transporting the cane to the *usine*, his net annual income from the sugar was $25.

This meager sum for less than an acre of sugar is, however, more than a neighbor earned on over 2 acres of bananas, on which he also grew 200 *pieds*. For these he received 7,000 francs ($20) during the year at the current rate of 5 to 25 francs the kilo, depending on the quality. Prices have been as low as this for three years. Even before, however, growing bananas on so small a scale did not pay. On the remaining quarter of the banana man's property he raises vegetables for his family of seven: yams, *choux*, tomatoes, peas, manioc, cucumbers, potatoes, taro, *bananes dures*, carrots, maize, onions, leeks, turnips, celery, and others.

Many of these people have enough vegetables for consumption, but not enough for cash crops. Both the men in the cases just described—the sugar grower with a minimal family and the banana grower with a larger than average household—are dependent on the plantation even for bare subsistence. They must buy many items of food alone. The sugar man works for the *usine* as much as possible— for 5 months a year, a total of 710 hours—for which he earns 81,566 francs ($233). His wife cuts cane for 48 days a year, earning 37,968 francs ($109).

To round out the picture, let us see what opportunities this couple has for additional income. There is the *allocation* ($15) for her two children on the basis of his earnings, although they do not contribute to the support of the children, who live with the man's mother. Their one valuable possession is a young cow, worth 20,000 francs, which can be pawned for emergencies; that is, an advance is paid at the animal's current value and the increase in value will be split with the man who provided the money. The cow must be kept on the *savane*, for 1 hectare per animal is necessary to feed it properly, and for this there is a charge. Formerly, the *habitation* allowed people to keep animals on its *savane*, but now it is using every bit of available nonsugar land either for its own pasturage or for planting mahogany. In 1941 and 1943 people were even allowed to plant on the uplands of the plantations.

The two families described are among the more comfortable of the people of the *quartiers*. Although others have as much land, they may be poorer because there are not as many wage-earning members to bring income into the family. Moreover, some do not find as much work at the *habitations* as the two families described, each of which has a man working at least five months a year; some can find only the equivalent of three months' work a year. An example of an indigent household is that of a widow whose older children have left. Only a son of fourteen and a grandchild for company remain with her. The father of the last child is legally responsible for him, but he contributes little because he has a family of his own and pays 5,000 francs a month rent. Last year he had only two months' work. The children who have left occasionally send a 1,000-franc note. The widow is not strong enough to do much cane cutting or water carrying and therefore does not collect much *allocation*. She barely manages to raise her vegetables. Others in the country, of course, are even poorer, for they have no land at all, but are only squatters.

The older people without exception describe their past as having been relatively prosperous, even though they had to work in the fields when only children. One woman of seventy-seven started work at the age of seven, earning 25 *centimes* a day; but in those days her mother paid only 1 franc a month for the land she rented from the *habitation*. In 1925 the pay was 1 franc 50 for a day's work; 3,000 francs was a fortune, the accumulation of ten years' salary.

Today, they say, even if one had the equivalent of such savings, one would still be poor. The franc has been stable since 1953, but in 1950 it was worth twice its 1956 value of 350 to the dollar, in 1947 three times that value, in 1946 five times, in 1944 ten times, and in 1939 twenty-five times.

In attempts to better their condition the *petits propriétaires* frequently strike. They are accused of moving elsewhere to work when on strike at one *habitation*. Early this year three men from one *quartier* were jailed for three months for their *gréviste* (strike) activities. Others were equally involved, but only three were caught. People have a right to strike, but it is illegal to keep others from working, which was the aim in these cases. The men say that they will strike again regardless of the punishment, and they are local heroes. They strike now not because they object to the day's wages for a day's work, but because under certain conditions it takes three days to accomplish one day's work, since a man or woman is paid by the amount done, not for the time it takes to do it. In other words, they object to piecework. Often the cutting is difficult because of abnormal conditions: hilly ground, wet cane, badly weeded fields, and the like. All claim that working conditions are worse today than in 1946 when they had the Collective Convention.

"Gens Casés"

The *gens casés*, whether they live in barracks or on small garden plots, must in most cases buy only at a designated store. Although the store is not company owned, the plantation deducts from wages all that the *gens casés* owe to that particular store, and no other store will give them credit. The *gens casés* must purchase more food than the *propriétaire*, for even when they have a garden plot it is not large, and they forage for whatever wild crops are available, such as breadfruit. As a result, the *gens casés* have less cash than other people, although they are assured of free lodging. If they work elsewhere or refuse to work when needed the general procedure is for the *habitation* to dislodge them. If it is a strike that prevents work the control is to remove garden privileges or to kill the workers' animals. During a prolonged strike, however, animal killing works the other way around, too, as retaliation.

On the other hand, the *gens casés* are assured of as much work as is available. Although mechanization has reduced the number of laborers needed on the *habitation*, the *gens casés* have not diminished, for the population has grown. It is estimated that ten times the workers needed for the amount of work done are hired each season, thus providing too little work for all.

PLANTATION WORK

On *habitation* Capesterre, where the *usine* is located, an analysis of the work records shows the estimate of ten times too many workers to be conservative. The *habitation* has 86 hectares planted in cane and 13 in bananas. The two basic techniques involved in raising cane are called *coupe la canne* and *attache la canne*: laborers work in pairs, one cutting and the other gathering and tying the bundles. Ideally, between them they do 20 piles in six hours. One pile is 25 *pacquets*, each of which consists of 10 *bouts* (pieces). Twenty piles is considered a day's work, the *tâche* (task), for which the cutter and the binder each gets a day's pay. Under difficult conditions the *tâche* requires two days, and the amount considered to be a just *tâche*, as we have noted, is the subject of strikes, political debate, and labor-management negotiations. The union will not permit a worker to do more in a day than a *tâche*, even if he or she is willing.

In addition to workers listed under *coupe la canne* and *attache la canne*, there are twenty other categories of work ranging from a groom for the horses to maintenance workers, from those who prune and fertilize to the transport crew responsible for shipping the cane to the *usine*. (I am not including the *usine* personnel.) *Habitation* Capesterre employs 679 persons to deal with its bananas and sugar. Of these workers only 2 have full-time, year-round jobs and are paid even if they do not appear for work and whether there is work to do or not. At the head of the hierarchy is the *géreur* (manager), a black man who lives on the *habitation* and supervises all work. Under him is the *économe*, an Indian, whose duties give an idea of the *géreur's* responsibilities: he apportions all work, supervises personnel, keeps pay records in ledgers. It is the *géreur* who decides who is to work where and at what. The *économe* earns 5,000 francs a week (about $14). Under him are five *commandeurs* who make 800 francs a day, nearly as much, but who only work eight months of the year.

Most workers receive 679 francs for each day's work (about $2.25), and everyone, including the executives, pays 6 percent of their salary for social security. The cutters earn a little more, 850 francs a day ($2.70), a salary which is equaled by those who load the piles into trucks. Only the chauffeurs earn more, 876 francs a day. The daily wage of the two carpenters is 800 francs. All others—water carriers, road workers, tractor operators—earn the standard wage of 679 francs.

During the five-month season from February 23 to July 31, 1956, 227 cutters were employed. Unlike the categories of work in which only a few employees are used (such as the two carpenters, the groom, the three animal feeders), most people work only a couple of days a week, although the range is from half a day to seven.

The work distributed after the *récolte* (harvest) is even thinner. Three weeks after the harvest the first of two (occasionally three) *sarclages* begins. This is the process of separating the cane plants from the straw. Between the first and second *sarclages*, plants killed by the tractors must be replaced. Then six workers fertilize the fields with ammonium and potash. Fertilizer is used again after the second *sarclage*. The first of these two processes yields one day of work to 588 people each time there is a *sarclage*. Fertilizing gives a day of work to 116 people twice during the year. Even less work is provided by the *habitation's* 13 hectares of bananas.

FISHERMEN

The 1,500 fishermen of the island are distributed chiefly on the south and west coasts because other places are too rocky and dangerous. An island estimate is an average catch of 40 kilos of fish a week (per fisherman) at 250 francs per kilo, which is $28.

In Capesterre there are 16 boats used by 50 men for a town population of 2,293, all but 2 of the boats being outboards. The *bourgs* directly to the south and the north of Capesterre are too rocky for fishing. Capesterre, then, is the east coast fishing center.

At 6:30 in the morning, still dawn, the people are all awake. There are sixteen boats covered with palm fronds on the sea wall.

The *matelots* (nonowners who fish) straggle down to the beach and uncover the *gommiers* (canoes); some begin to dig in the sea or search along the shore for the day's ballast of rocks. Six men drag each boat going that day down to the water, a shallow rocky cove with long, low breakers. In other *bourgs* the boats can set forth in the dark, but here it is treacherous—"the sea is *mauvaise*"—and the fishermen must wait for clear light. One man scoops water into the boat and dashes it against the outside. The seats are rinsed in the sea. Now twenty men have gathered, most of them sitting on the sea wall talking. Someone arrives with his sail wrapped in a bamboo mast and stretches it along the bottom of the boat. Others follow. "Holy Ghost," "Only God Knows," and "To You My Heart" are ready to leave.

They all have sails for emergency use, and the motorboats all carry an innertube for floating the motor in case the boat founders. Some men own nets, but this is not the season for them, and no traps were made this year.

By eight o'clock four boats are at sea. It takes about five minutes to get out beyond the four big breakers, and there is much concern for each launching. Five boats were left on shore today; some did not want to go, and others will go tomorrow if there prove to be enough fish.

The canoes, whose hulls are made in Dominica and insides finished by local carpenters, cost from 70,000 to 90,000 francs ($200 to $260) and weigh on the average 4 tons, the biggest, 10. The 15-horsepower Evinrude motors represent an investment of 250,000 francs ($714). It costs some 450,000 francs ($1,285) for a canoe, sail, motor, bait, and equipment. The fuel is paid for by the men, not by the owners, and the investment is a gamble, since on some days nothing is caught and on some it is too rough to venture out. The expenditure for gas is 20 liters to fish for *volants* (flying fish); 40 for *poisson rouge*; 60 at maximum.

Three men work every boat, each earning an equal share. The owner of the boat gets a share and the owner of the motor another share. If one of these is also one of the fishermen, he earns a double amount, but there are five shares to be allotted.

Eleven men are involved in ownership, the richest possessing two boats and two motors. He never fishes, but spends his time as a *commerçant.* Of the eleven, only three work as full-time fishermen, and a fourth, a *fonctionnaire*, sometimes goes out. Of the three, one is the only other possessor of two boats and two motors; the only *seine* (net) in town also belongs to him. Another of them owns one of the two motorless boats. Fishing, then, is a small industry for investment capital.

The maximum earnings per share are about 6,000 francs ($17) for one day's work. The average yearly income per share is from 100,000 to 150,000 francs ($285 to $430). About thirty, then, is the average number of days that fishermen can fish in a year. It would take a nonfisherman who owned a boat almost two years to get back his initial investment. The occupation is rendered even less lucrative because the fish are taxed at sale and a license is required for each boat at an annual expense of 40,000 francs ($115).

Making fishing equipment is one of the few remaining home industries (Capesterre has none of the others, such as hat weaving and basketry). The *fillet* for flying fish measures 14 meters 50 in length by 2 meters 50. It takes one man eight days to make it. Various kinds of traps are also made at home. Hooks are imported, as is nylon line.

It is August, and the good season is from May to July. Since there is a sellers' market, it is not important to beat the others in from the sea. Usually all boats come in at 4:00 P.M. with no competition among them concerning who will be the first to arrive. In August the *volants* are finished and there is not much besides *poisson rouge*. Five *volants* would now bring 100 francs, but in season it would take twenty-five of them to get the same amount. In November the season is not bad, and it takes three hours to reach the bank 50 kilometers away. In December and January the sea is too rough for any kind of fishing. From February through July a sail of only an hour or so is far enough to catch more than now. In the bad season, from the end of July through November, one must go out very far and use a line 100 meters deep.

When the boats come in a crowd gathers to help anyone who needs it. The fishermen of the first canoe help the next, and so on. The fish are already strung. They are carried to the marketplace by two men who hang them on a stick balanced on their shoulders. A conch shell summons the buyers to the marketplace, and the sellers display their wares in the empty butcher stall after the policeman weighs the catch, charging a tax of 5 francs a kilo, which is payable daily after the sale. Each canoe is allowed to keep 10 percent of the catch tax-free for consumption, and a small catch (such as that of the last boat in, with only 12 kilos) is not taxed, *"pour les encourager"* (to encourage them), explained the policeman. Occasionally a pauper will be handed a few little fish free. The average daily portion of the buyer is 125 grams.

For each boat two participants come to the market, one to weigh, the other to sell. Sometimes a wife helps. No extra money is made by performing this task. Some advantage belongs to the first boat in, even in this season, for there is only one wholesale buyer (from a large *bourg*) and the first one in sells more to her. If the fish are selling at 300 francs per kilo retail, she gets them for 250. One day, for example, the first boat in sold half its catch retail and the rest to the *marchande*. The others each sold their 10 kilos retail.

How many fish are caught a day by each boat (allowing for the 10 percent which goes for consumption) can be deduced from the tax records. The overall amount of fish caught in the *commune* can also be computed. From June 15 through August 1, 1956, there were 3,289 kilos (and the fishermen consumed about 330 additional kilos). For the ten days from August 3 through August 14 there were 490 kilos. During the month of August only three to seven boats went out daily, and the catch per boat varied from 10 to 250 kilos. During this same off-season fishermen and *marchandes* from a more northerly *bourg* and from St. Pierre came to Capesterre to sell.

A list of the personnel of each boat, which shifts daily, shows that no relatives work together and that only one son of a fisherman is also a fisherman.

OTHER OCCUPATIONS

There are little more than a dozen full-time artisans and specialists of various kinds, few highly skilled. The *usine* uses some, and there are a blacksmith and a cobbler. People must go to the capital for radio repairs, jewelry work, pottery, and the like, but there are many part-time carpenters, chauffeurs, masons, mechanics, and barbers. The highest-skilled artisan of the *usine*, the *bouilleur* or *chimiste*, is imported from British Guiana. The jobs requiring artisans are distributed to the population at large, most of whom claim some kind of skill. The arts and crafts are nonexistent.

Too many women are dressmakers to give much scope to full-time specialists, although there are some. Most women do their own laundry or have servants. The old professional *blanchisseuses* who braved the rushing torrents in Lafcadio Hearn's day are, therefore, extinct, together with the makers of creole headpieces and the *porteuses*. There is not much baking and selling of cakes by *marchandes*, for the *boutiques* and *pâtisseries* have taken over these functions.

Domestic help in the *bourg* earns 3,000 francs ($10) a month plus room and board. Some women go into Fort-de-France as *ménagères* or cooks, earning 4,500 francs plus room and board.

Food crops that are not exports are known as *vivrières*. In Martinique 1895 marked the peak of the *vivrières*—17,000 hectares were devoted to them. Since then there has been a steady decline: to 12,000 hectares in 1912, 6,220 in 1935, 4,200 in 1940. The government raised the area to 7,000 hectares in 1943, but in 1945 it was down again to 3,500. The decrease can be partly accounted for by the fact that bread replaced manioc at the end of the nineteenth century. The largest single crop among the *vivrières* today is yams, and they are grown high in the *mornes* where nitrogen is lacking in the soil; accordingly, the local market is small.

No fresh vegetables are sold in shops, and not everyone in Capesterre has land. There is, therefore, something of a local market. As we have seen, few *petits propriétaires* grow vegetables for sale, only the poorer ones from two of the *quartiers*. The women of Voltaire are too proud, they say, to bring their produce to market as *marchandes*. It is claimed that it is cheaper to import beans and rice from France than to raise enough food for the population, as it is said that salted cod (*morue*) from Canada is cheaper than developing the fishing industry.

It is against the law to sell on the street or to hawk wares because it would be impossible to compute taxes, so little of this is done. *Marchandes* must sell in the marketplace, and Saturday is the only day on which the local policeman collects taxes. On the other days only two or three *marchandes* come in from the *quartiers*, except at the end of the breadfruit season, when half a dozen come in, chiefly to sell the various cabbages (*choux*). The sellers, of course, are the growers; no middlemen operate here.

On Saturdays there are perhaps sixteen *marchandes*, each of whom pays 5 francs regardless of how much is sold. They arrive at eight and stay until noon. *Marchandes* also come in from the larger properties of a nearby *commune*. Even under these conditions of restricted demand Capesterre does not grow all it needs.

Following is a sample of market prices:

Product	Amount	Cost (francs)*
Chou blanc	1 kilo	30
Chou de Chine	1 kilo	25
Chou caraibe	1 kilo	40
Patate	1 kilo	25
Igname	1 kilo	50
Banane	1 kilo	50
Manioc farine	1 liter	160

*At 350 francs to the dollar.

A food allowance of 100 francs (15 cents) a day could buy the following:

Product	Amount	Cost (francs)
Morue (imported salt fish)	¼ liter	25
Cooking oil	1 *mesure*	22
Bread	1 *livre* (1 ft. long)	30
Breadfruit (1)	2 *livres*	10-50

Contrasted with this scale—the poor villagers live on even less—the following is the diet of the *pensionnaire* living on $40 a month: breakfast consists of soup, fish or eggs, fruit, bread, coffee, and milk. The main noon meal might start with salad or brain fritters followed by soup and then a meat or fish course. There is always an enormous plate of three or four root vegetables or bananas and also a tureen of kidney beans. This is all mixed together and eaten with oil and *piment*. Dessert is fruit, *conserves*, cake, or ice cream. The children of this house, however, eat mainly bread and a mash of vegetables, with meat served only when it is left over. The evening meal, served at 8:30, is always light: soup, fish, one vegetable, and dessert.

In the *quartiers*, old people without teeth eat only rice, *barbade* (custard), and milk. Breadfruit is never served at night, only bread, using $2\frac{1}{2}$ kilos for a family of nine. In the morning the family consumes 2 kilos of bread. There is no electricity at all in the *quartiers*, and the only approach to refrigeration is keeping something like a can of butter in a cold bucket of water. Beef, slaughtered once a week, lasts two days, but lamb must be eaten immediately.

Electricity was introduced in the *bourg* in 1945, but it costs 47 francs a kilowatt (as opposed to 17 francs in France), and only the *aisés* have refrigerators, which were introduced six years ago. The butcher shops do not use them. The hotel rents out space in a small one, and ice is shipped in bags of sawdust from Fort-de-France.

Another occupation, indicated by the menus, is that of butcher, although each one has another lucrative activity as well. There are six butchers in the *bourg* and one in each *quartier*. The *quartier* consumes only a single steer a week, whereas four to six are slaughtered in the *bourg*, each weighing from 200 to 300 kilos. Saturday is the day for beef; Sunday for pork only; occasional Wednesdays are for all animals; Friday (the day Saturday's cow is slaughtered) is for entrails. Lamb and goat are rare.

Each Saturday from 500 to 700 kilos of beef are sold in the *bourg*. Figuring 1 kilo for 4 people, some 150 people in the village, on the average, could eat meat once a week. Every part is sold at the same price, 300 francs a kilo, whether sirloin or hoof. Each Sunday twelve pigs are slaughtered, from 90 to 250 kilos in all. Not all butchers sell every week or even every month. It is an occasional occupation for which they pay a tax of 1 franc per kilo. In the month of April, during the strike, five butchers together sold the following amounts (in kilos): 841, 498, 38, 298, 618. This would be enough, if distribution were equal, for the *bourg* population of 1,001 to have 2 kilos of meat each per month.

Part Three

THE FAMILY

SIX

Life History
of the Household

We have set out to demonstrate Martinique as one of those societies with a nonelite subculture that characterizes most of its population. We have said that within this subculture, family organization differs from the standard Western family system, which is the dominant pattern and characteristic of the elite of the country. In chapter two we traced the broad outlines in the development of a nonelite subculture on the island, showing the effects of various influences on its emergence—miscegenation, emancipation, the economic hierarchy, differential association, settlement pattern, and so on. In addition, we illustrated the social stratification and race relations manifest today.

Part two portrayed the relation of one community to the total society. The round of life, the association patterns, and the social stratification of Capesterre revealed that few members of this rural *commune* belong to the elite. Most of the 3,871 inhabitants are what we have called associationally and culturally black, whether they be landless laborers, *petits propriétaires*, rich shopkeepers, *fonction- naires*, or professionals. Descriptions of economic activities and house types have further set the context for an analysis of family organization whose principles we shall examine in the next three chapters.

Margaret Mead has remarked that every description in anthro- pology, at least by implication, is a comparative statement. One does not bother to say that the natives do not walk backwards. In addition to comparison in this sense, I shall often throughout these chapters refer explicitly to contrasting or similar conditions seen throughout the Caribbean as evidenced in the literature cited in chapter one.

These studies of the Caribbean family suggest, if they do not explicitly state, that some form of matrifocality has been discovered in the deviant family system present in all areas so far examined. In all works mentioning the phenomenon (up to 1958), matrifocality is described in terms of the relative strength of the maternal over the paternal role in the nuclear family. Where the pure "grandmother family" exists, matrifocality is undisputed. But Raymond T. Smith doubts whether what appears to be a grandmother family is truly that over its entire developmental cycle. He finds, however, that matrifocality is even expressed within the conjugal family in Guianese villages.[1] Not only is it manifested in terms of a stronger maternal role, but he believes the whole structure to be shifted to the female side; that is to say, when nonnuclear relatives live in a household they tend to be related through the mother, and when outside children are incorporated into the household they are the children of daughters, not of sons. Smith explains matrifocality as a result of the absence of male status-defining functions in the social subsystem in which he identifies the deviant family.

Since in other areas observers have found matrifocality to be diagnostic of the Caribbean family, I shall discuss its relation to the family system in Capesterre. To anticipate my findings, I contend that there is no matrifocality in the structure of the stable conjugal family. Thus, Capesterre is different from the Guianese villages. On the other hand, the structure of the Capesterre family system permits nonconjugal families. One can find a woman alone with her children. Also present are three-generation families in which there is no resident father-husband in the first descending generation. Not only is such an arrangement a phase in a developmental cycle, but it can be a fully sanctioned permanent constellation. Then again, there are families in which the mother moves in with a series of men, or the latter move in with her, producing children who live with impermanent stepfathers; in such cases, these social fathers tend to be what Herskovits has called humanly and institutionally remote.

I contend, then, that the degree of matrifocality or patrifocality that characterizes the family in Capesterre is measured by the frequency of partner changing or the occurrence of the nonconjugal family. I do not find matrifocality a correlate of status-defining ability on the part of the male, nor do I find that it correlates with the man's economic role in the family. Further, the degree of stability in the conjugal household is also independent of the economic position of the family or the role of the male partner in the community.

Although Martinique has the same black and white polar values as British Guiana, the *commune* is stratified in terms of occupation, wealth, education, color, and family, all of which form a frame for status-defining functions. Since, then, neither matrifocality nor an undifferentiated social structure characterizes family organization in Capesterre, what are its principal features? First, let us look at parental roles in terms of authority.

Parental Roles

In Capesterre, as is generally true in the Caribbean, the individual, separate household is the common economic base toward which all its members contribute their money and labor. In the view of the local culture the household is the functioning family unit regardless of the relationships among the people within it. There are a few exceptions to this rule, such as the presence of a paying boarder.

We have seen that there is little division of labor in connection with agricultural tasks on the landholding of the *petit propriétaire*. Sexual division of labor in the household extends to such duties as child care, preparation of meals, cleaning, and care of clothing—all of which fall to the women; the men make repairs on the house. In shopkeeping or running a restaurant most of the work is done by women, although men can also do it. Either sex can be in charge of the P.T.T. or occupy any *fonctionnaire* position.

In the *quartier* the household is a dwelling surrounded by its own fields. The household on the plantation may be a separate structure, but usually it is part of a long house divided into separate compartments of single or double rooms. Generally, only in the *bourg* does more than one nuclear family occupy one private building, and even there it is rare. There are a few two-family houses, and occasionally a couple will move in with the man's parents.

Since the landholdings of a *quartier* man, at least those that he works himself, are generally contained in one parcel and his house is located on the same agricultural plot, the pattern Leyburn describes for Haiti is absent in Capesterre.[2] In Haiti a man may own several plots, and on each he may have a house and a woman, for he needs an overseer as well as a labor supply of children on each of his scattered properties.[3] Leyburn also reports settlements in Haiti like those in Dahomey, where there is a compound of separate huts—each with a woman and her children—ruled over or owned by one man. In Fond d'Espoir *quartier* two houses were occupied by mistresses of men living with their respective spouses on the same property.

In Capesterre, there is no rule governing which spouse's money goes for which debts incurred by the household. Sometimes it is the woman's earnings that are kept aside for luxuries like rum, Communion clothes, and school supplies, and the man's money that pays for food, taxes, and rent or purchase price. Sometimes the woman pays for all necessities and the man pays for luxuries, setting aside whatever money he wishes for drinking and gambling. Whether legally married or not, the couple can purchase their house and lot together or in the name of either alone. If a couple should set up a household and later separate, the property remains with the person who owned it before the *ménage* (extralegal union) or marriage occurred.

Unlike tne men in the community the Herskovitses describe in Trinidad,[4] and unlike those in the three villages Raymond Smith studied in British Guiana,[5] the male labor force in Capesterre is not migratory. In addition, because seasonal employment and the irregularity of it in the harvest season keep the man much at home, he is not physically or humanly remote. When the *ménage* is a long-term monogamous one the father interacts with the children with as much authority as the mother; and when he is not away at work all day this interaction is frequent. The affectional ties between the males and children are intense. Whether boy of five or old man, males fondle children as much as women do. As we have seen, the rural properties are very small and not much labor is required from children. As a result, the authority a man holds over his children is not applied in such a way as to lessen the affection or increase the respect felt toward him. The father does not treat the children with severe discipline. There is none of the "training in subordination" that Rhoda Métraux finds in Haiti,[6] and boys do not leave home to join gangs.

Although the French provincial family is a severely "patriarchal" one, such an attitude has not become part of the culture of Martinique; nor has the pattern of those British West Indian families that Simey describes[7] in the stratum where marriage is intensely Victorian in the sense that the women are completely subservient to the men. The possibility of such a relationship after a union is legalized is not a deterrent to marriage in Martinique. Marriage does not reinforce the low status of women as it does in Haiti, for in Martinique women of all classes work. Even the white aristocratic women, as we have seen, hold jobs in offices, open businesses as *couturières*, or become shopkeepers if necessary. Middle-class women are encouraged to become professionals or to have a business of their own, and lower-class women are expected to work. Unlike Raymond Smith's report for British Guiana, it is not the ideal in Martinique for the man to assume all economic responsibilities.

Raymond Smith points up correlations between the attitude toward the place of men and women and the power distribution within the household, showing that often it is the contrast between the man's ideal and his actual power which leads to separation of the spouses. While a man and woman are young, he says, the frequency of their interaction is at its peak. Since she cannot work, the woman is completely dependent. As soon as children arrive the spouses see less of each other and never go out in public together. The man at this stage is nearly cut off from interaction with his wife and children. The mother-wife's power grows with time until she becomes so contemptuous of her mate's wishes that she goes out to work. She does not earn much, but she no longer needs his support, for there are no little children. The children, as a matter of fact, can now provide for the mother, who even extends the boundaries of her motherhood and the power it brings by caring for her daughter's children. The feebleness of the father's role is described as the obverse of the mother's power.

In Martinique, there is no impossibly high ideal for the father's role. His actual role is greater than in British Guiana, yet this role is not the authoritative one that his economic leadership gives him in Haiti. The relationship of the man and his children is characterized by warmth. Children of the *fonctionnaire*, who is away all day, rush up to greet their father with kisses and hugs when he comes home. They eat together. Not only does the father play with them, but they come to him to ask him to change some order the mother has given them. He will ask them to recite poetry, to dance, to tell what they learned in school. In the culturally black classes the children have somewhat less of an opportunity to develop distinctive, let alone demanding, personalities, unless there is an only child. Although they are loved, they are not so encouraged to express themselves. A large group of eight children will stand quietly in the background as the parents talk or the guests come in. They are polite and unobtrusive. As they reach adolescence, they still show complete respect for both parents, but they participate in activities with ease and gregariousness. There is a Creole saying that describes the father's role: "*Le ou fini' tété maman, ou ka tété papa.*" (When you finish nursing Mother, you nurse Father.)

All children in all classes are loved at every stage of their lives. Moreover, when the "lap child" is getting more attention than the "yard child," much of this attention is given by the "yard child" himself or herself. Instead of feeling resentment, the child begins to identify with his or her elders. I have seen babies laughingly nearly pulled apart by little brothers fighting for possession to fondle them. Training in child care starts early. The *commune* has a nursery school for children of working parents, but when school is not in session all but the tiniest babies are left at home all day, the "old" responsible children of four tending those of two and three.

When a boy grows up and becomes a father he continues to feel affection for children—now his own—and there is no cycle which alters his place in a stable conjugal union. It is true, on the other hand, that however affectionate the father, the contact of the children with the mother is of even greater intensity and warmth, as it is in most societies. It is she whom children remember as scrimping to buy their schoolbooks, their fancy clothes for Communion. Even if the father's money makes it possible, it is the mother who shows greater concern. It is she who caters to the needs of infants, feeds the children, sacrifices for adolescent ambitions, listens to adult offspring's troubles. And although women work, often their work keeps them at home, for it is usually the female who is a shopkeeper, and the shop is in the home. A *couturière* also works at home. Even if the woman works in the cane fields, the man is likely to work more often. Thus, the children interact with the mother with greater frequency than with the father.

Close attachment to the mother, however, is easily extended to any mother surrogate. The very pervasiveness of love in this culture makes both parents less important than appearances would indicate. It is not only toward a person's own children that great affection is displayed, but toward any child within sight. With no regret, mothers often leave children permanently with relatives for no reason other than that it is convenient or that the relative has no children. When the mother comes to visit, such children watch her come and go with little concern, for they have been immediately swept into the same web of love from adults, small cousins, and neighbors that they had in their original home.

The subject of this easy transfer of affection is often a god-mother. Especially if a parent dies, the godmother adopts the child. Respect is paid to the godfather. Children will stop in to kiss him on their way home from school, but as one informant said, "A god-father is like a mere father, whereas a godmother is like a mother." Godparenthood is not so important and ritualized as it is in Spanish countries. Unless the parents are dead, godparents furnish no basic needs, nor are their obligations expensive, although it is ceremoni-ally important to have them.

The concept of matrifocality might be the outstanding feature of the family system if the nonconjugal household were the only type found in Capesterre, if the power structure in the stable conjugal household were the Guianese form, if only matrilineally related relatives lived together, or if only children of daughters and not those of sons were taken in by a grandmother. But since none of these facts is true in the Martinique example, I shall not consider matrifocality crucial in delineating the system. That it occurs at all is, as I have said, a function of the existence of nonconjugal families and whatever instability there is in conjugal relationships.

What I maintain to be distinctive in the system is the simulta-neous existence of family types that are usually found separately. This structure can best be examined by looking at several patterns. Let us begin with household composition, concentrating on the arrangement of relationships within the separate households, the duration of conjugal ties, and the developmental history of the household. I shall present the results of surveys made in the most recently formed *quartier*, Fond d'Espoir, supplementing them with data from other samplings when pertinent. The results of the Fond d'Espoir survey (eighty-one households) are based on a total sample. This is the least "aristocratic" of the rural settlements, the residents having acquired land only a decade ago.

HOUSEHOLD COMPOSITION

The material aspects of the household have been described.[8] In Fond d'Espoir the physical units range from the simple bamboo *chaumière*—a mud-floored hut measuring 8 by 12 feet—to a large, cement, five-room bungalow. Some of the large old wooden houses are as valuable as those made of cement. The occupants vary from shopkeeper to cane cutter, from plantation executive to odd-jobs man. Table 6–1 shows the nearly complete distribution of house types, illustrating the occurrence of each kind and the number of occupants in each.

Table 6–1 TYPES OF HOUSES IN FOND D'ESPOIR, OCCURRENCE OF EACH TYPE, AND NUMBER OF OCCUPANTS IN EACH TYPE

| *Number of Occupants* | *Types of Houses* | | | | | | |
	CEMENT	WOOD	STONE	STRAW WITH TIN ROOF	STRAW WITH STRAW ROOF	BAMBOO	*Total*
1	4	3		5	8	2	22
2	5		2	2	3		12
3	1	2		2	2	1	8
4	6	3		1			10
5	1	1			1		3
6	2			1	1		4
7	3	1		1			5
8	1			1	1		3
9				1	1		2
10	2						2
11		1					1
15	1						1
TOTAL	26	11	2	14	17	3	73

The following list is the same breakdown as in Table 6-1, complete, showing the frequency of the occurrence of various numbers of occupants in a house:

Number in house	Number of cases
1	22
2	12
3	8
4	11
5	4
6	6
7	7
8	3
9	4
10	2
11	1
15	1

81 households with 326 persons

The empirical occurrence of varieties of relationships within a household, in descending order of frequency, is:

Relationship	Number of households
Conjugal pair with children	27
Single men	18
Conjugal pair alone	9
Women with children	8
Three-generation family with grand- mother alone	5
Three-generation family with conjugal pair	5
Single women	5
Other	2
Grandparents with grandchild	1
Man with children	1
	81

Table 6-2 rearranges the foregoing data into a typological classification.

Table 6-2 TYPOLOGICAL CLASSIFICATION OF HOUSEHOLDS

Type of Household	Number of Households
I. Nuclear family alone (mates plus children of one or both)	27
Conjugal pair alone	9
II. Nuclear family with others (3 with grandchildren)	5
Conjugal pair with others	4
Grandmother with others	2
III. Women with children only	8
Men with Children	1
IV. Single men	18
V. Single women	5
VI. Nonmated pairs	2
	81

The first notable characteristic in these data is that the modal household contains or has contained a conjugal pair. (This is also true in Raymond T. Smith's communities.) This feature is visible only if in addition to counting those houses in which a conjugal pair exists at present, we count those persons with children, women alone, and others who have at one time or another formed a household which contained a conjugal pair. Of the 81 household heads, 62 at one time or another over their developmental sequence can be described as conjugal. (In Liberté *quartier*, 48 of the 71 have been conjugal.) Of the remaining 19 in Fond d'Espoir, 8 are young men whose aim in most cases is to live *en ménage* with a woman.

But note that eleven houses remain, some of which can be described as subconjugal or supraconjugal. In making this statement, I am not counting those who seem to be in part of a developmental cycle, but only those with whom, interviews revealed, such family types represent a permanent form. The reasons for the existence of these types will be unfolded as we proceed to describe cases in this and the following chapters.

As in British Guiana, the inception of the household often occurs after the birth of children. But child rearing is not the only motivation, as can be seen, even in so small a sample, by the incidence of childless couples moving together: eleven of the conjugal couples in d'Espoir had never had any children together or living with them, and certain unions are formed after the age of childbearing. Unions were formed by people aged twenty to sixty-eight years. In Voltaire there were three childless couples, which does not tell us how many more *ménages* were begun before children were conceived. The concept of conjugality is firmly established.

Children are likely to remain within the family of orientation until marriage or *ménage*. Frequently, however, young men (not women) leave home without any definite plans. They wish to live alone, even if only in a shed on the family property. A significant pattern can be seen in the fact that as many as four young men in Voltaire *quartier* moved out to become single household heads in this manner; in d'Espoir there are at present only two examples of this phenomenon (see Table 6-7), but others who have since started *ménages* began in this way. In every case, the motivation for leaving the parental house was difficulty in getting along with the *beau-père*, the stepfather.

Let us examine in some detail type II in Table 6-2, which includes the nuclear family living with others (five examples), the conjugal pair with others (four examples), and the grandmother with others (two examples). The presence of a grandmother per se may or may not indicate the classic grandmother family—a woman, her illegitimate daughters, and the children of the latter, the whole process having occurred without a conjugal union. I have observed several such families, mostly in the *bourg*, but none in d'Espoir. Although the situation lacks no prestige (one of the richest merchant families is such a grandmother family), it is statistically rare because the conditions fostering it are not likely to occur. First, there is a scarcity of women in rural areas, unlike the situation in Haiti where there seems to be a surplus. Second, as we shall see in chapter seven, there is a good chance of a grandmother family's being started if a woman comes into possession of a *maison paternelle*, an inherited house. Usually, however, a male heir keeps the house, his sisters having left to form *ménages*. But if a woman owns such a house, she will not leave it, nor will a man be likely to share it with her. Third, it is statistically rare for a woman's daughters not to live with a man at some point in their lives. But if one or more daughters bear children and do not leave home—because, for example, the daughter wishes to help the mother in a lucrative business, or because the daughter cannot find a status equal, or because she is crippled—a grandmother family will result.

Some households in d'Espoir are potential grandmother families. The subconjugal household (a woman living alone with her children) is always a potential grandmother family. An examination of some of the details of households where a grandmother is present will reveal several important principles. Before discussing them, however, I wish to define a few terms.

A *jeune fille* marriage is one in which the bride is considered a virgin. A marriage that occurs after a couple has lived together or if the woman already has a child is called *béni' péché* (to efface a sin). There are two types of illegitimate children, recognized and unrecognized. The latter is a child not officially acknowledged by a man; such an unrecognized child bears its mother's surname. Unmarried couples living together are said to have a *ménage*, and the individuals are often referred to as a *concubine* and its masculine form, *concubin*.

Now, let us start by looking at two households in which bilaterality is expressed by the act of a woman's taking in her son's child. In the first of these examples we shall also see a daughter who does not plan to live with a man, who remains at home with her illegitimate children, forming what I call the supraconjugal family. It is not only the classic grandmother family outlined by Henriques[9] and reported by Frazier[10] in the American South that is supraconjugal. The families we are about to describe are also supraconjugal because the economic base comprises three generations.

The first grandmother, whom we shall call Mme. Albert, aged seventy, was a *jeune fille* bride. A widow and the mother of ten children, she lives with a son of twenty-three; a daughter of forty-four; and two sons, nineteen and twenty-three, of that daughter, who has never lived with a man. In addition, another grandchild, St. Ange, lives in this household. St. Ange is the son of another of Mme. Albert's children, a man of forty-two. The grandmother raised St. Ange because the boy's father is not yet married and his *concubine* had too many children to care for one more. She returned to live near her own family, but did not take St. Ange to his maternal grandmother because the baby "loved his mother too much, and if he had lived close by, seeing his mother with other children, he would have grieved and become *rachitique* [literally, afflicted with rickets]."

The second grandmother who lives with the offspring of one of her sons is a woman of fifty-six who was legally married at eighteen. Although she is the mother of five legitimate children, it was not a *jeune fille* marriage, for she had had a child previously. After her husband's death she lived *en ménage* with one man for two years and then left him, having borne him a recognized son. She then had another *ménage* that lasted a year before the man's death; during this *ménage* she bore one unrecognized son. She has now been celibate for eight years "because of a religious conversion," living with this last son, fourteen, and the six-year-old child of a married legitimate son. The grandson lives with her because "One is lonely without children." Such a family is a truncated three-generation unit. The father, now married, of her recognized son contributes money to this household whenever he can, although his child has grown up and left. It is difficult for the woman to get more than three days' work a week during the harvest. Her house is a large, two-room wooden structure patched here and there with corrugated iron.

In d'Espoir there are three conjugal couples who have grandchildren at home in addition to one or more of their own children. One of these grandmothers lives with four of her twelve children, among whom is a daughter of twenty-three, whom I shall call Agnes. Agnes has four children, ranging from four months to nine years, indicating one of those rare cases of a girl's bearing a child at puberty. The father of Agnes's first child did not recognize him. Her next two were fathered by a married man. The last child is the daughter of a man with whom she did not get along well enough to live with. Agnes's mother confirmed the soundness of this decision: It is bad to live with a man if the two of you have "*histoires*" (scenes); it is better to remain at home. In other words, there is no disadvantage in Capesterre to becoming the founder of a subconjugal family—which this will be if Agnes's mother dies and the young woman continues to live alone. If Agnes inherits the house her chances of living with a man will be even less.

A woman who owns a house, however, does occasionally find a man to live with her. Agnes's mother (whom I shall call Claudine) has found three men to join her where she now lives, each acknowledging that the house is hers, that she is the *chef de famille*. This case is interesting in revealing how nonmonogamous a consistently conjugal family can be. A woman of fifty-two, Claudine was married in 1924 at the age of twenty, after having borne one child at home by another man than her future husband. From 1928 until 1934 she lived adulterously with a man, and because of this her husband left her. Then for seventeen years she lived with another man until he died. She has been living with still another now for the past five years; she has had no children by him.

Claudine's legal husband was the father of only one of her children (her third, which was the second child after her marriage). She was unfaithful to him while he was still with her, and this first *concubin* after her marriage was also the father of her first child; six of her other twelve children are his. Her next *concubin* fathered four.

All these children are considered legitimate, for they were born while Claudine was married to a man who did not dispute her claim upon registering them. The husband is now reputed to be dead. She never made him contribute to her support, "for one does not go to court for such a thing." Furthermore, he had always been poor. The present *concubin*, whose two unrecognized children are with their respective mothers, contributes to the support of the household with his wages as a cane cutter. He has relinquished his claim to his hereditary land in favor of his sister Eloise, who is living in a subconjugal family in the *maison paternelle*. Eloise's *concubin* takes care of the planting on her land and tends the cow and pig, while she weeds and fertilizes. She, too, works as a cane cutter, and they each make $2.25 a day, spending $21 a week for food for the family of eleven, which eats far more than they can grow. The household also includes a male cousin of the *concubin*.

Another couple, grandparents, have two boys of one of their

married sons from the son's first *ménage*, because the son would not leave his children to the mercy of the new stepfather. (Again we see the hostile stepfather theme.)

One grandmother of fifty-six (Justine) and her new husband have in their care the stepsons of her son because their mother and her new husband do not wish to be bothered by children. But the children visit their absent mother daily, eating in her kitchen at times. They call their mother "*Maman* Louise" and their stepgrandmother "*Maman*."

I have mentioned thus far only one collateral relative living in a household, the cousin of Eloise's *concubin*. Another household contains the woman's sister and her child. Two split examples are hardly enough to compare with Smith's findings that nonnuclear relatives tend to be related to the woman, but I believe this fact is irrelevant to establishing a case for matrifocality, since composition and distribution of power vary independently. Furthermore, I could not make a survey of such conditions because the houses are usually considered too small for many other adults to be present. One man in the *quartier* who is incapable of maintaining a household of any sort is not taken in by his family but sleeps in different places and is cared for by nonkin who can afford it. If relatives live with members of their nonimmediate family, I can see no organizational reasons for the balance to be on one side rather than the other.

People usually die before they are so helpless that necessity makes them join the family. As we shall see, old people prefer to live alone, some even moving to a small shack, leaving a young son in the good house. In Fond d'Espoir, there are only two households in which an old parent joined the conjugal pair. In both cases the old person—a father and a mother—is related to the woman rather than the man, and in both cases, as in British Guiana, the older person is not the household head. Occasionally, too, unrelated old people will share a house—the nonmated pairs in Table 6-2. Siblings of all three types also share houses, often presenting an obstacle to anyone's allowing a *concubin* or *concubine* to move in.

The persons of type III in Table 6-2—single men or women living with children—tend to represent broken families. Only a widower would live with his children. An unattached man would find someone to care for a child if the mother deserted it. In these split families, the people may or may not start a new *ménage*.

Another variation in household organization comes about when work demands that two households be maintained. This is likely to occur more often among the well-to-do, for example when two stores are owned, one in the *bourg*, the other in the *quartier*. In such cases the father may take some of the children with him.

MATING PATTERNS

Tables 6–3, 6–4, and 6–5 are samples from Fond d'Espoir of the ages at which people entered *ménage* or marriage, the number of *ménages* a couple has experienced, and the duration of the present arrangement. (The question marks indicate accidental omissions.)

For Voltaire, since the age pattern is the same as for Fond d'Espoir, Table 6–6 gives the number of children born before marriage to people who did not have *jeune fille* ceremonies, thus indicating the point in the life cycle of the family at which people decided to marry. This table also includes the number of outside children in the household.

Although the data are not complete, the pattern is clear. We find that only one woman entered a *ménage* at fourteen; three at fifteen; one at sixteen; and three at eighteen. Only two men started before twenty, the younger at eighteen. Five women began their *ménages* or marriages between twenty and twenty-three, and three men fall into this group. Between the ages of twenty-four and twenty-nine are six women and five men; between thirty and thirty-five, eight women and three men. The first *ménage* began when they were in their forties for two women and one man.

The proportions of people who start a *ménage* at various ages cannot be determined, the significant point being that in each decade of life from the second through the fifth people have their first experience in living together. Moreover, the number of cases in so small a group reflects the fact that they are all positively sanctioned. As we know from previous statements, young men generally feel that they cannot afford a *ménage* until they are well past twenty. The number of girls between fourteen and fifteen shows that men feel a responsibility for these early pregnancies—if they are themselves old enough, for it is not necessarily young men who have had affairs with these young girls. The large number of women in their

Table 6-3   UNMARRIED PEOPLE IN FOND D'ESPOIR

Present Age		Age They Began This Ménage		Duration of Ménage so far (years)	Number of Previous Ménages
MAN	WOMAN	MAN	WOMAN		
40	33	34	27	6	She had one; he none
35	22	31	18	4	Neither had any
30	24	29	23	1	Neither had any
?	40	?	35	5	Neither had any; he is now dead
30	26	18	14	12	Neither had any
?	38	?	37	1	She had another for 8 years; he had none
?	38	?	33	5	She had one for 13 years; he had none
?	28	?	21	7	Their first; he comes and goes
22	16	21	15	1	First for both
45	46	41	42	4	She had one for 11 years
?	37	?	27	10	?
?	39	?	34	5	Neither had any
35	?	33	?	2	Neither had any
39	46	28	34	11	?
39	?	29	?	10	?
?	65	?	43	15	She had one before
39	?	23	?	16	He has mistress simultaneously
22	16	22	16	½	Their first
43	?	36	?	?	He had one before for 10 years; she had one

thirties shows that the respectability standards are maintained by enough people so that it is not merely an ideal pattern.

These figures also show that most individuals confine their reproductive activities to very few people through a lifetime. Few are the people with as many as six partners with whom they have lived. This does not mean that the men who never entered a *ménage* until relatively late in life were continent. A large number say they had many women but no *ménages*. Nonetheless, the number of

Table 6-4 MARRIED PEOPLE IN FOND D'ESPOIR: *BÉNÍ PÉCHÉ*
(LATE MARRIAGES)

Present Age		Age at Marriage		
MAN	WOMAN	MAN	WOMAN	*Particulars When Known*
33	33	31	31	
71	52	43	24	She stayed a year; he has had three *ménages* since: one lasted 1 year; other two lasted 3 years each
48	?	29	?	
48	56	46	54	
80	?	60	?	
?	56	?	18	Three *ménages* before
74	61	67	51	His second marriage, after 24 years of *ménage*
?	77	?	41	She has had many since; widow
?	51	?	34	Widow
39	?	36	?	
28	26	25	23	
60	?	52	?	
56	?	27	?	She left after 18 years
41	38	29	26	
55	56	52	53	After *ménage* 22 years
45	?	42	?	After 20 years
40	?	37	?	After 10 years
40	38	37	35	
38	38	36	36	
43	?	41	?	After 12 years
43	?	40	?	She had children at home before
40	38	37	35	After 18 years
38	33	35	30	After 9 years
38	33	35	30	After 15 years
?	71	?	48	After 2 years
45	33	40	28	After 13 years
65	?	42	?	

pregnancies resulting from such experiences is relatively small. It is
those people who have lived in stable unions who have the largest
number of children. Population expansion, then, is related to the
factor of stability. It does not grow as a result of promiscuity. Of the

twenty *béni' péché* marriages in one *quartier*, almost half have some outside children, but no more than one or two. The stability of legal or common-law conjugal unions, although these unions are likely to start late, is a salient feature of the pattern. These findings contrast sharply with Simey's generalization for the Caribbean area: "Promiscuous sex relations are regarded in the West Indies as normal behavior."[11] Of some 270 households in a survey in Jamaica which he cites, not one consisted solely of parents and their children.

In summary, the stability of relationships in Martinique shows that matrifocality is not likely to be great, for it exists where the father is not permanent in the house. We have also observed that a father's mother as well as a mother's mother is likely to take charge of raising children whom the parents cannot keep, a practice that does not weight the structure on the maternal side as in British Guiana, where mothers have no control over the children of a son as they do over those of a daughter. Our data have now given us a picture of the composition, frequency, and duration of the conjugal household of Capesterre during its genesis and senescence.

Table 6–5 MARRIED PEOPLE IN FOND D'ESPOIR: JEUNE FILLE CEREMONIES

Present Age		Age at Marriage		
MAN	WOMAN	MAN	WOMAN	*Particulars When Known*
86	70	36	20	
?	48	?	23	
53	51	20	18	Annulled by man
46	45	28	27	
35	34	23	22	Man died this year
46	22	44	20	
?	51	?	34	
59	?	28	?	
68	?	38	?	
28	?	26	?	
40	?	28	?	
39	33	35	29	
46	?	19	?	
51	53	21	23	

THE NONMODAL HOUSEHOLD

As the data show, there are in addition to the nuclear family a number of individuals whose life histories indicate a departure from the mode. Of no cultural or structural importance are those who fall into a category of people incapable of any kind of stable conjugal relationship, or even of sexual intercourse. Here we find the mentally, emotionally, or physically ill. Here, too, are such personality deviations as the alcoholic, the homosexual, the impotent, the frigid. The culture views these phenomena in the same way that it views such personality traits as cruelty, undue quarrelsomeness, inordinate

Table 6-6   MARRIED PEOPLE IN VOLTAIRE: *BÉNI PÉCHÉ* MARRIAGES

Present Age of House Head	Total Number of Children	Number and Source of Children Before Marriage, If Any
26	3	2
30	3	2
32	7	3, including 1 outside child of each
34	7	7, including 1 outside child of his
36	8	5, including 2 of her outside children
38	6	2
39	4	4, including 2 of his outside children
46	10	4
48	7	4
48	10	5
50	9	9, including 2 of her outside children
50	6	2
52	5	0
62	12	5
62	9	9, including 1 of her outside children
63	4	2, including 1 of her outside children
65	13	4, including 1 of her outside children
66	7	7
68	6	6, including 1 of his outside children
68	3	3
74	2	2
76	1	1, one of her outside children
78	8	7

promiscuity. There are also a certain proportion of life histories that reveal fortuitous or idiosyncratic departures from the mode: The people in question may not have formed a conjugal household because of having loved one person who died, or from shame because they are crippled.

Patterns of cultural significance are revealed, however, in the nonconformity to the mode of a small group of seventeen single male households in Fond d'Espoir and eight in Voltaire. Table 6–7 gives particulars about this group, separated by age, and reveals the distribution of nonmodal traits.

A woman will seldom leave her family of orientation to set up a household alone, but there are several other sets of conditions under which women live alone or only with their children.

If a woman is left by her husband or *concubin* she is likely not to return to her house of orientation. Although such cases are, of course, conjugal at one point in their cycle, the attitude toward continuing to live alone, often with a definite disinclination to live with a man again, makes them examples of the subconjugal household. The principles involved in making the choice to remain a lone household head reveal the positively sanctioned nature of maintaining a nonconjugal household.

A woman who inherits a *maison paternelle* tends to become the founder of a subconjugal household. If a man moves into the house of one of these female heads, she remains the head, and the tendency is for a self-respecting man not to move in with her. We have mentioned this structural fact, and we shall look more closely at such a case in chapter seven.

Other examples of female household heads are old women who prefer living alone to joining their children. Although there are male heads in forty of the forty-three houses in which a conjugal pair are at the moment present, women are the technical owners in nine other cases, and in two the ownership is joint.

SEX AND REPRODUCTION

Based on a sample of 204 children born to 37 women past the age of childbearing, each of whom had at least 1 child, the average number of children born is 5 per woman. Four other women of this age group in the *quartier* were childless.

Table 6-7 SINGLE MALE HOUSEHOLDS IN VOLTAIRE AND FOND D'ESPOIR

Age	Particulars
20	Lives on family property in house of own because of *beau-père*
22	Eats with neighbor; left home because of *beau-père* (stepfather); has no children or lovers
22	Lives in *chaumière* on family property; has one child and visits his mistress who lives with her aunt
26	Lives on property of family, but alone because of *beau-père*; no children
27	Alone in house; no children; family dead
29	Has no children; lives with brother and brother's *concubine*
35	No children; has had a few affairs; afraid of women
35	Has had one *ménage* briefly; child with its mother
37	Many *concubines* come and go; no children
39	Four children with mistress he cannot move in with because she has *maison paternelle*; his brother sometimes lives with him, as does a stray drunk who is given shelter
40	Homosexual; no children
43	Mentally deficient; no children
44	Drunkard; no children
45	Drunkard; no children
46	Never had a *ménage*; no children
46	No *ménages*; homosexual; no children
53	Three unrecognized children, one with a *concubine*; divorced
56	No children; 15 years with wife; separated; none other
58	Two children; one *ménage* for 20 years; before that, many short *ménages*
60	With wife two years; separated; no others; no children
60	Five children with first wife, four with second; children live with his sister; wife works elsewhere, but they are together for vacations
62	Four children; she is dead; only *ménage* for both
65	A mistress comes and goes
65	One child elsewhere
70	Six *ménages* with one child each

The age at which women had their first child varied between sixteen and thirty-six: most women were in their twenties, but many started in their thirties; rarest were young mothers in their teens. Menopause seems to begin when women are forty-two to forty-six, judging from those women who were with one mate throughout this period but who have ceased to bear. People begin new *ménages* and marriages after this time, however, continuing their sex life until much later.

As I have said, married people have the majority of children. On the whole, those who change partners frequently have long celibate periods or have sexual intercourse at irregular intervals and do not have as many children. There are, however, a few monogamous couples, long married, who have only two, three, or four children, although these are people who use no contraceptives. I have no explanation for this relative infertility except when it was a late marriage.

It is interesting to see the distribution of how many children were born to each woman (not the number surviving) rather than the average number of children born. The following list gives the distribution among thirty-seven women in Voltaire who are over the age of menopause.

Women with 0 children	2
Women with 1 child	2
Women with 2 children	6
Women with 3 children	6
Women with 4 children	3
Women with 5 children	5
	24
Women with 6 children	3
Woman with 7 children	1
Woman with 8 children	1
Women with 9 children	3
Woman with 10 children	1
Woman with 11 children	1
Women with 12 children	2
Woman with 13 children	1
	13

In the rural areas very few women are acquainted with, accept, or buy contraceptives. Some women belong to a group whose small number of children indicates a limited sex life. Many women who have waited long before going *en ménage* or who have had a single, brief affair indicate that relative sexual abstinence is not uncommon. (Having pursued this idea with questions, my conclusion was verified.) The only reason offered is that many women are "cold," not very much interested in sex, not able to give themselves to more than one or two lovers in their lives.

The record of postmenopausal women in Fond d'Espoir shows the following:

Women with 2 children	3	Each with one mate
Women with 3 children	2	Each with one mate
Woman with 4 children	1	Late marriage
Women with 5 children	2	One with five fathers, the other with two
Women with 6 children	3	Two with one father, one with three
Woman with 7 children	1	One mate
Women with 8 children	3	One, two, and four mates
Women with 10 children	2	Each with one mate
Women with 12 children	2	One father; four fathers
Woman with 15 children	1	One mate
	20	

Of the 145 children born, only 11 died before reaching maturity.

As house density shows, privacy is rare. Even where there is enough room—most houses have two or three rooms—people find no objection to sleeping three and four in a bed. The only people consistently bothered by this are grown sons who do not get along with or are jealous of their stepfathers.

As we have seen, some sons remain at home until marriage or *ménage*, and some in their later twenties build a house of their own, usually a *chaumière*, on the family property. If they have enough money, or if their parents have died, they have larger houses than the *chaumière*, and they usually ask a woman to live with them. Often the invitation to live together is like a proposal of marriage in that the couple has not yet had sexual intercourse.

Parents, whatever their own reputation, are uniformly severely strict with their daughters, screaming at and beating them if they show any signs of meeting men. Rather than through verbal instruction, children learn of sex through observing their parents, who often sleep on the floor in the same room with them or sometimes with only a curtain separating the parents' bedroom from the rest of the house. Everyone thinks the standards of sexual behavior and courtship are much more lenient than formerly. Nevertheless, this parental generation reports frequent sex experiences beginning at the age of twelve; but only one pregnancy of a girl as young as fourteen has occurred in d'Espoir within memory. A few cases are rumored about a young girl who had a baby and her parents pretended it was theirs and registered it as the real mother's sister. These children grow up calling their real mother by her first name and respecting the grandmother as their mother.

I have heard people say that in the past young girls would become pregnant, having been seduced in the cane fields, and as the pregnancy became increasingly visible they would pretend they did not know what had happened. And the mother would also keep questioning the girl as if there were some doubt about what had occurred. On the whole, however, there is less reticence with children than formerly, and young adults are very relaxed in their attitude toward sex, making frequent jokes about it, enacting suggestive pantomines, teasing one another. Parents are affectionate before their children, calling each other *chéri, chouchou, doudou*. There is none of the formality that exists in British Guiana, where a man calls his wife "Mistress Brown."

At the same time, however, those women who become pregnant at home before going into *ménage* generally report that their mother was angry. This is not always true, depending on the status of the lover. But when angry, a parent is likely to beat the daughter or make so many *histoires* that the daughter must leave home. She might move in with a grandmother or godmother or aunt. Some continue to stay despite the *histoires*, as we have seen by the number of supraconjugal families. Furthermore, the anger subsides rapidly, and after a girl has made such a *totoblo* (*faux pas*; literally, a type of fish) several times, no notice is taken of it and her pregnancies are positively sanctioned—provided, of course, that she does not have the reputation of being promiscuous.

The anger expressed about an unsanctioned pregnancy is similar to the attempt to keep daughters from being seen with a man before any serious plans are made. It is reminiscent also of the Mexican practice of the groom's forcibly kidnapping the bride from the father. In none of these cases would it seem that the intention is to prevent the inevitable or the expected, even the desired. It is the sanctioning of the eventual state rather than the resistance to its inception that is important for the ultimate structure of the family.

Raymond T. Smith interprets the practice of sending the daughter with her first pregnancy from the house as affirming the mother's power in the household when a member threatens her position by being her potential equal, a mother. But in the absence of matrifocality in the conjugal household of Martinique the practice could mean, on a more operant level, that it is a disgrace to go with a man not respectful or respectable enough to provide a house, the desire not to be involved with people of lower status. A mother is not likely to be angry about her daughter's pregnancy if the man is capable of taking her *en ménage*, although ideally a marriage would be preferred. But if it is obvious that the daughter has no personal qualities that would make her chances unusually bright, the mother's indignation is cooled within a month.

No one today values technical virginity, although a man marrying a *jeune fille* may prefer that she be a virgin. In the past, after the wedding night, he would report to the bride's mother whether the girl was really a virgin, but there has never been any ceremony of examining the sheets for proof in Martinique. I heard of one instance in which the husband reported to the mother that her daughter had indeed been a *pucelle* (virgin). The mother laughed and said she was rather surprised.

Under no circumstances, however, can a girl afford to have the reputation of being promiscuous. To have many children by as many men is not necessarily considered promiscuous, for her intentions could have been sincere with each and the relationships simply did not work out. But if a woman will have "one-night stands," that is all she will ever have in her community; no one will wish to go *en ménage* with her, for she cannot be trusted.

As we have seen in chapter five, truly respectable or ambitious or unusually attractive young girls will not see a man at all except at a heavily chaperoned dance. Even after the formal engagement it is difficult for the couple to get parental permission to see each other alone. Meetings must be secret, and some women are not willing to risk such meetings unless they are sure their social position will keep the man's interest even if he may lose some interest in her after he knows he can have her. In short, all courtship is secret until the baby arrives, or the *ménage* is set up, or the engagement is announced.

Occasionally, a love affair starts when a man passes a girl on the street and secretly hands her a letter in which he writes that he has always admired the girl, that he finds her pretty, that he needs her. She answers him by letter, saying (if she accepts) that she will meet him at an appointed place. If she rejects his advances, yet respects him, she ignores the letter. If she dislikes him, she will insult him, saying in extreme cases, "Go make love to your mother!"

Many men promise marriage and deceive the woman, who then seeks another fiancé. Some women change men on the basis of who provides the best presents, but they are on their way to losing social standing. It is chiefly in the *bourg* that the promiscuous girl is found, and in the *bourg* that a man has his several affairs, for in the country such behavior is hard to hide and so disruptive that negative sanctions stop it. The young bachelors of the country must go to the towns or the city to find women, for they are bachelors chiefly because they cannot afford to set up a *ménage*, and few country girls can be tempted. If a girl falls in love with a bachelor, however, he can win her over. But respectability and security motivate more women than love or sexual desire, and as a result few women are promiscuous, and many live for years without any sex life at all. As we have seen, not a few have an affair and a child and then never again have another man. The sex ratio in the country is influenced by the fact that many girls go into the city to become maids,[12] and it is the women who usually leave the *quartier* to marry.

Prostitution is extremely rare. This leaves many young men without a sexual outlet more than a few times a year when they go to a dance at a *fête* where "*les poules*" are found, or when they persuade married women to let them risk sneaking into their houses while their husbands are away, a rare occurrence. The women, on the whole, are faithful. Not only do the men demand fidelity, but the typical Martinique wife is described as a *maman poule*, a mother hen, a better tender of children than sexual partner.

The attitude of the *Béké* toward the behaviorally black is that they are all promiscuous, that they "make love like cats," that they all go off to the cane fields at puberty and never come out. This is partially substantiated by the fact that any *Béké* can have any black woman quite willingly. There is always a joking relationship between *Béké* men and the lower class, chiefly sexual in nature. A *Béké* stereotype of the older black male is that he is so tired from his hard work that he is not very virile, that he shows little interest in sex unless the woman takes the initiative.

The acculturated and educated all know of birth control and claim to have access to it in the form of pills, injections, and condoms, and when it is important to them they practice it. Some also try the rhythm method. But seldom do they find the prevention of children desirable from any point of view. Several acculturated women told me that after their family has reached the desired size, they will take injections against conception. The less acculturated often despise the use of contraceptives. Some use a "*capot*" only if they have contempt for the woman or mistrust her. However poor, young girls see no reason not to become pregnant. "Babies are *poupées* [dolls]," explained one. "They're the most interesting thing in life. What can you do without one?" If asked their ambition, most girls will answer that they only want to be a mother. Rarely do they speak of love. By the same token, a man speaks of physical desire or of finding someone with whom he will not have *histoires* more often than of *amour* (love). Men usually think of their wives in terms of "the-mother-of-my-children," and they do not feel that the man is required to be faithful, although opinions vary widely on the question of whether affairs should remain indefinitely hidden. When a man is tired of his wife, often she has no idea of it, for he keeps up a pretense for the sake of the children.

Divorce is sought only under the most drastic conditions, and among the poorest the expense—60,000 francs—precludes it. Only under the most difficult circumstances will married couples separate. Since most marriages are contracted after the two have lived for years *en ménage*, most people are sure beforehand that their marriage will be compatible. Of the fifty marriages that took place in Fond d'Espoir, only six couples have separated.

This subject brings us to the next chapter, in which the relation of marriage to the family will be examined. We shall see that marriage is conceived of as an institution separated from the values that influence those aspects of family organization which determine how children are produced and reared. This separation makes possible the various family arrangements already revealed, arrangements permitting, as we saw, the positively sanctioned existence of other families than the conjugal.

NOTES

[1] Raymond T. Smith, *The Negro Family in British Guiana* (London: Routledge & Kegan Paul, 1956).

[2] James G. Leyburn, *The Haitian People* (New Haven: Yale University Press, 1941).

[3] Guy Dubreuil, in an unpublished manuscript, reported that in a community of banana growers in Martinique he found that some peasants do have separate plots with a woman and household on each. This banana-growing region is considerably richer and includes larger landholdings than Capesterre.

[4] M. J. Herskovits and F. S. Herskovits, *Trinidad Village* (New York: Knopf, 1947).

[5] Raymond T. Smith, *Negro Family in British Guiana*.

[6] Rhoda Métraux, "Some Aspects of Hierarchical Structure in Haiti," in Sol Tax, ed., *Acculturation in the Americas* (Chicago: University of Chicago Press, 1952).

[7] T. S. Simey, *Welfare and Planning in the West Indies* (Oxford: Clarendon Press, 1946).

[8] See chapter three, pp. 85–89.

[9] Fernando Henriques, *Family and Colour in Jamaica* (London: Eyre & Spottiswoode, 1953).

[10] E. Franklin Frazier, *The Negro Family in the United States* (New York: Dryden Press, 1948).

[11] Simey, *Welfare and Planning*, p. 83.

[12] Nearly one quarter of all employed women (8,000) were domestic laborers in 1961.

SEVEN

Marriage and the Family

Malinowski once made the following observations:

> In all human societies ... there is universally found what might be
> called the rule of legitimacy. By this I mean that in all human societies a
> girl is bidden to be married before she becomes pregnant. Pregnancy
> and childbirth on the part of an unmarried young woman are invariably
> regarded as a disgrace. ... I know of no single instance in anthropologi-
> cal literature of a community where illegitimate children, that is
> children of unmarried girls, would enjoy the same social treatment and
> have the same social status as legitimate ones.[1]

It was about the same time that the above lines were written
that Herskovits began the investigation of communities where no
such rule of legitimacy prevails.[2] This was among certain New
World Negro communities of which Martinique has many examples.
In some Caribbean areas, people seem to be ashamed of illegitimacy;[3] but in other regions, such as the American South, Frazier
says: "[the people] appeared completely unconscious of any violation of the mores in having children outside of marriage ..."[4]

My observations in Martinique concur with Frazier's statement,
and the people feel this way not because some substitute for
Western marriage that is equally rigid has developed. We do not
find 100 percent illegitimacy according to Western terms and a high
degree of some other form of legitimacy which the local culture
considers to be marriage. In other words, I did not find what Dom

Basil Matthews reports for East Indians in Trinidad, namely, that they had "ceremonially valid but legally unrecognized marriages."[5] The extralegal unions in Martinique are not ceremonially validated in any way. There simply is no rule of legitimacy. The rarity of such a phenomenon can be seen not only in the light of what Malinowski said in 1927, but in the light of what Lévi-Strauss wrote in 1956:

> If there are many different types of marriage to be observed in human societies ... whether by exchange, purchase, free-choice or imposed by the family, etc.,—the striking fact is that everywhere a distinction exists between marriage, i.e., a legal group-sanctioned bond between a man and a woman, and the type of *permanent* or temporary union resulting from violence or consent alone. [Italics mine.][6]

I emphasize the word "permanent" to point up the fact that even if common-law marriage is called a differential ideal in Capesterre, even if the union is stable, this arrangement is not like that of the traditional societies which Lévi-Strauss and Malinowski have in mind.

In chapter six we examined the actual forms of the family, citing examples of three-generation families with no conjugal pair present in the middle generation, in which there may or may not be a conjugal pair in the grandparental generation. We also cited cases of women living alone with their children, not as divorcées do in the West, but as a group-sanctioned type of childbearing and child-rearing unit. In addition, we saw numerous cases of conjugal families, both with and without developmental histories involving the other two types. Furthermore, those families larger or smaller than a conjugal grouping exist not only as parts of a developmental cycle but as permanent, expected constellations. Despite their rarity, therefore, I say that a model of family structure in Capesterre shows the simultaneous existence of the conjugal, the subconjugal, and the supraconjugal family.

This model as well as other organizational characteristics— boarding children out, including outside children in the household together with the children of the current spouses, the fluidity of conjugal unions, the value placed on children—have a correlate. I maintain that such a structure with such organizational principles is the counterpart of the absence of a rule of legitimacy.

To illustrate the ongoing processes in forming *ménages* and marriages, I shall discuss in this chapter how marriage is articulated with the family system. I shall examine the values that replace a rule of legitimacy and illustrate what I maintain to be the attitude of the people toward illegitimacy, or rather toward the nonlegitimate nature of their family system.

TYPES OF CONJUGAL UNIONS

According to law, a fully legal union may be cemented by a civil act without a religious ceremony. When the Catholic sacrament is desired, however, the state demands that it be preceded by the civil act as well. So few Protestants exist in Martinique that the policies of these churches, the evangelical American sects of a fundamentalist cast, need not be considered in this discussion. Within the basic form of the French Catholic ritual, there are four subtypes of marriage ceremonial that have cultural importance in Martinique.

First, there is the *jeune fille* ceremony, contracted by a couple who have at least never lived together and when the woman in the eyes of the church is a *pucelle* (the term "*vierge*" is reserved for the Mother of God). The man's moral state is not considered. Such a marriage takes place at 11:30 in the morning or at 4:00 in the afternoon at what is called a benediction nuptial and is marked by a *cortège, chants, cloches* (a procession, songs, and bells), and is traditionally followed by a *fête* at the home of bride or groom.

Another type of church wedding is conducted only in the presence of two witnesses. It occurs at 6:00 in the morning, accompanied by no procession, no bells, no special notice. This is the only type of church ceremony open to women who have lived "in sin."

The mission marriage, like the dawn ceremony, is for the purpose of *béni' péché* (the remission of sin), and is accompanied by no special festivities or honors. It differs from the dawn ceremony in that a number of couples are married simultaneously.

The fourth subtype of marriage ceremonial is *au lit de mort* (on the death bed). In the history of the *commune* there have been seventy-five death-bed marriages, not a few of whose participants have recovered.

Only the Catholic missions have arrived in Martinique, and each of the five has stayed for a few weeks in each *commune*, conducting spectacular parades. There were boats filled with offerings, viewed by hordes of devotees overcome with an emotional fervor that filled the *matérialistes* with disgust. With the processions, songs, preachings in the streets and in the countryside, the people experienced for the first time the kind of religion that is well known in the British islands. Each mission is remembered for its characteristic color. The first one came in 1923 in *robes noires*. In 1938 they arrived in *robes marrons*. The Mission de la Madone came from Africa in 1948. Only the latest two, in *robes blanches*, went from house to house, in 1953 and 1955. Some people think the great influence of the missions was owed to the fact that the priests were more *instruits* (learned) than the parish priests.

The mission influence in Capesterre can be measured by the number of marriages performed in mission years compared with a nonmission-year average of 9, ranging from 2 to 29. The first mission had the greatest impact—149 marriages ensued. In 1938 and 1948 only 20 and 31 couples, respectively, responded; but in 1953, 73 were married by the mission. Finally, the anticlimactic mission of 1955 drew 17, for the previous mission had taken care of most couples.

The missions are not interested in marrying young people who are not yet living together, but in cementing already existing relationships. For this reason, in addition to its appellation *béni' péché*, it is called *raccommodage*, the mending of a piece of torn material.

In Capesterre there has been only one purely civil marriage not later blessed by the sacrament. It was contracted by a phenotypically white civil servant, well educated, but whose mother was a *cultivatrice* and whose father was a *Béké*. To have celebrated the marriage with the usual *cortège* would have identified him with a group of which he was not culturally a member. On the other hand, he was not accepted associationally by any group except that of his mother. The isolation was sufficient for him to marry in a civil ceremony, as many of the elite of the capital do when they marry white French people.

This man could have taken the course of the nontraditional

marriage followed by two very young mulatto schoolteachers, the only simple church service any *jeune fille* ever had in Capesterre within anyone's memory. They married at the nine o'clock Mass instead of having a special nuptial Mass. Attended only by their two witnesses, these rebels wore only everyday dress and held a simple family dinner for ten afterward.

The one remaining type of marriage is what the British call common-law marriage. When a *ménage* has endured for six months a spouse has the same rights of inheritance as a legally married mate. But culturally, to live *en ménage* is not considered the same as marriage, although a woman will refer to her *concubin* at times as *mon mari*, my husband, and he to her as *ma femme*, my wife. In speaking of other people's relationships, however, they will usually designate them as *concubines*, not spouses. To say that two people are *en ménage* means that the two are living under one roof and that one of them is the household head. The terms *concubine* and *concubin*, however, are also used to describe the participants in a faithful monogamous arrangement in which the couple do not live together in one house. One or the other or both may still be living in their family of orientation. The culture also recognizes the distinction between the relationship of two unmarried people and adulterous *ménages* or relationships. The term *maîtresse* is generally restricted to the woman who is married to or living with one man and who has an affair with another. A mistress is also a single woman whose lover is married or *en ménage*.

INCIDENCE OF CONJUGAL TYPES

Among the eighty-one households of Fond d'Espoir, fifty represent unions characterized in the past or present by legal marriage. Of these fifty marriages, all had been *ménages* except sixteen in which the brides were *jeunes filles*. In Voltaire, of the seventy-one households, forty-seven couples are or have been legally married; of these twenty-two brides were *jeunes filles*.

Insurance company statistics concerning *locataires* who collect the *allocation familiale*, representing 14,000 mothers with children under fifteen, show that only 30 percent are married. Revert's estimate of marriage among marriageable persons is 50 percent.[7] My statistics on the two *quartiers*, representing 152 households of which 97 contain legally married persons, give a percentage of 63.8. According to Henriques, in Jamaica, where he says the highest illegitimacy rate in the world is found, 54 percent of Jamaican mothers were married, according to the census of 1943.[8] Leyburn says that "Nowhere else in the Western world has there been so little actual marriage in proportion to the population as in Haiti."[9]

Marriage rates cannot be accurately obtained from census data, which give a static picture; nor can they be deduced from a survey unless the latter has historical depth. As we can see from the tables on pages 141–144 in chapter six, marriage tends to occur late, and any interpretation of marriage patterns deduced from the number of illegitimate births would be inaccurate, at least for Martinique. The number of illegitimate births later legitimated in a century of records kept by the town hall of the *commune* is 883, not counting the 391 children legitimated during the two big mission years. That there are twice as many illegitimate as legitimate births suggests that such births are positively sanctioned, but it does not tell us how marriage is articulated with family organization.

Illegitimacy does not indicate instability of conjugal unions, since, as we have seen, married women can have legitimate children by many fathers. The situation is different from country to country; for example, under English common law, late marriage cannot legitimate children already born. We can also tell from the town hall records that many mission marriages did not legitimate children. Although not all children are necessarily legitimated when a couple marry, it is the rule to do so, and the fact that many couples did not indicates that children were not born to these persons or that legitimacy is not of any consequence to them.

A census analysis ignores another important aspect of the situation, the distinction within the category of illegitimate births between those whom the father recognizes and those whom he does not. We can, however, obtain this information from the *État Civil*, the registries in the town hall. To take three years at random, we see (and it is an accurate reflection of the whole) that although illegitimate births outnumber the legitimate, recognized children usually outnumber the nonrecognized. The illegitimacy rate here is 67 percent.

Status	1934	1941	1948	Total
Legitimate	50	44	32	126
Recognized	42	67	65	174
Unrecognized	18	10	51	79
Yearly Totals	110	121	148	379

LEGAL ASPECTS

A man need not live with a woman to recognize one of her children, but if he lives with her he is forced to recognize her children unless he wishes to go to court to dispute paternity. Both to dispute paternity and to insist on recognition, as well as to sue for support in the latter case, are not considered worthwhile. Social pressure alone in most cases guarantees that a man will meet his obligations if he can afford to do so. In the past, it is thought, men would often postpone recognition, waiting for a sign that the children resembled them; but now, with the *allocation*, a man will not hestitate to recognize a child whether it is his or not.

By law, recognized children inherit along with legitimate children from the father.[10] Unrecognized children, then, are at a disadvantage, although they are their mothers' legal heirs. A legitimate child has a right to an equal share with siblings of both the mother's and the father's estates. A recognized child of a man who later marries a woman other than the child's mother automatically loses his or her share of half the father's estate, that half belonging to the man's legal wife; on the other hand, he or she is bequeathed a share of the mother's property.

A case involving conflicting rights between legitimate and illegitimate children can be extremely confusing should it ever reach a court. Upon the occasion of major legal reform on this matter, which took effect in 1972, some of the intricacies of the Napoleonic code were reviewed by Flora Lewis.

> The new law abolishes the difference previously drawn between "natural children" of unmarried parents and children born of adultery .... The new law provies that "anyone who had sexual relations with his [the child's] mother during the legal period of conception ..." must pay support. But mothers who "engaged in debauch" are excluded. .... The law also eliminates the "presumptive paternity" of a married

woman's husband when the child is born more than 300 days after an order of non-conciliation is issued in a divorce case, whether or not the divorce is granted.[11]

The surviving spouse in a marriage has the use of half the property of the deceased until the estate devolves upon the legal heirs. A common-law union involves the same rights. Many men think it better not to have legal heirs, to be free to leave property to whomever they wish, which is the case if there are only unrecognized children. During life, no spouse can alienate his or her property without the other spouse's written consent. A spouse of either sex owns half of all the other acquired before marriage.

If a number of marriages are contracted by the same man, the children of his first wife lose half of the father's half of the estate with each succeeding marriage. A discarded common-law wife, unlike an abandoned legal wife, has no legal claim upon a man's property; such a law works as well regarding a man's claim upon a woman's property. The inheritance tax favors legitimate heirs: 80 percent if illegitimate; 40 percent if legitimate.

Naming customs conform somewhat to inheritance practices. A child carries the family name of the man who recognizes him or her, whether it be the biological father, any unrelated man, or the mother's husband. If no man recognizes a child, the child bears its mother's surname. If a woman is married and her husband is alive and does not dispute their assumption of it, her children bear her husband's name regardless of paternity.

The reluctance to marry cannot be clarified by pointing to bureaucratic barriers. The mechanical aspects of getting married are not a deterrent. Unlike the Haitians, the people of Martinique do not fear officialdom in general. They are, as we have seen, accustomed to coming to the *bourg* to register *allocation* claims, births, deaths, tax reports. They are all—except for an occasional old person—literate.

Economic Aspects

With the exception of female teachers, I have never met anyone of any degree of wealth who felt it an economic necessity or advantage to be married. Direct economic pressure to marry exists in only one occupation: a female teacher must maintain the official ideal of morality by marrying if she either lives with a man or bears a child. Only under these conditions can a female teacher maintain her job (that is, if anyone registers a complaint). Such pressure does not affect a male teacher. Contrary to practice in Trinidad, in all other occupations married persons do not get preferred employment, for the priest has no influence in obtaining jobs; [12] and unlike conditions in Jamaica, no communities in Martinique were organized by church groups whose sale of land was contingent upon marriage. [13]

There is an indirect advantage in being married if the goal is to obtain bank credit in the city. A banker is likely to favor the possession of Western standards, but marriage per se makes one no better a credit risk. On the other hand, unlike Haiti where the land tenure makes marriage a disadvantage because a man needs several wives, in Martinique there is no conscious disadvantage in being married.

Contrary to alleged conditions elsewhere, there is no correlation between marriage and economic standing within the *commune*. We have described how poor the average household is in the *quartiers*, and we have seen how many of these families form legal unions. Conversely, in the *bourg*, the richest shopkeeper may be living *en ménage* with a *concubine*. The restaurant-owner's family, for example, is a classic grandmother family.

PRESTIGE

In pursuing the reasons why the nonelite have persisted in their departure from Western marriage norms and the extent to which this "deviation" correlates with differences in the organization of the family, let us examine self-image and prestige.

In Haiti, the gulf between the elite and the nonelite is much greater than it is in Martinique. According to Leyburn, the priests are so few in the country, the population so large, Western religion so little penetrated, that the only peasant marriages that occur are those precipitated at the insistence of "children aspiring to social prestige." [14] In Martinique, I met no children who seemed to care whether their parents were married. At the *lycée*, where the most mobile of the young are trained, no one with whom I discussed the matter said there was a difference between the married and the unmarried state. There are stories of children who snub their country parents on the city street, but marriage would not make the old people more acceptable to the elite. Not one of the couples encountered in the *quartiers* married because of the influence of their children.

There is no social disadvantage whatsoever in being illegitimate (if recognized), which is not to say there is no disadvantage in being nonelite. Although the elite marry, no one has ever confused being married with elite status. As we have seen, education is the one means at present for reaching this rung; but such channels are few and crowded, so this influence is slight. Contact with whites and the elite are few in the rural districts and not of the sort to provoke imitation.

RELIGION

It is through religion that marriage as a concept is becoming more pervasive. In the next chapter we shall see how religious ideas became incorporated with more basic values. These more basic values will be described later in this chapter. At the moment let us examine the religious attitude of the *commune*.

We have already seen how many marriages were precipitated by the mission in Capesterre (not all *communes* in Martinique were reached by the mission). The percentage of married people, therefore, may be higher in Capesterre than elsewhere. However, we must ignore such a statistical appearance of the incidence of marriage and inquire into the meaning of marriage among the people.

Religion in a less heightened form than that of the missions is a permanent part of the life of the *commune*. Unlike the situation in Haiti, there is a priest for every few thousand persons. In Martinique, not only is everyone a church member who attends at least once a year or so, but the church goes out to influence the people in their homes. The Legion, a group of churchwomen, try to persuade people to marry as they go on visits from house to house. Through these women the priest sends for children to appear for their religious instruction if the parents have neglected to send them. The priest keeps track of his flock by means of a list of baptismal names.

All children receive instruction that carries them as far as their first Communion, and all people are buried by the church. Marriage is the only sacrament in which there is no automatic participation. The Herskovitses make the same observation for Toco, Trinidad:

> The sense of dependence on the conventional church is strongest in relation to christening and death, rather than marriage . . . or confirmation, which are valued chiefly as prestige-giving ceremonials.[15]

According to the Herskovitses, this differential response is an important reinterpretation of African behavior. Those aspects of African religion (such as burial) pertaining to tribal deities with cult centers have been referred in Toco to the established denominations; on the other hand, the intimate household practices, including marriage, have continued outside the churches.

The priests differ with one another in their diagnosis of the inhibition to marriage. They blame factors ranging from the climate to a man's hesitation in making a woman his equal; from a man's preference for spending his money on gambling rather than on a marriage to fear of the required medical examination. Most priests are metropolitans and some believe that the men of Martinique avoid marriage because they want several women at a time. The most pertinent motivation here would be the desire for plural wives; but as we have seen, the patterns of family life, even when there is no marriage, are largely conjugal and relatively monogamous. The lone young male household heads are likely to become conjugal. Although the priests have no real insight into the situation, they are accustomed to dealing with the verbalized rationalizations offered by the people, such as "We are not ready yet," or "We cannot afford a *fête*."

All priests agree that the church does not wish to force the issue, that (even though the priests cooperated with the missions) it is not good to coerce the people. The doctrinal rationale behind their stand is that those not ready to marry would become adulterers, and this is far more sinful than concubinage. Inheritance would also become a legal problem if adultery were more widespread, since children born to adulterous fathers cannot be recognized. In strict Napoleonic codes, prior to reforms in 1972, even a mother is "unknown" on the birth certificates of such children.[16]

The clergy are also in agreement that *les Martiniquaises* are "bad Catholics." In many *communes* only one man to ten or fifteen women attends Mass, and only a small proportion of the women attend on any given Sunday. In one *bourg* in the process of being created around a church, only one-sixth of the population attend regularly, again mostly women. According to policy, all persons are encouraged to attend, although only virgins and married people can take Communion. Most people laugh about the men, saying that even the married ones are too sinful to take Communion.

Even in the face of threats of the devil's imminent arrival, voiced by both priest and Legion women, the people shrug and say, "We will get married when we are ready." Threats are no goad to immediate action, nor is the catechism. People have varied reactions to statements about the fiery fate of those who live in sin. In the first place, there is the plan to marry at some time in the future—"when we are ready"—and the danger is not thought real. Furthermore, the pattern of late marriage indicates that possibly the normal chain of events involves late marriage, that the only difference between Western practice and here is the timing. But this is not completely true, for the existence of mission marriages alters such apparent regularity of pattern, and many couples part before they marry. Moreover, people are not at all concerned about the sinfulness of early unions if they legalize the final union. The *au lit de mort* wedding always offers a last resort, although no provision is made against sudden death that leaves no time for expiation. Is Hell believed to be the fate of such people? Few are so orthodox, for more prevalent is a strong, pervasive belief in a kind of fatalism, a predestination. "Why would *le bon Dieu* punish us like that if He made us sin in the first place? Nothing happens that God has not willed. Just as He has willed us to be *malheureux* [to live in misery], He has willed that we live like this. The catechism? *C'est plutôt pour les enfants.* [That's for children.]"

These are the attitudes of people who are living or have lived *en ménage*, whose parents or children may have died before marriage. The orthodoxy of belief among those women who have had *jeune fille* marriages is impossible to assess. However, the attitude of the men who have married *jeunes filles* is indicated by the fact that nearly all had other women before.

Outside the church the idea of sin is totally separated from a concept of the disgraceful. The roots of these religious attitudes will be taken up in the next chapter. The "real" reason for not marrying, everyone will say, is that no one can afford the obligatory *fête*. So far, only the mission-stirred fervor has released people from this obligation. The overt appeal of the mission marriage is its cheapness. But in nonmission years there are no cheap marriages—it is not done. From cleric to elite poet, from destitute cane cutter to village lawyer, all say that the rarity of marriage is because people cannot afford the *fête*.

The "Fête"

Before pursuing marriage patterns on the level of values and the social arrangements that embody them, let me give an eyewitness account of a *fête*, a *jeune fille* wedding of two young people born in the same *quartier*, each the offspring of *petits cultivateurs*. I shall then present some data on the expense of *fêtes*, for this is central to the folk interpretation of our problem.

The bride—Ma'Lou, a *couturière*—and the groom—Monplaisir, a *usine* mechanic—arrived at the church at four o'clock in the afternoon in one of five cars hired for the occasion. They walked up the nave amidst a procession consisting of six little girls between the ages of five and ten, dressed in floor-length pink satin gowns, and a little boy. Among the several witnesses was the mayor, in top hat and black suit. Following were two old men; two old women; one young matron of honor wearing a blue afternoon dress; and three young men who, like the groom, wore tight black double-breasted suits. The bride was in white silk with train and veil. Including the principals, there were seventeen members of the wedding.

Not many spectators appeared in the church. They were for the most part a miscellaneous group who, like me, happened to drop in. Only a handful wore their good clothes, the rest remaining in everyday madras kerchiefs or straw hats and old ankle-length skirts; the young preferred modern house dresses. Aside from the bridal party, there was only one man in the entire church. He turned out to be the photographer.

One of the old women in the procession was the groom's mother, but the bride's mother, although not sick, was not present. No one else thought this remarkable. The mother is usually there, they said, but not necessarily, explaining that she probably had something else to do. This seemed a baffling "custom" in view of the importance that I was led to attribute to the event.

The service itself, marked by no local idiosyncrasies, lasted about half an hour. Then the entire party reentered the cars and drove to the house of the bride. A large group of women had gathered outside the church and others were looking on through the windows along the main street. I did not see any more until nine o'clock that night when I went to the *fête* with a group of local friends from the *bourg* who did not know the couple personally, but attended because of me and because their status gave them an automatic invitation.

We drove up through a heavy rain and sloshed through the mud walk across a field to the house of the bride's family. A neighboring relative had also prepared her house for the occasion. Both families had built a bamboo canopy across the front of the wooden houses, and in one house the partitions and the furniture had been removed to make a 20- by 20-foot ballroom.

The rain stopped for awhile and the hundreds who had been crowding onto the terraces and into the houses scattered around the yard. The people I came with, my hosts, stood silently by, speaking to no one. Then occasionally they would kiss relatives. But few people spoke. The women formed one group and milled around very silently; the men, another, standing and looking. The only guests apparently at ease and chatting were older couples. It was such people to whom I spoke.

On the temporary terraces, tables were laden with rum, wine, champagne, fancy cakes, sandwiches. Food and drink were passed continuously to some two hundred people for the six hours that I remained. When I arrived, the orchestra was eating dinner. When they finished, another group moved in to eat. Then the dancing started, the seven-piece orchestra continuing with fox-trots and tangos and meringues until dawn. The older people stood around the tables, the old men telling jokes and talking politics, but the young people communicated with one another only while dancing.

A young man I had met came over to me on the terrace and said he would like to dance with me, but since I had come with someone, it would not be proper, that it was not done, that people who came together were couples. I explained that I was an exception, and we danced. But despite this formula, which several repeated to me, I observed many people changing partners. In the beginning only men introduced by my host danced with me; but as the evening went on, others would come up without a word and we would dance. The dancers were packed as tightly as at any New York nightclub—and the height of chic among rural men is to wear a woolen jacket. Some of these young men said this was the first rural *fête* they had ever attended, that such affairs are more properly held in the *bourg* where there is not so much mud. Although the city boys sneered, they had come far out of their way to go to the reception of people they did not know.

During the dancing I was ushered into the other house, and with some dozen other people I sat against the wall. In a moment the bride and groom sat against the wall with us. No one talked. The *nouveaux mariés* occasionally exchanged a whispered comment, a smile. Wine and cake were passed. After about ten minutes someone raised a glass. There were a few mumbled felicitations, we drank, sat a few more moments, then my hostess said that we should leave to give others a chance to greet the newlyweds. We returned to the dance through the crowd of old men obviously enjoying themselves. On the way I asked to be introduced to the mother of the bride. She was in the kitchen; she had not felt up to the formalities of serving city people and going to church.

When it was time to leave, our chauffeur came in for a few dances. I wanted to thank my hosts, but I was told that no one does that here: one just quietly leaves, unobserved, as did the bride and groom at some time during the evening.

This, then, was the *fête*, the pivot of all those values in which this societal segment differs from the general Western pattern of which it is a part. The table on page 169 lists the expenses involved in a *fête*.

The prices are arbitrarily chosen, for they may vary. For example, the *pâtés* for after-dinner guests, allowing ten to a person, range from 10 to 50 francs a *pâté*. Rum is 240 francs a bottle;

Item	Cost (francs [350 to $1])
Publication of the banns in the *mairie* ten days before the wedding	90
Publication of the banns in the church for three Sundays	5,000
Medical certificate and X-ray	1,000
Birth certificate	65
Five cars at 1,500 francs each (partly paid for by the guests)	7,500
Dinner for *cortège* of 12	20,000
Orchestra at 5,000 francs per musician	35,000
Ten *pâtés* per person at 50 francs each	25,000
Clothes (for bride)	22,000
($330)	115,655

champagne, 3,000. Cakes can be 1,000 francs each. The orchestra can cost 75,000 francs. The wedding dress can be anywhere from 5,000 to 10,000 francs for the making alone; the material from 200 to 500 francs a meter, and from 6 to 10 meters are bought. The veil of 10 meters is 500 francs a meter. Shoes are 3,000 francs, and stockings from 500 to 1,500 francs.

There are no rules about who pays these expenses. Often the families share them. But the groom usually buys the living-room furniture, with the following traditional necessities: table, buffet, chairs, tableware; the cost for the most respectable is usually about 200,000 francs ($570). The bride's family buys the bedroom staples for about the same amount. Sheets range from 1,500 to 25,000 francs each; mattresses from 8,000 to 15,000 francs.

Of course, the style of the wedding and the furnishings (and the latter are a corollary of the former) are variable. As one old lady put it: "*On ne se marié pas sans fête. S'il n'y a pas de pain doux et du champagne, il y a de tambours et de rum.*" (One does not marry without a *fête*. If one has no cake and champagne, there are drums and rum.) But if the rum is for too few people, the purpose is defeated, for one only got married in the first place for the *fête*. In questioning different people, I got the impression that to spend the family's yearly income is not too unusual, and the storekeepers claim that people go into debt to them for four and five years because of the *fête*. A man in the *quartier* with 10 acres, one of the relative *aisés* of the country, spent 450,000 francs ($1,285) on his son's marriage. In addition, the groom spent 125,000 francs ($357) on his dining room. At his own wedding this man's expenses were shared equally by his parents and those of his bride at a *fête* for fifty people.

One of the poorest couples in the *quartier* spent 30,500 francs ($87) at their *fête* after a long *ménage*. Someone called this not a wedding but a conversion after so many years. They had none of the expensive furniture of the couple discussed above.

Another couple, after a mission wedding, spent 125,000 francs ($357), their year's wages. They felt a greater sense of social obligation because they had no children for whom baptismal *fêtes* had been given. On the day they decided to marry they had 500 francs (a little over $1) between them. They pawned their cow for 20,000 francs, and since the bride's mother was dead her godmother gave 10,000 francs. Friends and relatives brought cake and wine. About fifty people attended.

Baptismal *fêtes* cost about the same amount as the weddings: from 30,000 to 40,000 for the poor; about 150,000 for families with two working cane cutters; and 450,000 for the *aisés* and rich. The old people say there were not many marriages before the missions because everyone wanted "to receive their friends," and most people could not. During a mission, however, *fêtes* are not expected because they would be impossible; several members of one family might be married the same day. Furthermore, the guests would have to spread themselves too thin through a *commune* where perhaps twenty-five couples had been converted.

On the surface there might appear to be a connection between economic standing and being married instead of living *en ménage*. In the first place, people said when they were not married that it was because they could not afford the *fête*. Then, in attending a *fête*, I learned that they were indeed expensive, and that although it could be lavish or not, it still represented a poor couple's yearly income. However, it was not much more expensive, I was told, than a baptismal *fête*, which was mandatory for each child. In reality, though, the latter is much cheaper. To the poor couple giving a simple affair the two are the same, for they have no orchestra, no automobiles, no elaborate dress for either occasion. But to the *aisés*—or to those who choose to spend as much as the couple whose wedding I attended—there is no comparison between having people in at a baptism and the wedding party described. This couple might be in debt for five years.

It did not seem true that people refrained from marriage because they could not afford it, even if the marriage was considered only a *fête*, and clearly marriage was a *fête* rather than a sacrament alone, for anyone could afford the latter. Only the destitute, the paupers, seemed truly not to have a yearly income which would be acceptable as a sum to spend on a marriage *fête*. Within this framework of conspicuous waste, I concluded that anyone who could afford a *ménage* could afford a *fête*. I further corroborated the impression—a hypothesis now—that the expense of the *fête* was not a deterrent to marriage by observing that many obviously *aisés* people had been living together for years simply *en ménage*. There were obviously other than economic principles at work. The problem involved explaining these as well as discovering why a marriage was synonymous with a *fête*.

STATUS EQUALITY

In making my survey and talking about the subject, since there are too few weddings even within a five-year period to show regularities deduced by observation alone, I discovered my next piece of the puzzle; namely, that not all people *did* consider marriage to be a *fête*. No sooner did I learn that "We are not married because we cannot yet afford a *fête*," than I found that some people had married without a *fête*. Again it had nothing to do with economic standing. The reaction to people who had done so varied: some were scorned, some were excused by their fellow *quartier* dwellers. My task was to study all cases and public opinion about them—those who remained unmarried because they would not marry without a *fête* yet could not "afford" one; people who married without one; and couples *en ménage* who were neither pious nor poor.

The stories of both mother and son in one family reveal identical considerations. She is a prosperous, respectable restaurant owner. Although she is light-skinned, her *concubin*'s family disapproved of his marrying her because her family was not so distinguished as theirs; furthermore, she already had one child. They lived together for many years until his death, he meanwhile fathering several children in the *bourg* with various mistresses.

One of their sons met a *cultivateur*'s daughter. "*Tout de suite il l'aime.*" (Love at first sight.) But he did not ask the girl to live with him. Not only were her parents poor, the "*conditions sociales*" (a frequent expression) of the two families were different. She came from "*les peuple bas,*" meaning that they had no education, ambition, dignity. The old mother did not speak good French, and at funerals they held *veillées*; nor did they have a proper table to set. In short, the girl was "*mal élevée,*" behaviorally black. The son, a *fonctionnaire*, saw her secretly, and she became pregnant, which is often precipitous, as we have seen, of a *ménage*. But he did not wish to have one. Nevertheless, when the girl's mother drove her out of the house and the girl came to the boy's house, public opinion demanded that he provide for her. The girl's family considered the event a *totoblo*, a *faux pas*, a disgrace. The boy's mother grumblingly gave the girl shelter until the son rented a house for her in a nearby *bourg*, where he lived with her most of the time.

A few months before the birth of the second child he met a shop clerk, abandoned his *concubine*, and moved in with the new one. Because of his position, the first woman sued him for support and won the case; she had no pride, and he was rich. Her parents took her back with open arms. She had lived *en ménage* and her child was recognized. No longer was it a *totoblo*.

Both *bourg* and *quartier* are filled with such cases. People live *en ménage* with no intention of ever marrying because of status inequalities, often expressed in color differences, although not always, for light color can be the result of a recent mixture involving a woman of low status; in such cases the child has none of the advantages that miscegenous unions produced in the past.

Henriques has observed a similar phenomenon in Jamaica, where educated black women are often spinsters because they will not marry down in terms of education, and light men will not marry them. In Jamaica, he points out, there is also a prejudice against professional women. In Martinique, on the other hand, it is the best *mulâtres* families that are likely to have *vieilles filles* (old maids). These women will not marry down, nor will they even marry up, although such opportunities are rare. In Capesterre one of them once fell in love with a white man, a planter who had lost his money. He wanted to marry her, but her father would not permit it on the grounds that he was able to place himself in the white man's position, and if the *Béké* married her they would both be outcasts. Such people often identify themselves with the white group, feeling the same family pride.

Mulâtre women who have not found status equals to marry do not always remain *vieilles filles*. They sometimes become involved with educated blacks, but they will only live *en ménage* with them; there is no possibility of marriage. In Capesterre a black dentist has lived for some twenty years with a phenotypically white *mulâtresse* of excellent background but no advanced education. Their children feel no stigma whatsoever; on the contrary, the family is among the social leaders.

Another case is provided by Mme. Renault, who could not marry some of her lovers because they outranked her, and who would not marry others because wealth had given her too much mobility to lower herself. This woman is a prosperous *commerçante* and property owner, the mother of highly respected children. Among them are a physician living in France with a white wife, a successful baker, a daughter living *en ménage* with a plantation executive, a daughter married to a government clerk, a son who is a schoolteacher, a son who is a local factory mechanic, and an unmarried daughter living at home with her who has two recognized children but has never lived with a man. This last daughter makes the family fit the classic grandmother pattern. She now runs her mother's business.

The father of three of these children was a local tax official of high standing who later married his social equal. Interestingly, his three children are the most successful of Mme. Renault's children (the title Mme. is honorary). It was through his money that Mme. Renault, poor and uneducated but beautiful, started her successful business.

The other four children had more modest fathers. One was a chauffeur; his son is the factory mechanic. One was a schoolteacher, whose daughter is the one living at home. The *instituteur* and the daughter married to the clerk are the offspring of a fisherman.

One of the principles behind the paradoxes of verbalized values, then, is status equality. It is not only expressed in cases of the good old *mulâtre* families, but throughout the *commune*, and it has always been like this. Père Labat reports that in the beginning of the colony slaves would marry only within their own category.[17] Within the slave population the rankings were: first, the house servants, who knew the European ways best; then the *Nègres à talente* (skilled workers); beneath them were the *Nègres à culture* (field hands); and at the bottom, the *Nègres pièce d'Inde* (recent arrivals from Africa). The measuring stick was obviously the degree of European acculturation, and the means of diffusion was primarily from servants who were close to the white family, particularly the "mammy" or *da*, as she is called in Martinique.

The same principle operates among the groups differentiated on the basis of their *quartier* residence. The people of Fond d'Espoir, those only recently risen above the status of *gens casés*, say that the people of Hauteur Pelée, who have owned their land since 1902, do not wish to marry them. Why not? For the same reason that the people of Fond d'Espoir do not wish to lower their status by forming alliances with the *gens casés*. They say it is not wise after struggling so hard to own land to go down in the world again. Of course, this ideal of absolute equality is not carried out in reality. I discovered many inter-*quartier* liaisons, but not many marriages. The ideal is not, on the other hand, to have *quartier* endogamy, but to import a mate (usually a woman) from a similar *quartier* in another *commune*, which may be called *quartier* exogamy.

Just as slaves married only within categories and the *quartiers* are ranked, so also are individuals ranked within the *quartiers* as well as throughout the *bourg*. The records of a dozen decades in the town hall, giving the occupational status of the *mariés*, show that teachers marry teachers or big *commerçants*, skilled workers marry *couturières* or their equivalent, and *cultivateurs* marry *cultivatrices*. The *État Civil* also gives the marital status and occupations of the parents (if they are alive at the wedding date) of the bride and groom. From 1825 to 1835 the record also mentions conditions of servitude. After that date, no other listings have been preserved until 1866, after which the record is complete except for the three years following the eruption of Mont Pelée in 1902.

From such data we have documentary proof that status through occupation influences the selection of marriage partners, and we can tell that marriages are contracted among the lower echelons on the same basis. Although marriage has never been exclusively an elite phenomenon—there were always a few rare slave marriages—it was primarily so. In the earliest records, those of 1825, only two marriages occurred in Capesterre, both between whites. The grooms came from Bordeaux, and one of the local women was the celebrated one for whom a *quartier* (fictitiously Voltaire) is named. Her descendants are now colored. There were no marriages in 1826 and only three *Béké* weddings in 1827. In 1828 the first marriage involving a *fille de couleur libre* (a freed colored woman) appears. There were two such marriages among the eight of that year; in both, the participants were all listed as *propriétaires*. Within the next few years several marriages were listed with no decipherable information except that two of them involved persons whose parents were unmarried. Two couples within the ten years from 1825 to 1835 legitimated children who had already been born. The records next show that from 1866 until the present, the number of marriages per year, with the exception of the mission years, has remained at a constant rate.

Let us take 1953, a mission year in which seventy-three marriages took place, as a good random sample of the expression of status equality among the lower classes. Of fifteen female servants,

2 married mechanics
1 married a stoker
2 married chauffeurs
5 married fishermen
1 married a carpenter
2 married *cultivateurs*
1 married a mason
1 married a *journalier* (day laborer)

The five fishermen are near the bottom of the ranking system, as are the two *cultivateurs* (no occupation except that of cane cutter) and the *journalier*, who is like a servant. Eight of the fifteen men, then, are obviously of the same status as a servant. The stoker and the mason have very little work and thus are as poor as the others. Although the records do not show whether the mechanics and the chauffeurs are full-time employees, my investigations confirmed that they are poor, landless, part-time workers from the *bourg*.

Of three *couturières*, a higher status than that of servant, one married a *distillateur* and one a shoemaker, both skilled occupations as much above the maids' bridegrooms as the *couturières* are above the maids. The third married a mechanic, who may or may not be steadily employed.

Among the forty-six *cultivateurs*, forty married *cultivatrices*. Of the remaining six, two married maids, one married someone with no occupation given, and one married a woman listed as *sans profession*, meaning that she could be of any status whatever.

Of the fifty-three *cultivatrices* in the pool, forty, as we know, married the *cultivateurs* listed above. Of those remaining, two married fishermen, one married a butcher, one a carpenter, one a barrelmaker, and two married mechanics. The butcher, we know, is of higher status, and among the other occupations some may also be higher. Other years have shown exceptions, too, for example 1950 when a teacher married an electrician. On the whole, however, the equality is remarkably consistent.

As we have said, status inequality is no insurmountable obstacle to living *en ménage*, but obviously the *ménages* tend to follow status lines, since most of the above marriages were *béni' péché*, meaning that the couples had already lived together. When parents object to plans for living *en ménage*, the children in almost all cases go against parental wishes: "*Tant pis pour la Maman*" (too bad for Mother) is a frequent comment. But objections to marriage are generally heeded, since a *fête* is a mockery, a contradiction in terms, in the face of hostile public opinion, and the opinion of the neighbors is not likely to differ from that of the parents.

As these figures and facts clearly demonstrate, marriage is not restricted to the higher economic ranks: fifteen female servants, forty-six *cultivateurs*, and so on. On the other hand, as we have seen in other examples, not all well-off people marry. We have sketched the cases of Mme. Renault, the *commerçante*; the dentist; the rich restaurant owner and her son.

We have seen that status equality overrides financial standing and that marriage by and large correlates with status equality. But not all equals who live together marry each other. Let us see what other principles are involved in the articulation of marriage with the family.

CONVIVIALITY

When there are no status barriers to marriage, other factors may override the motivation to marry. Some of them also govern the choice of mate when a person goes into *ménage*, for in terms of daily behavior, marriage and *ménage* are ruled by identical expectations, at least in a short-range view, although the *ménage* can be easily dissolved and no social obligations are involved in entering it. Setting up a *ménage* is not marked in any way by family or community: there are neither presents nor congratulations, neither toasts nor announcements.

Some of the considerations that play a part in the decision to live with someone are those that would be true in any society. But, as we shall see, conviviality is elaborated in Martinique in a way that is by no means universal. Perhaps its greater importance stems from the fact that no other pressures keep a couple together.

If a man is not forced into *ménage* because of social pressure to help provide for a woman who has borne his children, he wonders first whether the woman will be faithful, whether she is the kind of person to whom he wants to be tied down, however temporarily. The woman's concern is with the man's stability, whether his character equips him to have power over her children. In Martinique, the demands of the sexual division of labor have not been so elaborated as to make conjugality an automatic preference. Still persistent is the knowledge gained in the days of slavery that a woman is capable of raising her children alone, and that it is sometimes desirable for her to do so. When she hesitates to live with a man, she may also be waiting for something better to come along.

People often explain that such-and-such a couple will not convert their *ménage* into a marriage because they have too many *histoires* (scenes). The value involved in all such considerations I shall subsume under the term "conviviality." The moral and emo-

tional expectations that go into making up the household are most
clearly revealed in a number of folk beliefs that spell out the ideal of
conviviality, a concept closely allied with another Martiniquan
theme—hospitality. To get an insight into these patterns, let us
examine the *quimboiseur*. Although the *quimboiseur* is disappearing, it is said, he remains in symbolic form the crux of many values,
or rather, the values remain even though they are not now so
frequently expressed by referring to the *quimboiseur*. Such forces
were probably always more symbolic than existential.

THE "QUIMBOISEUR"

The *quimboiseur*—healer, poisoner, man of magic—is, says Revert,
a French folk figure. The word, an informant explained, comes from
the Creole pronunciation of the French for "Here, drink!" (which is
"*Tiens, bois!*"), a characteristic pose for the magician. A number of
people claim to have met or known *quimboiseurs* very well within
their lifetimes, but most of the young people have only heard
rumors about certain people. At present only one man in the
commune is reputed to be a *quimboiseur*; others say he is only a
séance practitioner, what the British islanders call a "lookman," who
according to Herskovits represents an African reinterpretation.
When the lookman gives prescriptions for magical remedies, they
are usually taken to the pharmacy. Not having the occult ingre-
dients, the pharmacist pretends to have them, selling something
harmless and making money the while. Certain priests will not
hesitate to give the best medical advice when necessary, indicating
their inspiration to be magical.

The *quimboiseur* in his darker guise would be hard to study. So
secret are his maneuverings said to be that only a few will admit his
definite existence, for he has long been illegal. Nor is his illegality
counter to the beliefs of the police, who are ashamed of and angered
by his survival in their modern world. Since they know the *commune* intimately, when the police feel this way they can stop the
quimboiseur or drive him far underground. Young educated people
see through him completely, they say. But the slightly less acculturated, though equally educated, harbor a flicker of wonder about
him, like urban Westerners who talk of psychic phenomena. Actually, nearly every *Martiniquais* believes in the fortune-teller.

Even if he is stamped out by the police, however, the *quimboiseur* flourishes in another way. He is difficult to find not so much because he is secret but because he does not usually exist as a participant in all those activities attributed to him. "He" is, above all, a supernatural explanation for certain kinds of events like sudden death and some forms of antisocial behavior. It is the content of this system which reveals a number of family attitudes.

If there is discord within or between families, it is because the *quimboiseur* has caused it. He can be paid to work his mischief, but now generally it is only his own evil nature that motivates him gratuitously. People cannot be sure that the author of a situation is a *quimboiseur* unless they go to one of them, who explains events in this way to satisfy his clients. The victim or onlooker usually has no idea who the distant *quimboiseur* is, but believes the information.

If the witch or sorcerer wants to promote discord between a man and his wife, he might ask the husband to have a drink with him (*prendre un punch*), his classic mechanism. The *quimboiseur* would then keep the glass from which the husband had drunk; then the *quimboiseur* might throw it into the fire, thus bringing about the desired effect. The husband, upon going home, becomes quarrelsome, makes *histoires* with his wife, whereupon the woman's parents want her to leave him, even if it is a prestigious marriage. Everyone believes it is generally better to live *en ménage* for many years than to marry hastily. All parties must be completely sure that the *ménage* is a convivial one.

Notice that the *quimboiseur* is doubly connected with hospitality-conviviality patterns. He works his evil in the context of social drinking, but it is the antithesis of values embedded in drinking together that he creates. In short, so destructive are quarrels considered that there are supernatural explanations for them.

I describe the model for the drinking and hospitality patterns as a link in the historical chain in chapter eight. To anticipate my comments, these patterns seem to be copies of aristocratic eighteenth-century lavishness and polish, for some people even have a visual memory of the first act performed by planters upon receiving a friend after an arduous, dusty carriage ride: a drink is offered.

This ubiquitous routine is perhaps the most standardized pattern in the whole country. When someone calls at no matter how rich or poor a house, the host's first words are, *"Un petit punch?"* To refuse is generally a sign of ill will, reminiscent of the days when poisonings were frequently suspected. To judge by the frequency with which the early priests preached against drink, the suspicion might be thought to have some validity. However, patterns of credulity are involved here.

Today there is no spontaneous image of the *quimboiseur* with his *punch rangé* (poisoned drink) that prompts a visitor to refuse a drink, but it is *"mal élevé"* for a man to reject one. Women may be excused, but if they refuse rum, a soft drink or a mixture of beer and soda (*parnache*) will be pressed on them. As pointed out in chapter four, even if a workman comes to a *fonctionnaire's* house on an errand he must be offered the punch, and in every kind of house it is brought to him in an identical decanter on an identical tray, mixed with the prescribed sugar syrup and a squeeze of lime. This same workman would never be invited to the *fonctionnaire's fête*, but he must be offered the drink. In field work that involved visiting many homes in a day, my impression was that the unbelievable hospitality must be a great burden to them. It took me awhile to perceive that normally, without a foreign guest, the occasions for paying calls— hence for consuming large amounts—are not frequent, as I have explained in describing association patterns. I shall later connect this hospitality and the occasions for and frequency of invoking it with a major function of the marriage *fête*. It is only important to establish here that to be inhospitable is as much a *totoblo* as for a woman to have her first unrecognized baby.

In addition to causing *histoires*, the *quimboiseur* is invoked to reveal and express the social criticism brought about by a man who leaves his *foyer*, abandoning his children and woman. A man who thus evades his obligations is certainly not responsible for so heinous and rare an event: no man would do this voluntarily. Only a malevolent influence could explain it. And if a man should leave his family for another *concubine* when it is not a mutual agreement with his spouse, the act must be more than the motiveless mischief of the *quimboiseur*: the magician was provoked by the new *concubine*. The parents of a *jeune fille* would use this explanation should a man change his mind about marrying their daughter because he suddenly discovers the "character" of his mistress to be more suited to his own.

Despite his criminality, people are afraid to do anything about a *quimboiseur*. The suspected magician never openly admits his part in some distant event that people, wondering if he is guilty, come to tell him of. He only smiles and nods, allowing the whispers to impress possible future clients, I was told.

When a man beats his children, a *quimboiseur* has nothing to do with it; but if he hits his wife, the rumors start. People used to seek a supernatural provocation when grown children were disobedient, but only the *moins cultivés* (less cultured) would think so today. A man's sexual indifference to his wife, however, is caused by the *quimboiseur*; but if she is indifferent, another man is suspected. (Perhaps this is a case of *cherchez l'homme* [look for the man].)

It is unnatural for a man to leave his own mother to live in the house of his *belle-mère* (mother-in-law). The whole society supports his mother in going to a séance to discover the reason for such weird behavior.

Sexual deviations like homosexuality, however, are considered *malpropriétés* not caused by *quimboiseurs*. The *comères* (homosexuals) are teased and ridiculed, but men indulge them frequently enough, especially if the *comères* have money. Some have attempted marriages, but their insistence on sewing and cooking usually drives their wives back home.

Another symbolic expression of values, an effective negative sanction in itself, is the *bois-bois*, seldom seen now because illegal. The *bois-bois* is a dummy resembling a person who has aroused disapproval. When the effigy is burned at *Carnaval*, the culprit is ridiculed. The punishment is still carried out secretly when a man abandons a wife for a *concubine*, when a woman abandons her husband, when a widower marries a very young girl. Before 1902 a *concubine* would be burned in effigy for leaving her lover, but now only a wife is so scorned; the *concubine* is punished by verbal rebuke.

When a man of forty marries a girl of eighteen a mechanism of good-natured ridicule is used: shell horns are blown outside his house on the wedding night. To end the rite, the groom invites his tormentors in for a drink.

SOLIDARITY

If a couple are status equals, and if they have lived together compatibly for many years, the question then becomes whether to spend money on a *fête*. I asked one man why he had held a *fête*, turning his seven-year *ménage* into a marriage; he could, instead, have transformed his *paille* house into a *ciment*. His was a mission marriage. He answered: "*Les Martiniquaises sont très critiqués.* If a friend comes, you have to give him a punch. If you don't give a dance, it's the same thing as not offering a drink."

In a culture where large groups are not entertained except to celebrate a *rite de passage*, and where such gatherings are the only expressions of *esprit de corps*, by means of which individuals validate their belonging, the *fête* is a sign of in-group membership in good standing. Those who feel the obligation of entertaining the group were in the past only the few who could do it in the grand manner, even among the cane cutters. Now with new channels of attaining positions of leadership through political activities and status through landownership or occupational advance, the poorest people also aspire to such roles. Although the mission permitted marriage without the *fête*, the social leaders who marry in this way also give *fêtes*. Again, I repeat: these social leaders are not necessarily rich—they can be very poor.

Let me sketch in the attitudes of people who believe they must give a *fête*.

A man in the *quartier* had married a few years before, although it was not a mission year, and his wife had been a *jeune fille*. They did not have a *fête*. His reason (given me) for the marriage was that "religion is more important than waiting until you can afford a *fête*." He is phenotypically very light, without any education, and married to a black girl half his age. He had fathered both recognized and nonrecognized children before his marriage, so evidently had not been quite so "religious" before.

At the next house the couple had lived *en ménage* for twelve years, and told me they did not intend to marry until they could have a *fête*, until they had accumulated more money. I asked what they thought of the above case. They answered:

Yes, that is the kind of man who marries without a *fête*. He had to go all the way to [nearest large *bourg*] to do it. He wouldn't dare do that kind of thing here! We would mock him forever, but we don't bother with him. He's too unsociable. If one of *us* did such a thing, no one would leave us alone. . . . Do you know what happens when someone who is too cheap to give a *fête* dares go to one of our *fêtes*? He can't say, "Pass me the wine." If you aren't married, you can feel at home at anyone's party. But if you are *malin* [scheming], then you can't open your mouth. You might as well not go.

I found another marriage that had taken place without a *fête*, again not during a mission year. I asked what people thought of this couple. "*I mallé sans son, sans trompette. Un gros sel. I fai' un totoblo.* (He married quietly, without music. A large grain of salt. He made a *totoblo*.) Both large-grained salt and the fish are things no one eats or serves if he or she has any pride at all. They are marks of stinginess or unawareness, indicating a hopeless failure, like a Bowery bum in America.

As another told me, "You never want to make a *totoblo*. They won't speak to you on the street. And they'll make up songs about you at *Carnaval*":

Terrogène mallé
Sans le rien
Terrogène mallé
Sans le sou.

(A man named Terrogène married without anything, without a sou.) Terrogène was so angry when he heard the ditty that he went all the way to the metropolitan *gendarmerie*. The author of the song explained that Terrogène was, so to speak, projecting, that no one had mentioned his name at all, that the words were not "Terrogène," but "*Rien de gens*" married without a sou. (No men marry like that.)

Clément also married without a *fête*. "Yes, he married on Christmas," said a neighbor. "He did it to save the money he would have had to spend serving lamb." On Christmas only pork is served. Nor did he even give a large pork party, but only entertained his family. Clément was as absurd as a man who would go to his own wedding in a borrowed suit; there is a joke about such a fool, who had to allow the owner of the suit to make love to the bride.

People who make these *totoblos* "don't even know how to bring up their children," the conversation continued. A woman explained to me that

Sometimes a parent won't beat a child because he doesn't want the other parent to be more loved. But this will not do. This is foolish behavior. When other parents beat children, you beat your children. When everyone sleeps, you should sleep. If you don't punish children they grow up like the *mals élevés* on the streets of [the *bourg*]. And they are the ones who grow up to make *totoblos*.

All of this was said by a woman who has six children out of wedlock. She has lived with her *mari* for years. Not one of the children was a *totoblo* with no man to recognize it or to want to live with the woman. I asked her if she intended to marry. "Marry?" she asked incredulously. "We work only three months out of the year. And we have six children . . ." Then softly, "I have no intention of leaving my *mari* [husband]." When he came in from work he kissed her fondly, kissed the youngest child, and offered more rum all around. After the visit he walked home with me, and I gave him some rum.

But not all who married without a *fête* are guilty of *totoblos*. One popular man was excused because he had had so many children, with a *fête* for each baptism, that no one thought him *malin* when he built a house for his marriage instead of having the *fête*. But for those who are well-liked, omitting the *fête* is an expression of alienation from the group. Then the behavior is criticized as *gauche*.

There are, however, a few who deviate from the conventional not because they are inadequate in some way, but because their superior status permits them to indulge eccentricities. Examples of such couples are the two schoolteachers mentioned in the beginning of the chapter who had a simple wedding, and the phenotypically white, well-educated man who had the civil ceremony. In other words, the existence of elite values is recognized, and some people are entitled to possess them, to be "natural" heirs to such customs. But others are not, and there is unanimous agreement on who is a delinquent equal and who is superior. However, superior status alone will not excuse a man from *fête* obligations. Although in some places in the Caribbean the desire to marry[18] is itself evidence of pretensions to elite group membership, this obviously is not true in Martinique.

M. Pierre's acceptable excuse for having a marriage without a *fête* suggests the basis on which allowances are made. He is a popular member of the *quartier*, married into one of the best local families. A phenotypically white *mulâtre* with seven years of school, he was trained in a respected if nonelite skill for which there is no longer any demand in Martinique, that of *distillateur*. He is now a cane cutter, but the above factors give him as high a status as anyone in the *quartier* and entitled him to marry into the rich black family that he did. It is not, obviously, color alone that is determinative, for the man who committed the *totoblo* detailed above was as white as this man, but behaviorally only a cane cutter and educationally lower than most of the blacks. The pariah also has personality qualities that negate that mobility his color might have given him. M. Pierre married without a *fête* during the depression of 1939. Otherwise, his wife's family—he is from elsewhere—would have demanded one. At the time, he went through the ceremony instead of living *en ménage* because marriage is "*plus social*. It puts one on another level [*un autre rang*]."

Opposed to this unusual situation, let me describe one of my first visits to a rural couple living *en ménage*. M. Thomas is the father of seven of his *concubine*'s nine children. He has no other children, and although he has had many women, this is his first *ménage*. One of the children bears the *concubine*'s name even though M. Thomas is the father, because he neglected to recognize it on time; recognition after three days costs 10,000 francs. This man's total lack of knowledge of acculturated values enabled me to grasp the concept of marriage as it must have been in the past in a plantation area.

He said, upon my instigation, that "Marriage effaces carnal sin from the soul." At the time, I thought this would indicate an acquaintance with Western standards. Moreover, he considers himself to be religious. They live in a poor *paillotte* with a leaky straw roof, but others no richer than they have been married. His answer to my direct question was that he did not have the money to marry.

"But it doesn't cost any more to marry than to live like this," I countered. "The priest will marry you free."

"But I have no money for it," he repeated as if I were ignorant, as I was.

"But it's free, isn't it?" I persisted.

He laughed. "Furniture is free? A *fête* is free?"

"But if you are religious, you marry without a *fête* or furniture, don't you?"

I could elicit only question-begging: "But I am too poor," and he listed his miseries. He is a mechanic who has not worked since 1942 because he is sick with parasites.

To such a man, my idea of marriage was only a small part of it. Obviously, marriage was not anything without the part that costs money. It was neither impatience nor reticence that kept him from conceptualizing it my way.

In the beginning I had the same kind of problem with a woman because of my "hardening of the categories." Not at all poor, living in a large wooden house, Mlle. Narcisse, in her forties, is the mother of four children who are recognized by her *concubin*, who lives in his own good house nearby. I had absorbed the idea that to people like her as well as to M. Thomas, to whom she is related, marriage was a *fête*, no more, no less. She told me that she keeps house for her *concubin* and stays with him when he is sick, but that they will not live together, let alone marry. When I asked her why, she said, "*Naturellement*, I am not married because I live here alone." She pointed to a house that to my eyes was older than the others, a different kind of architecture, but not so rich as the cement houses; her *concubin* was very well off, a plantation executive.

When I did not understand, she said, "But this is the *maison paternelle. Les blancs* never abandon *la maison paternelle*." But why couldn't her *concubin* move into it with her? "Because he is a big man with a good job and a good house." Why couldn't she leave it and move with him to another *quartier*? "Would Count X leave his *maison paternelle*?" she asked incredulously, the very model of colonial aristocracy. Her paternal grandfather was a white man and had left the family a large piece of property which now amounts to only one quarter of an acre for each heir.

Finally she explained to me, realizing that my country was really isolated, that for a man to move into such a house gave the woman too much authority, and no man with self-respect would do so. "But there are no problems," she said. "Isn't it simple to live so close together? It isn't as if we had to walk from one *morne* to another to see each other."

Very well, self-respect and paternal houses are more important than living together. But why not be married and continue to live in separate houses? "It is inconvenient to marry," she said, "but we must marry when sure of each other, because some day I want to be able to take Communion. But *le mariage est l'esclavage* [slavery]," she continued. "Here, if you marry, you marry forever. The church has no divorce. To divorce is worse than not to marry. It isn't because I want my liberty that I don't marry. *Mon Dieu*, no. *Les personnes vagues* [irresponsible] want their liberty. Promiscuous women want their freedom. There isn't anyone who respects them."

Mlle. Narcisse got up and strode up and down as if she were on the road, showing me how she behaves when one of these women who want their freedom passes her. "They are *mals élevées*," she said, stamping her foot. She pursed her lips in a mask of distaste and said coldly, "*Bonjour*." She then tossed her head and stamped off, saying, "That is all you say to them, '*Bonjour*' and no more. These *mals élevées* make me angry and *I* will have nothing to do with them." The emphasis on the "I" clearly placed her among the Mrs. Grundys of Capesterre, as indeed she was.

Marriage, as a concept dissociated from respectability, has its roots in a past partly remembered by old women still alive. One of them said, "No one disapproved of living *en ménage* unless the man drank or gambled or beat the woman. My mother was married, but it was rare, and she didn't know who her father was. Today marriage is easier, but life is harder. In the old days, the priest didn't teach much about religion. We didn't understand it. Now many people learn religion and get married. But then, when you married, you had to invite *everyone*, more so than today . . ."

The people who are married by the missions without having had a *fête* as well—or without legitimate excuses for not having one—are in a different category from those who do not have the mission as an escape. The mission seizes people at the last minute without notice and, as they say, there is usually no time for a *fête*. It is a good opportunity for people who have become religious, even momentarily, or for those who are not in agreement with what I shall call the *totoblo* set of values, for various reasons. But some of the real in-group also criticize the mission "*victims*," as one put it. One person married by the mission was addressed by an old friend as "Mlle. X." "Call me *Madame*," said the newlywed, "I am married now." "Oh," replied the friend cattily, "I didn't happen to notice you in the procession yesterday."

The unmarried *cultivatrice* who told me this story explained that most people feel there is no individual honor in this mass service.

> And there is no dishonor in being called "Mlle. X." After all, it is your baptismal name. And when you are baptized, it isn't a mass [production], is it? It is you alone who get the honor. And it's the baptismal name that's the most important. It's the name you keep after a divorce; it's your name on legal papers. . . . The mission is impersonal. It's only a name-changing ceremony. And there's no time for a *fête*; it's a *douboullon mariage*. [This expression derives from a hash with fish that is thrown together fast.] All you've done without a *fête* is *béni'péché*, which has no charm.

KINSHIP AND MARRIAGE

The people involved in these *ménages* and marriages are related to one another in ways that vary from *quartier* to *quartier*. I found several cases of the sororate, a few cases of stepfather-stepdaughter matings, and also cousin matings. Young cousins often have sexual experiences together, and if a child results no one feels any sense of guilt; but cousin marriages are not preferred, although the church will make dispensations for them. In one *quartier* I was told, "The whites marry their cousins to keep the property together, but we blacks don't often do it." This informant spoke of a *quartier* to which only two families returned after 1902, and ever since have married chiefly endogamously. No one feels it to be immoral. Second cousins are considered only the most remote relatives, and marriages occur frequently among them.

It is not too unusual to find the following jumble of relationships: Jeanne was Pierre's mistress. Jeanne had two daughters by another man. Pierre took the two as mistresses and married one of them. He had children by all three women—mother and two daughters. Pierre then slept with Jacqueline, an unrelated woman by whom he fathered two children. Pierre's brother Paul married Jacqueline and recognized her two sons by his brother, officially making his nephews his sons.

When a stepfather becomes sexually involved with his *concubine*'s daughter, the mother behaves as if the daughter were simply another woman. The mother is not morally outraged, but tries to see either that the liaison stops or that one of the two leaves the household. Public opinion is rather to laugh at such things than to be shocked. The daughters involved, if they consider it proper to speak of their sex life, do not hide the identity of the man anymore than if he were totally unrelated. However, stepmother-stepson relationships are deplored: "One has more respect for a stepmother."

The stepfather's attitude is expressed in the Creole phrase: "*Moin pas ka nourri' chouval ba officier l'armée monté.*" (I do not nourish a horse for another cavalry officer.) The *beau-père* does not mind raising a pretty stepdaughter for himself. Each of the three persons who told me these tales said he knew of half a dozen cases, but no one would tell who was involved except the guilty parties, for "*Les Martiniquaises n'aiment pas les médisances.*" (We do not like to say evil things that are true.) I heard of only one case of real father-daughter incest. The reaction to it was only that such things are crimes and one almost never hears of them.

NOTES

[1] Bronislaw Malinowski, *Sex and Repression in Savage Society* (New York: Meridian, 1927; 1955 reprint), p. 187.

[2] M. J. Herskovits, "The Negro in the New World," *American Anthropologist*, 32, No. 1, 1930.

[3] Dom Basil Matthews, *The Crisis in the West Indian Family* (Jamaica: University College of the West Indies, 1953).

[4] E. Franklin Frazier, *The Negro Family in the United States* (New York: Dryden Press, 1948), p. 94.

[5] Matthews, *Crisis*, p. 10.

[6] Claude Lévi-Strauss, "The Family," in Harry L. Shapiro, ed., *Man, Culture and Society* (Oxford: Oxford University Press, 1956), p. 268.

[7] Eugène Revert, *La Martinique: Étude Géographique* (Paris: Nouvelles Éditions Latines, 1949), p. 476.

[8] Fernando Henriques, *Family and Colour in Jamaica* (London: Eyre & Spottiswoode, 1953).

[9] James G. Leyburn, *The Haitian People* (New Haven: Yale University Press, 1941), p. 187.

[10] See p. 90, note 11 for Horowitz's correction of this assertion. He says that it is not true, according to the formal code; but the ethnolegal norm is as I heard it from a local "lawyer."

[11] Flora Lewis, "French Reform of a Napoleonic Law Gives Illegitimate Children Full Rights." *The New York Times*, August 5, 1972.

[12] M. J. Herskovits and F. S. Herskovits, *Trinidad Village* (New York: Knopf, 1947), p. 177.

[13] Cf. G. E. Cumper, "Labour Demand and Supply in the Jamaican Sugar Industry 1830-1950," *Social and Economic Studies*, 2, No. 4, 1954.

[14] Leyburn, *The Haitian People*, p. 188.

[15] M. J. and F. S. Herskovits, *Trinidad Village*, p. 302.

[16] Lewis, "French Reform of a Napoleonic Law."

[17] Père Jean Baptiste Labat, *Nouveau Voyage aux Îles de l'Amérique*, 1722 (Paris edition: Duchartre, 1931), II, p. 63.

[18] Matthews, *Crisis*.

EIGHT

Historical Links
and Chains

That the rural middle class as well as the urban lower class in Martinique remain unacculturated to Western marriage patterns suggests that it is the folk-elite continuum rather than economic class or rural-urban factors that is determinative. This chapter will explain why there is no rule of legitimacy among the people in the nonelite subculture. In those remote *quartiers* where the *totoblo* society has encapsulated folk family values most vividly, as in Capesterre, we can find clues to historical origins. But is this "explanation"?

It seems as safe as it is empty to say that all history "caused" the present. Nevertheless, there are dangers in specifying. Herskovits believed the specific historical determinant of family patterns in New World plantation areas to be primarily the African heritage; others, slavery, regardless of the provenience of the group; still others, deprivation of property and status and their ecological frame.

I shall consider the history of the *quartiers* in terms of the freed people who existed contemporaneously with slavery and look specifically at the attitude to Western religion, the only force currently attempting consciously to change nonelite attitudes toward marriage.

Slaves and freedmen, it seems, associated religion only with recreation, hardship, or rebellion. The latter two connotations have been removed, leaving little more than a void. More meaningful to women than to men, as we have indicated, even in their view the church today represents primarily a focus for gatherings, a feeling that cannot be communicated to their sons, who know they will have the drinking bars or *débits de la régie* instead when they grow up. There is also the foxhole type of faith that lasts the duration of a crisis. Only a few show a deep, constant interest. Sincere and acculturated belief is more widespread in the *bourg*, and here the church activities are a greater part of social life. Religion is also a predominantly secular frame for expressing family solidarity or showing conspicuous consumption during *rites de passage*.

But there is little interest in the content of religious doctrine. Most men are cynical and scoffing about the women's interest in church ("a place to show off clothes"), and "a priest is a man like me only with skirts to hide under" expresses a consensus. Men will recount tales of priests' love affairs, but this does not make religion false (a foreign rationalist concept); they think church laws should be changed. There is no feeling that dogma or laws are sacrosanct or absolute: "The catechism is for children"; God will not punish what must be or what is. Such fatalism makes it possible to show little supernatural concern for the fate of dead sinners. What must be and what is have always been so widely divergent from priestly words that a mechanism soon developed for not being bothered by the logical incompatibilities of the West. Paradoxes are even a theme in the culture: a person is Freemason and Catholic simultaneously; a God-fearing Communist; a *"matérialiste"* participant in séances; an atheist defined as "one who believes all religions"; a respectable unmarried mother; a pious sinner.

All early European observers witnessed much "superstition," at first African and then in Schoelcher's day folk beliefs "like [those of] a French peasant."[1] The *sortilèges*, ghosts, and curses were indistinguishable from generalized Old World patterns. Even the *quimboiseur*, who is a "sorcerer more or less. a curer," is derived from seventeenth-century France.[2] The attitude that prevailed toward formal religion is illustrated by one slave's answer to a priest who said, "Honor God, and He will make your manioc grow." The practical skepticism expressed was: *"Temps perdu*, Père B. If I hadn't planted it, it would never have grown."[3]

Magic has today been largely severed from most practices which would interfere with modern standards of health. For example, hot bricks are no longer placed on a pregnant woman's abdomen. Anyone responsible for permitting a birth to occur outside a hospital is arrested. With magic removed from all life's dangerous situations, there is no strong emotional clinging to it. The *quimboiseur* had a renaissance in Hearn's day,[4] when even educated mulattoes went to him; but now, survivals of such beliefs tend to be secret. Anyone who attributes death to the work of a *quimboiseur* must whisper the opinion, for all acculturated people are ready to report him or her to the police. People will recount their experiences with magical poisoning only when out of the *bourg*. Magic, science, and religion are one, for science has been legally imposed as technology without any teaching of the principles of scientific method. Locally educated people will say that syphilis is spread by the tongue of a female dog. Magic has been muffled not because it is irrational, but because most practices have been replaced by substitutes with prestige value; and religion has never had a separate existence.

The inception of this religious situation was brought about not only by superficial instruction, but also by a split in attitudes toward religion held by four factions in French society: the king's government, the plantocracy, the Jesuits, and the parish priests. Some of the conflicts acted out on this battleground were: Should there be slavery? Should Christians be slaves? Should Christian slaves marry? The progression reveals the answers found to all questions but the last, for the church never attempted to answer whether a Christian family could really exist among plantation slaves. Nor did they wonder whether the men whom they authorized or forced to marry slaves had the desire or incentive to protect their wives and children, and if they did, were there the means?

Ultimately most of the answers were dictated by economic events. Even within the ranks of the clergy, those French prelates associated with the king who opposed slavery on humanitarian grounds were easily silenced by biblical supports for it. A *curé* of Fort Royal summed them up when he argued that no law, divine or human, opposed slavery; furthermore, only soul-saving, not material things, were important.[5] "Let them suffer," he said of the slaves, "for this brings consolation." It was a better life than in heathen Africa. Not only was slavery for the obvious good of all, it offered the slaves the opportunity to model themselves on Christ, for they could obey the master as God. St. Paul suggested these words to the *curé*, and before him Noah had said, "Cursed be Ham; may he be the slave of slaves of his brothers." Emphasis was always on the resignation of one group rather than on the charity of the other. Schoelcher heard one priest ask a slave which Commandment ordered him to obey the master. No one but the priest knew the answer, which he announced to the whole church: "the fourth, Honor thy father and thy mother." The folk-to-be did not absorb a passion for rational consistency.

If assimilation has been more complete in Martinique than in some other places, it is not because the slaves were treated any more humanely as a result of Catholicism. In 1848 it was l'Abbé Jacquier who led the crusade against emancipation, and Peytard says the French planters were as "cruel and immoral as any."[6] Schoelcher, after a tour of plantation colonies, observed that the French inflicted worse punishments than the British.[7] Even New Orleans, where the church had a "nigger heaven," reflected the French island plantation system:

> They form some legitimate marriages, but are completely abandoned to the state of nature, vilified, scorned, almost without knowledge of good or evil, should we be surprised that the dissolution of their customs be such that for 50 sous a husband cedes his wife to another for eight days? This mixture of the sexes produces . . . an immorality and a frightful concubinage to which the planters, who are really responsible for it, shamefully close their eyes, because it enriches them. The children of their slaves belong to them and there is on each *habitation* a main building where all these little *créoles* are raised with much more care on the part of the interested proprietor than on the part of their mothers who are generally indifferent to the fruit of their entrails.[8]

The floggings, mutilations, death sentences, tortures were the usual extremes.

So little religious opposition was there to slavery that it was through his pious fervor that Louis XIII was persuaded to support it; it was the best way to Christianize the Negroes.[9] To the king, colonization itself was initially started only for the purpose of conversion, but had the slaves not been given religious membership by fiat, it is unlikely that there would have been many conversions. Du Tertre reports that the missionaries, who won over only 20

Caribs in thirty-five years, were not very active with the 15,000 slaves. In short, there was little difference between the lives of the Catholic slaves who were baptized at birth and those of the British and Dutch slaves who were baptized at death because of misgivings about enslaving Christians.[10] The difference in Catholic areas came later, when the fact that everyone was of the same religion prevented an additional dimension of social cleavage.

The planters approved of converting the slaves insofar as religion could make them docile. They formed the official island attitude, well expressed in a memo to the king dated 1777:

> Religion, by the sanctity of its principles ... must direct its first attention to the Administration. .... It is above all by the check that it imposes on the slaves that slavery ... can be maintained ... [for they] are equally insensible to honor, shame or punishment.[11]

Nonetheless, the priests and planters were constantly embattled over the manner of spreading religion. One conflict centered on the connection between Sunday markets and church attendance. The Code Noir ruling forbidding Sunday markets was reversed the same year, reflecting a triumph for the planters. Until very recently, when the *boutique* made its appearance in the country, one of the strongest incentives to go from the *quartier* to the village was the market. The planters deemed it wise to keep church attendance to the minimum possible, not only because large groups were dangerous but because of the production time lost. In 1652 it was necessary to legislate the priests' desire that slaves not work on Sundays and *fête* days; in 1664 the planters were fined 120 pounds of tobacco for preventing the slaves from attending Mass on these occasions. There was little to be done about the lunar calendar, but in 1787 the king was persuaded to obtain permission from Rome to reduce the *fêtes* to ten a year. This measure helped make up the loss of forty extra workdays a year when the planters could no longer prevent church-going.

The form of worship as well as the time it took bothered the masters. In 1704 an ordinance forbade assemblies and dances during divine service. Nor could there be any more "beating of the *tambour* during the religious service or after the setting of the sun ... ; it was one of their favorite distractions."[12] The slaves' imitation of the whites' *fête* processions was another danger. In 1753, an array of 15,000 to 18,000 men dressed in costumes portraying royalty and paraded with wooden guns. They were well behaved, says Peytard, but the governor used a minor dispute as an excuse for forbidding the parades in the future. Later they were reinstated with the participants in ordinary dress. The priests were determined to encourage this sort of religious participation, and when the planters again threatened to forbid it, the priests demanded payment for each slave who did not attend.

It was in fact difficult to contain the large groups, and there was at least one major plot (which misfired)to take the island during the Christmas Mass of 1748. Moreover, religious gatherings, reported Moreau de Saint-Méry,[13] were the excuse for many activities; the slaves covered their meetings "with the veils of darkness and religion in order to gather at night in the churches which become thus the refuge of fugitives and even a place of prostitution."

The religious life of the slaves was further confused by the conflict between the Jesuits and the parish priests. The former, who were finally expelled in 1763, would encourage the slaves to dress as *curés* and to conduct their services without the knowledge of the parish priests.[14] They would also defer baptism by refusing to accept the slaves' choice of godparents. Ordinances were passed to correct this tendency. The secular magistrates also objected to such Jesuitical practices as public penance, during which the people would kneel for the entire Mass; at the end all bastards would be baptized at once.

Siding with the planters, the governor advised—in a letter of 1764 to the minister—not to spread a religion that made the slaves critical of their lot:

> Sane politics and the strongest human considerations are opposed to it ... The safety of the whites demands that the Negroes be held in the deepest ignorance. ... I have arrived at the firm belief that it is necessary to lead the Negroes like beasts.

"Deepest ignorance" was the only possibility through these years of mixed interests. A new arrival from Africa would share a hut with a Christian slave and would live and work side by side with French *engagés* while they still existed. It was in this way that folk beliefs were Europeanized. To the planter's advantage, Africans absorbed a veneer of French culture, which was deepened by imitating the domestic servants, who copied their manners from the aristocrats. Religion was not a prominent part of the patterns they imitated; but at the same time, African ideas were scorned.

There were so few priests that the clergy could scarcely find time to teach the catechism to house slaves in the city. The priests "live completely with the masters instead of with the slaves."[15] Even when the masters were forced to encourage church attendance, the church was often too far for regular travel.[16] In 1715 chapels were built on the plantations, a safer measure than having hundreds of slaves gather in the *bourg*, but the priests suppressed them the following year. A demand was made in 1840 to have a priest at least once a month in the dependencies of the parish. But, says Schoelcher, "As for religious instruction, it is nothing . . . as everyone knows, one of the prejudices of the country is that the instruction of the blacks would be a new danger for the whites."[17]

The quality of religion as Schoelcher saw it is shown in the following passage:

> The churches teem with Negroes and above all with Negresses; they constantly have the name of God in their mouths, they regularly make the sign of the cross when they are sick or begin a new undertaking; but they do not know what they say, or what they do. They have superstition instead of religion. They do not understand God, and He is used almost like a charm.[18]

He saw one woman who ordered a Mass to learn the identity of a thief; another for the safe arrival of her lover.

Schoelcher's statement applied in 1845. In the 1880s Lafcadio Hearn observed that the poor in the cities and towns liked going to church, but that to the people in the country religious symbols were only "fetishes." The church, he said, suffered in the rural areas for two reasons. The first was that these were the places where revolutionary sentiments existed, and the political journals mocked the church. Second, the church had always been identified with the whites. Religious schools were (and are today) racist, and when universal suffrage was instituted the rich and their church lost power.[19]

As for behavior within the churches during the days of bond-age, the slaves were divided into three classes: those who were baptized, instructed, and married; the baptized unmarried; and the catechumens. The first, dressed in surplices, supervised the others. Everyone admitted that the services were for the purpose of preventing *marronnage* (escape), poisoning, and abortion. The culprits were placed on their knees and did public penance, receiving absolution at Easter. So severe was the attitude of organized religion that in 1718 one slave was sentenced to death for drunkenness in order not to incur the loss of his soul.[20] Prayers twice a day were part of the punishment of prisoners.

Whatever the discrepancies between religious policy and most Western standards, the church was consistently in favor of marriage. By an ordinance of 1664 the planter who prevented either marriage or baptism was fined 500 pounds of tobacco. The masters never prevented baptism, but they always opposed marriage. The Code Noir of 1685 tried to enforce keeping a mother and her immature children together, but it was not until 1845 that the clergy dared attempt outlawing the separation of the husband from the family, so important was it to planters to sell men and women separately.

Marriage was a symbol of great meaning to the government as well as to the priests. In 1848 the director of the interior said at an official dinner:

> They sent me eleven men who presented me with their wives and asked me . . . to thank the Republic . . . Farewell my friends. When you wish to manifest your joy, cry: "Long live work, long live marriage . . ." You must work and marry in order to obtain the recompenses of the other life. . . .

The officials thought marriage would help prevent the liberated slaves from leaving the plantations.

Marriage again appeared as a symbol of worthiness after freedom came, when the government was faced with its first problem—Should the ex-slave be given the franchise? The delegate from France recommended that the vote be restricted to those who could read or were married, thus "offering more than others a greater guarantee of capacity or morality."[21]

Schoelcher says of marriage among the slaves:

It is very rare that the Negroes are legally married, for the simple reason that marriage would fetter them to disorders of which they are used to being free, or rather because deprived of all knowledge of social principles, incapable of raising their slave mentality as far as the moral aim of this formality, they abandon themselves by instinct to concubinage as the most natural estate. . . . A libertinage without check is the only compensation left to the slaves as the price of the brutalization in which they are maintained. Legitimate unions are rare among them: the masters, far from favoring them, place every obstacle to it [says another observer quoted by Schoelcher].[22]

Schoelcher also observed that the men on the plantations did not feel jealous of their women, but rather got tired of them.

In Bourbon, which Schoelcher considered "the most civilized and humane" of the French colonies, it was forbidden to separate legally united partners or to take a young child from them. "But even in this colony . . . legal marriages between slaves are excessively rare." In reading Schoelcher we must replace nineteenth-century sentiments and concepts with new ones, but the facts are essentially there, and at times even psychological insight as well as moral indignation. How could a slave feel affection, he asks, "under these conditions: When a white slaps his face, he must remain silent . . . their condition puts them in a state of perpetual hostility with society."[23]

Although exhortations to marry have never been effective in Martinique, all observers report that some marriages took place during slavery. One motive for these occasional weddings was that for many years all gatherings with dancing and drinking were forbidden unless special permission was obtained; a wedding was the excuse for permission, for the priests would object if planters refused. That a marriage could occur without a *fête* even today seems meaningless to most of the people, as we have seen. Drinking and dancing were often described as the favorite diversions of the slaves. If marriage was an excuse to have such a *fête*, it is clear why the two became associated. Moreover, the habit of celebrating a marriage lavishly was reinforced in other ways. An ordinance issued in Guadeloupe in 1772 is revealing: "The tumults and indecent shouts of the *blancs* and above all of the Negroes after the celebration of marriages, force the *curés* to administer this sacrament only at night."[24]

Testimony to the popularity of slave dances and assemblies is that they were heavily policed from the beginning of the colony and in 1654 were prohibited under pain of death. Evidently they continued in practice, however, for the laws keep renewing their prohibition. In 1678, for example, a historian reports a large assembly of *Nègres au mariage*, gathered from all *quartiers*, at which an infantry lieutenant was insulted. The *conseil* then once more forbade any assemblies of Negroes. He described the custom as gathering in the houses of the principal *bourgs* "in imitation of the free men, giving one another meals, public dances, with a disorder and confusion characterized by the most frightful license." [25]

> As for me [says an author in 1786], I do not hesitate in deciding that one cannot be too much in favor of marriage among the slaves. I have before my eyes several examples of men who marry nearly all the *Nègres* of their plantation and who have a great quantity of . . . slaves . . . who surpass those from Africa, whose type is becoming rare. . . . It is very rare that the slave husband and wife come from different masters; therefore [the ordinance preventing this] is useless. [26]

As we have seen, the slaves resisted marriage insofar as it was presented as a ritual of a religion that they found neither compatible nor understandable. Furthermore, what one white man, the priest, suggested or exhorted, another authority figure, the master, discouraged. The master's motive was not only his desire to sell slaves separately or to keep the slave ignorant of ideas which would make him rebellious, but also his desire to gain sexual access to slave women. A planter even today recently resisted mechanization of his plantation for the same reason: "Why would I want to lay my hands on machines at night instead of soft flesh?" (A white man reported this to me.) Only 2 of the 69 manumissions that took place in 1831 were men, and the women were all between the ages of sixteen and twenty-one. [27] Of the 2,326 colored people who had received their freedom by 1788, 1,538 were female. [28] "It was not uncommon for a rich man to have many 'natural' families; and almost every individual of means had children of color." [29]

A slave woman saw no advantage in marrying another slave, since her only mobility lay in becoming the *concubine* of a white man. Even today, I was repeatedly told, most rural families prefer their daughters to be a white man's mistress rather than a black man's wife.

Insofar as the concept was accepted, marriage was part of a celebration. But such a celebration required first the possibility of a monogamous union. Slave life presented obstacles not only to marriage, but to stable free unions. One force against the endurance of relationships was the unequal sex distribution on any given plantation, since more women than men were given liberty and moved away. Such facts coupled with the strictures on interplantation gatherings would lead to polygynous patterns, which must have been reinforced by the standard French behavior of the eighteenth century. So entrenched was polygyny that often legitimate wives became the godmothers of their husbands' *mulâtres* children.[30]

> Today the situation has not greatly changed [says Hearn in 1888]: and with such examples on the part of the cultivated class, what could be expected from the other: Marriages are rare:—it has been officially stated that the illegitimate births are 60%; (75 to 80% would probably be nearer the truth . . .)[31]

The following sentence sums up many of the forces at work:

> Later in the eighteenth century, when hospitality had been cultivated as a gentleman's duty to fantastical extremes,—when liberality was the rule throughout society,—when a notary summoned to draw up a deed, or a priest invited to celebrate a marriage, might receive for fee five thousand francs in gold,—there were certainly many emancipations.[32]

It is in these private emancipations, I believe, that the pattern was set for the family values that characterized the total emancipation of 1848.

From the beginning of the plantation system settlements were created in the hills above the *habitations*, the *étages*, which consisted of households with female heads. The "visiting husbands" gave their women much more prestige than any married woman possessed. The children of the mixed unions had no model for marriage provided by their parents; consequently, when church teachings were made accessible to all, after emancipation, the concept of marriage became an overlay on the older pattern, in which *la fille de couleur* valued her freedom. According to Hearn, "*les filles de couleur* . . . these women whose tints of skin rivalled the colors of ripe fruit" became so popular as to undermine the European family institution completely. "That which only slavery could have rendered possible began to endanger the integrity of slavery itself: the institutions upon which the whole social structure rested were being steadily sapped by the influx of half-breed girls."[33]

La fille de couleur who supplanted *la belle affranchie* (the beautiful freed woman) was motivated by a "desire to please." Her emotions, says Hearn, were winning but superficial except for her maternal affection.[34] But after the colonial crash she became less submissive. Her lover was likely to emigrate, her life became more difficult, and "she no longer enjoys that reputation of fidelity accorded to her class in other years." Nor could her existence any longer be said to be made up of "love, laughter, and forgetting."[35] Her lovers left her destitute and marriage or *ménages* became possible.[36] "The man's personality," Hearn says, "was never generous and loving like that of the woman."[37] The male slave was not worth much compared to the female, and he always cost less to free. Labat[38] describes the slave man at the beginning of the eighteenth century as deceitful and violent. The male *mulâtre* had not worked with these blacks for a whole century before emancipation. During that period the cultural patterns leading to mobility could only have been transmitted by the women.

NOTES

[1] Victor Schoelcher, *Esclavage et Colonisation* (Paris: Presses Universitaires de France, 1948), p. 93.

[2] Eugène Revert, *La Martinique, Étude Géographique* (Paris: Nouvelles Éditions Latines, 1949), pp. 167, 169.

[3] Schoelcher, *Esclavage et Colonisation*, p. 93.

[4] Lafcadio Hearn, *Two Years in the French West Indies* (New York: Harper & Bros., 1890), p. 181.

[5] Schoelcher, *Esclavage et Colonisation*, p. 119.

[6] Lucien Peytard, *L'Esclavage aux Antilles Françaises Avant 1789* (Paris: Librairie Hanchettes, 1897), p. 169.

[7] Schoelcher, *Esclavage et Colonisation*, p. 54.

[8] Ibid., p. 35.

[9] Peytard, *L'Esclavage aux Antilles*, p. 168.

[10] Père Du Tertre (pseudonym), *Histoire Générale des Antilles Habités par les Françaises* (Paris: 1667–1671), II, p. 503.

[11] Peytard, *L'Esclavage aux Antilles*, p. 181

[12] Ibid., p. 182.

[13] Ibid., p. 190.

[14] Ibid., p. 191.

[15] Schoelcher, *Esclavage et Colonisation*, p. 95.

[16] Peytard, *L'Esclavage aux Antilles*, p. 179.

[17] Schoelcher, *Esclavage et Colonisation*, p. 120.

[18] Ibid., p. 93.

[19] Hearn, *Two Years in the French West Indies*, p. 180.

[20] Peytard, *L'Esclavage aux Antilles*, p. 180.

[21] Schoelcher, *Esclavage et Colonisation*, p. 22.

[22] Ibid., p. 61.

[23] Ibid., p. 63. Schoelcher is the beloved symbol of freedom in Martinique. He was the governor at the time of emancipation.

[24] Peytard, *L'Esclavage aux Antilles*, p. 181.

[25] Ibid., p. 261.

[26] Ibid., p. 357.

[27] Hearn, *Two Years in the French West Indies*, p. 333.

[28] Revert, *Martinique*, p. 39.

[29] Hearn, *Two Years in the French West Indies*, p. 326.

[30] Ibid., p. 325.

[31] Ibid., p. 327.

[32] Ibid., p. 325.

[33] Ibid., p. 324.

[34] Ibid., p. 330.

[35] Ibid., p. 335.

[36] Ibid., pp. 330–332.

[37] Ibid., p. 334.

[38] Père Jean Baptiste Labat, *Nouveau Voyage aux Îles de l'Amérique*, 1722 (Paris edition: Duchartre, 1931), II.

NINE

A Model of
the Family Structure

Martinique as a total society has developed a subculture in which family organization differs from the dominant picture. Differential association in the *communes* has produced a family structure represented by the model of conjugal, subconjugal, and supraconjugal households existing at one time in the same social subsystem. This model is the corollary of an absence of the rule of legitimacy. In the place of such a rule, other values that express family organization have emerged in Capesterre—status equality, conviviality, ingroup solidarity expressed in hospitality obligations, among others.

To recapitulate the sequence of events that led to the absence of a rule of legitimacy in Capesterre, let us recall the early history of the island. An African population was severed from its roots, all its major adaptations becoming dysfunctional in a new environment whose patterns it could not absorb in their traditional form. A section of this population—slave women—sometimes gained upward mobility when they lived in subconjugal families in the hills. Some of their offspring were led directly to the elite sector, like the father of Alexandre Dumas *père*, who became a Napoleonic general. Those who remained in the *commune* had no opportunity to become acculturated to elite values. At no time did they lose prestige by having no rule of legitimacy, and in the beginning marriage was a deterrent to mobility for the people of color.

Given that people in the rural *commune* are outside the system which associates marriage (in the form of a rule of legitimacy) with prestige, the only other source for learning to value marriage is religion. In Martinique acculturation to Christianity has bypassed the Christian concept of marriage. Whereas the conjugal family of the West with its rule of legitimacy is derived from an earlier European supraconjugal family system, the economy and ecology of the *commune* never made this phenomenon functional in Martinique.

We shall now add the variety of family organization found in Capesterre to the others in the literature and compare separate aspects of the family. Table 9-1 shows that in the terms that have been discussed in the literature, there is no apparent combination of specific referential characteristics common to all families in these various regions.

MATRIFOCALITY

Let us examine the dominance of the mother. The extreme of matrifocality occurs as a modal type, in the form of the grandmother family, in certain communities of the southern United States. Frazier,[1] unlike Henriques,[2] has taken life histories and knows that the form is not only part of a developmental sequence as it is in British Guiana. In Martinique the grandmother family is also a permanent structure, but very rare. We cannot tell from the data the extent to which this bare minimum of a family is a lifelong constellation in Jamaica, but we know it to be at least, as also in Martinique, a prominent phase of the developmental cycle.

Regarding that aspect of matrifocality which Raymond T. Smith describes as the diminution of the male's interaction over time in a conjugal household, such data are not even hinted at in the other studies. But in Martinique, as I have attempted to show, the conjugal family if stable is only bilateral in distribution of power. Everywhere that the man is present he is the *chef de famille* as a *de facto* as well as *de jure* leader. A man's refusal to live in a woman's *maison paternelle* reflects the French concept of paternal authority.

In the British Guiana community, Raymond Smith finds that the distribution of power which he calls matrifocal is echoed in house-

Table 9-1 CHARACTERISTICS OF FAMILY ORGANIZATION IN VARIOUS REGIONS

Area	Community	Internal Stratification	Predominant Composition	Marriage	Matri-focality
Jamaica	Low-class sugar parish; more female than male workers	No full-time specialists; no economic or occupational differences except non-local shop-keepers and teachers	Concubinage (faithful)	Feast for respect; women fear ill-treatment; men fear women will not work	Male dominance only in Christian family; grandmother transmits folk-ways
British Guiana	Three postemancipation coastal villages; nucleated corporate farming and plantation		Prehousehold keepers, followed by common-law conjugal households	Feast; marriage a rare act of conformity to upper-class values	Mother over time becomes more and more the power center
Toco, Trinidad	Isolated rural district; shares, rectors, plantations, migratory	Differential status, enterprise, striving to rise	Keeper unions unstable	Married people often separate and become keepers again; need supernatural sanction for family	Matriarchal family disappears in economically favored households; humanly secondary role of man

Area	Community	Internal Stratification	Predominant Composition	Marriage	Matrifocality
Haiti	Nucleations of 100 peasants who own scattered plots	None	*Plaçage*; little faithful concubinage because surplus of women	Only rarely, when children aspire to prestige; feast	Woman manages household, but man owns it and chooses her
Martinique	Plantation *commune*	Specialists; ranking	Faithful concubinage	Feast; rare except for missions; much late marriage	Equal in conjugal households
United States, South	Plantation and work for freedom		Faithful and legal	Often	Man has power; buys wife's freedom
	Dispersed independent farmers		Common-law; no stability	Rare	Grandmother family
	Isolated rural nucleated		Stable common-law	None	Mostly patriarchal
	Nonisolated, nonnucleated		Grandmother; some conjugal, usually temporary	None	Matrifocal

hold composition; that is, the relationships of persons in the households are such that he calls the whole society a structure shifted to the female side. This he labels the crucial structural feature of the society.[3] In chapter seven I have shown that in Martinique the grandmother is likely to take in children of her son as well as those of her daughter, and a man or woman adopts children of his or her brother as well as sisters' children. Thus, in Capesterre, unlike in British Guiana, cross-cousins do come under the control of one woman; and unlike the situation in Trinidad, second-cousin marriages are contracted. Furthermore, the temporary households formed during vacations are as likely to be in the house of the man's parents as the woman's.

In Martinique, as in all Caribbean regions on which we have reports, kinship and residence frequently do not coincide because of the practice of adopting children—the British "caretaker" children; the *'ti moun* of Haiti; the *kureki* of Dutch Guiana. Everywhere these children are more often relatives or godchildren than an unrelated neighbor's offspring, and their relationship to the household head is an important diagnostic of laterality. In Martinique it shows no matrifocality.

The above remarks do not, of course, apply to families that are not conjugal or to families in which the husband-father changes frequently. But in relatively stable conjugal families there are no structural resemblances to or retentions of even a partially unilineal society, and bilaterality applies to the *gens casés* as well as to the landed *propriétaires*. It is as much a part of the behavior in the most recently settled *quartier*, Fond d'Espoir, as in Voltaire, where property has long been a possession. It occurs despite the fact that family labor has no economic importance.

Matrifocality in any ot its many faces is highly variable over the Caribbean. It can increase or decrease with landownership; it can increase or decrease with women's independence. In British Guiana, the lower-class woman is for most of her life the most economically dependent of any women in these areas. Yet it is there that her power is described as so great that it shifts the family structure to the female side. It is there, except in areas where the grandmother family is modal, that her power is at its maximum.

On the other hand, where the woman's interaction with her

children and mate is closest to that of African polygyny, in Haitian *plaçage*, the man is not described as losing power; rather, it is the man who is undisputed leader. The Capesterre woman, as in Haiti and contrary to the woman of Guiana, is expected to work. She has more status than her Haitian counterpart, but does not have the complete emotional power over children that Haitian *plaçage* permits. Let us not forget, however, that the household with a female head does exist as a positively sanctioned, expected occurrence, and what we have said about the conjugal household does not apply to such families.

The sources are so written that it is difficult to examine the variability of internal status differentiation. M. J. and F. S. Herskovits refer to it.[4] Where they find matrifocality they also describe the upward striving and a developed concept of ranking, which they attribute to Africa, but which shows that in another vocabulary the men must have status-defining functions, however conceived. Even if the Herskovitses' data are considered insufficient for judging status differentiation in Toco, Capesterre shows conclusively that the nonelite can exist in a differentiated subsystem. I have documented the ranking system in chapter four, and the men clearly have status-defining functions. Not only are there channels for wide occupational differentiations, but family background is a basis for differentiation. The residents of an old *quartier* have superior status to the *arrivistes* in a recently settled neighborhood. A landowner is *ipso facto* superordinate to the *gens casés*. A man with education and professional status is outranked by a lighter-skinned woman from a preemancipation family. People unequal in status will live together but tend not to marry. Although there are not many associational opportunities for expressing status differentiation, it is expressed whenever possible, and always when marriage is involved.

Raymond Smith's argument—that matrifocality is the obverse of an undifferentiated subsystem, that the former is "explained" by the latter—would lead to the expectation that matrifocality would be absent in Capesterre. Before we explore his hypothesis in Capesterre, however, it is important to say that Smith believes the functional relation he found in British Guiana—between matrifocality and an undifferentiated subsystem—to be important because matrifocality, according to the evidence of the literature, is supposed to be the crucial characteristic, the central attribute common to all families of the type we are calling "the Caribbean family" whether it be in Scotland or Peru.[5]

We have seen that Capesterre shows a deviant family in a nonelite subsystem. Martinique, then, would appear to belong to the class of societies to which Raymond Smith's hypothesis should be pertinent. Yet, as we have maintained, Capesterre has status-defining functions for the male as well as for the female. What does such a finding do to the Smith hypothesis?

First, let us assume that matrifocality *does* exist in Capesterre in some form, even if not in the tautologically obverse form that is part of the Smith hypothesis. If matrifocality exists in Capesterre, it clearly cannot be explained by undifferentiated status and the rest of that concept.

It is possible to argue, to save the hypothesis, that Martinique is a society of a different type. To take this position would be to choose a functional relation in one or more societies as the criterion of a social type. But this would be begging the question. It would not explain family deviation, but only one form of it. It would mean that any functional relation, no matter how limited its distribution, could serve as an explanation. The alternative is to say that Raymond Smith's explanation lacks generality, that it fits local conditions examined by him, that it may fit other societies as well, but that it is not the universal correlation that explains family deviation in the Caribbean and other areas where like symptoms are found.

Let us say, on the other hand, that matrifocality does *not* exist in Capesterre and that it is not, therefore, surprising to find the absence of what correlates with it. If matrifocality does not exist in Capesterre, then Smith errs on the count that matrifocality is the constant in the Caribbean family.

We have seen that each author has a separate referent for what can be called matrifocality. (Not all authors use that particular term, but it is better than "matriarchy" or long synonymous phrases.) There is no doubt of the existence of matrifocality when the modal type is a grandmother family. But does some other single form of matrifocality exist throughout the Caribbean area? The example of Capesterre alone would show that Raymond Smith's types of matrifocality—power distribution in the conjugal household and composition—are not universal. As I said in chapter four, the degree of matrifocality in Martinique is a function of the incidence of the nonconjugal or weakly conjugal family. If a woman has many mates her children will tend to interact more with their mother instead of with a succession of stepfathers. They will tend to have enduring relations with their mother's family instead of the family of an absent father or a current *concubin*.

We can say, then, that Capesterre does not have a matrifocal family organization insofar as stable conjugal unions are involved, but that it is matrifocal insofar as unstable conjugality or nonconjugality are part of the social structure, as we maintain them to be. To judge Capesterre as patrifocal merely because the relatively stable conjugal household is modal would be, I believe, to ignore the crucial aspects of the system. We have seen, furthermore, that stability as well as legal and ritual marriage within the subsystem are not correlated with status differentials or economic differences. That portion of the population, then, that displays matrifocality in its family organization cannot be explained in any terms that we have found in the literature.

MARRIAGE

Let us briefly review modes of explanation, although, as we see, each author singles out different aspects to be explained. Except for the Africanist school, most people hold that regardless of the history of a group, a family pattern will not persist unless it is a functional adaptation to ongoing forces, which these students outlined for past periods both during and after slavery.[6] Ecological explanations also fit this view.

Seeking a more general statement that would also cover those cases with other historical antecedents, the latest analysis, just reviewed, suggests a correlation between matrifocality and certain features of stratification.[7] In this approach, matrifocality becomes by default the organizing principle of the family when males have no status-defining functions, a situation that occurs when a group occupies an internally undifferentiated position at the bottom of a stratified society.

Each of these theorists has a different view regarding marriage.

Since none considers the problem an integral part of his or her analysis, their views are not in all cases derivations from their major orientation.

According to M. J. and F. S. Herskovits, "Marriage is not only a prestige phenomenon in terms of social or religious values, but equally, if not more importantly, has to do with economic stability and position."[8] Because of poverty and the desire to change partners frequently, they continue, there are more "keeper" (common-law) families than any other kind, and they are unstable.

Simey observes for the West Indies in general: "The married state is something quite extraordinary, only open to those in higher walks of life, well endowed with worldly goods."[9] He points out that the practice of late marriage is a common one, and the deterrent is in part that marriage is identified with higher social standards in which an entirely different and severely "Victorian" domestic behavior pattern is expected. The women are afraid that men will become hard taskmasters if they marry them; the men are afraid the women will cease to work and will demand servants.

According to Raymond Smith, "The conversion of a common-law marriage into a legal union often serves to validate . . . [the] new power distribution [in which men have a minimum of interaction with the family], and the care with which men address their legal wives as 'Mistress' is illuminating in this respect."[10] He further observes that marriage is meaningless from the view of economic security or domestic relations; nor are people concerned with improving their status through marriage, since the whole class has an undifferentiated status, for to do so would conflict with the social structure. "Its [marriage's] real significance is an act of conformity to the 'respectable' values . . ."[11] for marriage is conceptualized as an upper-class symbol.

Regarding the *fête* in its connection with marriage, Henriques observes that a marriage without one is no marriage at all. Leyburn[12] mentions the expense of a feast as a deterrent to marriage. Raymond Smith reports that people with money who do not entertain at a marriage are accused of being vampire witches, and the entertainment demands a dance for the whole village. He also states that the decision to marry has nothing to do with being able to afford the *fête*. The nonlegal nature of most of the ties, he says, reflects a reluctance to establish a conclusive bond, and is in accord with the primary emphasis on mother-child relations instead of on conjugal relations.

Only Herskovits has found salient African retentions in the marriage ceremony. The people of Toco, Trinidad, who came originally from Tobago, have family shrines, and the ancestral dead are invoked at a marriage for the welfare of the descendants.[13] There is even a vestige of bride service: the suitor helps the girl's family with their farming.

We have seen that not only is marriage articulated with the family differently in Capesterre, but my interpretation of its relation to the family system is differently conceived. Most aspects of this situation require separate modes of description. For example, the idea that marriage is a *fête* has a model in eighteenth-century European behavior. Nor is it at variance with African practice as long as such memories persisted. That the *fête* was even functional under slavery has been shown as a possibility in chapter eight, and that other aspects of marriage remained dysfunctional during slavery has been amply demonstrated by many authors, notably by Frazier.

The model for status equality was firmly rooted in French culture, where concubinage was a structural feature. We have seen (chapter two) how color became an ingredient of status differentiation, but factors that once enabled the *mulâtres* to acculturate to the dominant society are no longer operative. The land is almost completely occupied. Education is now open to everyone, but the resulting occupational roles have almost reached a saturation point. Today, whatever kind of structural whiteness[14] that can be achieved in such a cradle-to-grave community as Capesterre leads (with few exceptions) to nothing but associational blackness. This fact in turn maintains the social arrangements that perpetuate the *totoblo* society.

In Capesterre, women and men come together publicly chiefly for *rites de passage*, and they allocate their earnings accordingly. The extent to which distribution and consumption are focused on the *fête*, and by whom, is shown in an examination of who does or does not marry and for what reasons, in the past as well as the present. In the distant past, marriage always entailed a *fête* and was very rare. Few took these hospitality obligations upon themselves. Now the responsibility is becoming more diffuse. Marriage in the early days was a superstructural pattern imposed on designs for living totally unlike those of the elite West or tribal life. We may assume that the values which today override marriage were the core of that society: conviviality, cooperation in raising the young, indiscriminate love of children—all originally on an economic foundation of bare subsistence, but where children were not considered a burden.

Marriage as a hospitality obligation was countered by another goad—mobility. Mobility was often furthered by the unmarried state. Capesterre, as we have seen, was settled in part by planters' *concubines* who created a privileged land of visiting husbands. Here we find another and converging model for the respectable unmarried mother and the grandmother family as preferred forms. Marriage in the subsystem has never become the business arrangement which in French culture was separate from the romantic attachment to *concubines*. This is the partial base for conviviality values not found in French bourgeois society.

We have also seen how religious conceptions of marriage remained an alien and only partly assimilated superstructure—that magic, science, and religion became one in the world view. Martinique has been a fluid culture, catching up with its own past in some sectors (religion is becoming more conventional in rural areas) while that past is disappearing among other individuals. It is a snake swallowing a body that never defined itself in the original molds. Some people are for the first time reaching marriage through Catholicism (the missions) that is merging with secularism (among Communist intellectuals). The elite have accepted marriage while completely bypassing religion as a motive.

Marriage today is many different things to different people, and sometimes several things to one person at the same time. The following conceptions are manifested, but only if the requirements of status equality and conviviality are met:

Solidarity expression in terms of hospitality obligations
Magical exorcism
Social acculturation without religion
Religious grace and Church acceptance

At one pole in the subsystem marriage is the vehicle for acting out solidarity expectations by means of a *fête*. At the opposite pole marriage is completely independent of the *fête*. The latter shows freedom from the *totoblo* society, which can result from deviation in an antisocial direction, or acculturation toward the elite.

Such, in summary review, are the differences and similarities to be explained. Let us put them in a fresh perspective.

A New Approach

In the past, each theory has sought to displace its predecessors, but has proved in turn, I maintain, not to cover all known cases, a requirement of any hypothesis. (Of course, such a procedure would demand a rigid definition of what constitutes a case.) By suggesting still a new approach to the problem of the "deviant" family, I am rejecting no previous modes of analysis except insofar as they purport to be nomothetic. In other words, what I discard as explanation I believe should be retained as what Kroeber calls "descriptive integration," as connections between the family and ever-widening aspects of its context. For this is what we mean by "understanding" if not "explaining" a problem, still a part of the social sciences if only as potential evidence for later generalizations.

Furthermore, all modes of analysis should be retained because there is always the danger that a true explanation will be uninformative, like saying that disruption without acculturation leads (under specified conditions) to nativism. In this paper I have already correlated family organization with its cultural antecedents; with its relation to other structures in the society; with the influence of production and labor. With the qualification, then, that I do not suggest my explanation as the substitution for analysis, but that I consider it a conceptual condensation, I shall now outline the only correspondences I have discovered to cover all cases. I shall isolate the arrangement of parts I call family structure and link it with a factor on a different level of analysis. I shall make a synthesis of a structural model and its associated values, calling the procedure "explanation." As for *explanation* in the sense of accounting for the genesis of a pattern, we can only pursue the correlations of descriptive integration mentioned above, emphasizing different ones for different areas, for none of them apply to all. In Martinique, I have traced historically how an absence of the rule of legitimacy came about, but this specific historical explanation will not cover other areas.

In an attempt to gain a new perspective on family structure in the Caribbean, let us begin with Lévi-Strauss's classification of families in the ethnographic record, a taxonomy based on the broadest possible diagnostics.[15] Human societies, he says in effect, have family systems that are either conjugal, subconjugal, or supra-conjugal. Each segment of a society has only one type at a time as the florescent form, so to speak; that is, not broken down.

The conjugal family, characterized by a mated pair alone as the child-rearing and economic unit, is standard chiefly in two types of society: (1) the simplest societies with a minimum of surplus and a strict sexual division of labor; and (2) the modern West.

The subconjugal family, in which the woman alone is responsible for childrearing, occurs only when a society has met such disaster that its traditional institutions have been destroyed. Lévi-Strauss cites the Emerillon Indians of French Guiana as a case.[16] It was this type of family that was developed under slavery in Afro-America.

Most of the world has known the supraconjugal family as ideal, a household or child-rearing unit involving relatives other than a mated pair. Anthropological literature is replete with analyses of such family systems—the *susu*, the joint family, the stem family—in which the children have a specific place despite the possible brittleness of conjugal units. Lévi-Strauss suggests that rather than calling this supraconjugal group the "extended family," we should call the Western family a "restricted family,"[17] because our Western institution is derived from our supraconjugal European past.

The basis for the supraconjugal and conjugal families is the fact that marriage is a group—not an individual—affair. Without examining such broad considerations irrelevant to this paper, let us see how the Caribbean family fits this classification.

The unique feature of the Caribbean nonelite subsystem is that it possesses all three types of the family simultaneously. This structural feature may be expressed in the life cycle of individual families as they develop, each going through all stages. Or it may characterize the *profile* of the subsystem; that is, each form can represent a permanent lifelong structure side by side with lifelong households of different types. From this point of view, it does not matter whether the families described by Henriques and Simey are parts of a developmental sequence or not.

To illustrate, if a mother lives alone with her children, temporarily or permanently, her family can be described as subconjugal as long as it is part of the social structure, an expected behavior rather than an accident or a failure to achieve the ideal. If one or more of her children remain at home with her, and together they raise the children of the next generation, the household has supraconjugal features in that a nonconjugal relative shares child-rearing responsibilities. Another supraconjugal arrangement is that of a conjugal couple one of whose children, whether remaining at home or not, leaves his or her children to be raised in the family of orientation.

A model of the Caribbean family, then, is one which includes all three Lévi-Strauss types simultaneously, whether independently or developmentally. As I have explained, this kind of generalization requires the use of a concept of social structure that includes regular behaviors other than modal. We are only beginning to document the empirical combinations that the model is capable of producing. The manner in which *modal* distributions of compositional emphases, variations in power centers, and the like will vary from region to region, from one community to another, will depend on an infinity of possible combinations of factors. Among such factors are degree of status differentiation, intensity of land shortage, proliferation of specializations, amount of cooperative labor needed, sex ratio resulting from location of work opportunities, channels for mobility, criteria of status differentiation, solidarity of the community, cultural isolation, integrity and nature of previous culture brought to the subsystem, foci of the contact situation, bases for association, legal motivations, agencies of control, economic influence of the church, and others.

With this plethora of protean variables, it is difficult to discover correlations among them capable of general application, as some students of the Caribbean have attempted. Limited correlations are functional interdependencies within a given whole. They cannot pass as general explanations for the range of samples that are available.

To ask why each community thus far described fits my suggested model rather than the type of correlation involving the variables just mentioned involves a corollary to the model. The corollary is the rule of legitimacy as discussed by Malinowski[18] and Lévi-Strauss.[19]

The model operates as it does (the structure of all these subsystems is the same, although expressed in different modalities and developmental emphases) because there is no rule of legitimacy. Or rather, there is no rule of legitimacy because the social arrangements are as the model describes them. We have, then, the axiological (pertaining to value) heads and the structural tails of the Caribbean family.

In all those societies that I shall call traditional, the rule of legitimacy dictates that marriage (a group-sanctioned bond) and the production and/or rearing of children must coincide. Just as Lévi-Strauss explains kinship systems in terms of the exchange of mates based on a rule of legitimacy, we could explain how the Caribbean model operates on the basis of the mere absence of such a rule. In either case there are limited possibilities that can be deduced. Why different types of traditional systems arose in some places and not in others is a problem often dealt with in anthropological literature.

Why the rule of legitimacy is absent in Caribbean societies is a historico-functional problem for which there is yet no general explanation that would apply to all cases, if we include those cases mentioned by Raymond Smith that have a different historical background from the New World plantation areas (the Moche of Peru and a lower-class Scottish family system). High illegitimacy rates found in many Latin American areas with still different histories[20] further complicate the problem. In chapter two and chapter eight I have described how the absence occurred in Martinique. Frazier has done the same in great detail for the American South.[21] When all such histories are available for all the regions in question, it would be a good problem for a future study to seek common features. It is beyond the scope of the present treatise.

Let us go back for a moment to the concept of social structure as including nonmodal behavior, the only fruitful interpretation in a society whose very structure is the mingling of several types of family systems which normally appear separately. In chapter one we saw that the concept of structure as used in this paper is a structure derived from a specific series of social arrangements. It is these arrangements that are crystallized as values by human groups. Therefore, since there are alternative structures, there are alternative ideals and expectations. No Caribbean subsystem is characterized by its own single substitute for Western legitimacy. Their only concept of legitimacy is that of the West, which they have not completely internalized. They have *low rates* of legitimacy, not a total absence of it. Only the latter would indicate a totally separate system. But the presence of some form of legitimacy does not indicate that they have a *rule* of legitimacy which is broken only by delinquents. An illegitimate child is not, as they would say in Martinique, a *totoblo*, a shameful *faux pas*. We do not say that the individual Caribbean subsystem has no value grammar of its own—we analyzed a variety of one in chapter seven—but simply that it lacks a single family ideal governed by the rule of legitimacy found in traditional societies. The nonelite culture is a *tertium quid* which neither conforms with elite values nor is in origin or development a totally autonomous emergent.

To delineate the structure only by the modal is a sound method in a traditional society. And to treat Caribbean subsystems like traditional societies is consistent with the general view that such cultures should not be described as internally disnomic, but only as symptomatic of disnomia in the total society in which such a subsystem could develop. Most authors regard marriage as an ideal not normally realized—for no apparent reason. Raymond Smith does see marriage as a separate value of another system; to him common-law marriage is a differential ideal. But my interpretation sees no one ideal, even a differential one. Marriage and its absence, legitimacy and its absence, conjugality and its absence are all variants in expected behavior, alternative ideals, each of which fits a different set of circumstances.

Such ideals grow out of the structural possibilities. Even the conjugal household is different from such a household in societies in which conjugality that stems from the rule of legitimacy is the governing principle. With or without marriage, conjugality and child rearing do not have to coincide in the Caribbean subsystem.

Not only is conjugality not the sole ideal, it is sometimes a violation of sanctioned behavior, as with the *maison paternelle*.

Again, as the modalities of structural features vary from region to region, so too will the specific values be differently systematized. But as long as there are multiple, mingled structures, there will be multiple, mingled values. In the absence of a rule of legitimacy, both structure and value system are determined by the duration and frequency of mating relationships and the ability of other persons to rear the children. The absence of a rule of legitimacy does not carry with it implications of any specific household type, or distribution of power within it, except that it does make possible the subconjugal household. To the extent that this facet of the possibilities is realized, matrifocality can be predicted. Other types of matrifocality may or may not be present. Matrifocality, then, is a derivative of the model and its corollary.

If we look at the family system purely synchronically, we notice several givens in what Homans calls the external system; that is, the environment, social or otherwise, that sets the frame for whatever the human group does within it. (In a factory, one of the givens of the external system affecting a group of workers would be the wage system.) "We must," says Homans, "assume a certain state of affairs at the beginning of our exposition the existence of which we can account for only at the end." [22] The internal system is "the elaboration of group behavior that simultaneously arises out of the external system and reacts upon it." [23] To analyze these givens is a separate problem beyond the scope of this book, but the causality implicit in ecology, economic history, and land tenure has already been discussed.

The first given is the absence of the extended family or unilineal descent group. Hence there is no context in which the rule of legitimacy would acquire its usual economic functions that are correlated in tribal societies with bonds of cooperation and exchange. On the other hand, strict conjugality is not the functional necessity that it is in the severe environments of most hunting-and-gathering societies. A sexual division of labor is preferable but not mandatory, and it is seldom fully developed.

Another given is a strong neolocal preference. Some of the factors producing this value also create obstacles to the goal, such as close living quarters and the reflected poverty.

Given also is the sanctioning of the fruits of any sexual behavior, even in the face of such nonpermissiveness and negative valuation of promiscuity as are found in Martinique.

We have seen how in the internal system every eventuality within these external conditions has been systematized. Either the mother provides for her children within her family of orientation, or, if she has left, she either keeps the children or gives them to others. A conjugal house can precede or follow either alternative. This household either remains or splits, becoming part of a family of orientation or a grandmother family of sorts. The development of the household after this point is influenced by the factors of age, death, and the decisions of the household children.

We have seen how such a system developed in Capesterre and how it is articulated with the concept of marriage. Our nomothetic approach to the problem (the model and its correlate) reveals nothing of such descriptive integration, but the whole value system is representative of what can develop in that rare occurrence in human societies, the absence of a rule of legitimacy.

SUMMARY

Social organization is directional activity that involves systematic choice. I have analyzed the choices involved in entering marriage or *ménage* in Capesterre as they are planned in conformity with selected ends, or values. We have seen that the forces against marriage are all those prior concerns of the *totoblo* society, which are different from the values of the dominant society as they impinge on the creation and rearing of children.

Whatever specific form these values take in different regions or communities, and however they alter over time, they allow for the child-rearing system to express structural differences from those found in a society that makes marriage synonymous with child-rearing units, whether conjugal or extended. I have shown how some of these values run through various contexts in the subsystem; how they touch upon consumption habits, hospitality patterns, association; how they harmonize with magic, science, and religion. We have seen examples of the meaning, concept, and vocabulary that accompanied the nonelite family as it emerged as an institution.

The importance of analyzing marriage in the subsystem is its illumination of principles that add up to the absence of a rule of legitimacy. The structural correlate of the absence of such a rule is, I maintain, the distinguishing feature of the Caribbean family, namely, the simultaneous existence of three family types that usually exist separately: the conjugal, the subconjugal, and the supraconjugal. Throughout nonelite subsystems, conjugality can exist before, after, or during child rearing. It can also exist independently of children, or not at all.

NOTES

[1] E. Franklin Frazier, *The Negro Family in the United States* (New York: Dryden Press, 1948).

[2] Fernando Henriques, *Family and Colour in Jamaica* (London: Eyre & Spottiswoode, 1953).

[3] Raymond T. Smith, *The Negro Family in British Guiana* (London: Routledge & Kegan Paul, 1956).

[4] M. J. Herskovits and F. S. Herskovits, *Trinidad Village* (New York: Knopf, 1947).

[5] John Philip Gillin, *Moche, a Peruvian Coastal Village* (Washington, D.C.: Government Printing Office, 1947). See also C. S. Wilson, unpublished dissertation (Cambridge University, 1953).

[6] Cf. T. S. Simey, *Welfare and Planning in the West Indies* (Oxford: Clarendon Press, 1946); Henriques, *Family and Colour in Jamaica*; and Frazier, *Negro Family in the United States*.

[7] See Raymond T. Smith, "Culture and Social Structure in the Caribbean: Some Recent Work on Family and Kinship Studies," *Comparative Studies in Society and History*, 6 (1963).

[8] M. J. and F. S. Herskovits, *Trinidad Village*, p. 84.

[9] Simey, *Welfare and Planning*, p. 85.

[10] Raymond T. Smith, *Negro Family in British Guiana*, p. 148.

[11] Ibid., p. 179.

[12] James G. Leyburn, *The Haitian People* (New Haven: Yale University Press, 1941).

[13] M. J. and F. S. Herskovits, *Trinidad Village*, p. 177.

[14] See chapter two.

[15] Claude Lévi-Strauss, "The Family," in Harry L. Shapiro, ed., *Man, Culture and Society* (Oxford: Oxford University Press, 1956).

[16] Ibid., p. 271.

[17] Ibid., p. 273.

[18] Bronislaw Malinowski, *Sex and Repression in Savage Society* (New York: Meridian, 1927; 1955 reprint).

[19] Cf. chaper seven, pp. 154–155.

[20] See Dom Basil Matthews, *The Crisis in the West Indian Family* (Jamaica: University College of the West Indies, 1953), p. 13.

[21] Frazier, *Negro Family in the United States.*

[22] George C. Homans, *The Human Group* (New York: Harcourt, Brace & World, 1950), p. 93.

[23] Ibid., p. 103.

Epilogue

One of the few benefits of publishing a dissertation long after it was written is that answers to criticisms can appear at the same time. Of course, not all reconsiderations revolve around criticism of my own notions, and I can tie my data into some of the later interests.

Let me turn first to explanations for the phenomenon of the Caribbean family that have been offered since Raymond T. Smith's belief that it is accompanied by the absence of status-defining functions for males. The principal ones are migratory wage labor (Solien 1959);[1] absentee male labor (Kunstadter 1963);[2] and poverty per se (e.g., Moynihan 1965,[3] Rodman 1966,[4] and Jayawardena 1960, 1962).[5] Jayawardena also shows that poor Hindus are not matrifocal, however, because males perform ritual functions.

All these packages, I claim, are clearly overgeneralizations of local Caribbean modalities, or variations on a larger theme which cuts out most of the societies in the Caribbean. An example of projecting from circumscribed patterns is Raymond T. Smith's analysis[6] of the power balance of Guianese conjugality, with male power dwindling as the household cycle ages, which is clearly not found in Carriacou, where Michael G. Smith shows how a man has a wife and a concubine,[7] or in Martinique, where we saw fairly stable conjugality. Correlates offered, therefore, illustrate only geographically limited functional interdependencies, which may or may not be spottily repeated elsewhere. Thus, another level of analysis is required for discovering a principle that generates all variations at least currently found in the record.

It is fruitful, I believe, to begin by confining the field of inquiry to a single culture area, and only later explore worldwide distributions of some trait cluster such as migratory labor, unwed mothers, or whatever. Otherwise, we cannot differentiate homologous, parallel, or convergent adaptations. It seems fruitless to attempt semi-grand theory before this.

Kunstadter's paper embodies many of the pitfalls of such attempts, and shows how making an issue of a peripheral trait excludes what the author set out to explain. Taking his inspiration from Solien's dissertation, he hooks onto the "consanguine" family, considering it to be congruent with matrifocality, which is in itself an error, as Solien points out.[8] Consanguine, says González of her own work (under the name of Solien), may or may not be matrifocal, since it refers to blood kin, not to domestic groups or affinal relatives. "It is one of the structural features of matrifocality," she says, "that, given a conflict, a man is more likely to turn to his mother . . . rather than his wife, or . . . the mother of his children . . . [The] crucial point in . . . the consanguineal household is that the effective and enduring relationships are those . . . between consanguineal kin."[9] (Only 45 percent of her Black Carib sample may be so characterized.) Focality to González is "measured by female stability, role dominance, and authority patterns," all of which appear only with bilateral kinship.[10]

Kunstadter lumps as consanguineal the matrilineal Nayar and the Western merry widow, bypassing by his criterion most modal Afro-American patterns. Evidently he uses his *explicans* (namely, absentee males) for determining the choice of phenomena to be explained. He says he rejects my approach because an absence of legitimacy fails to account for the Nayar (*sic*), as if there were any reason for including them. Moreover, he finds my whole thesis "tautological," as if I had discovered that unwed mothers were caused by an absence of weddings.

Unwed Mothers

Just as Kunstadter's category omits most of the characteristics in question, it is also erroneous to identify the Caribbean puzzle with all forms of illegitimacy. Illegitimacy is an interesting subject, but not germane to creating the model required. For example, although the Wapisiana of South America have zero illegitimacy because they consider cohabitation as marriage, and everyone presumably cohabits;[11] and although the Tiwi of Australia[12] preclude illegitimacy through the practice of instant widow remarriage and infant betrothal, these facts do not distinguish or illuminate the Caribbean family. Moreover, ignoring the particulars of a historical or ethnic complex creates the errors of the prefunctionalist theorists.

Some writers think they have eliminated the reality of distinctive ethnic patterns by such reasoning as Jane Kronick's in Roberts's *The Unwed Mother.* Referring to all quantitative studies of illegitimacy made before 1962, she says:

> I do not wish to quarrel with the historical accuracy of Frazier's account ... The ... data, however, appear ... inconsistent with this theory [that a Negro subculture accounts for Negro illegitimacy] ... Families of Eastern cities, which are predominantly Negro, indicate that illegitimacy occurs only in ... about the same proportion as among the white ADC [Aid to Dependent Children] population, [about $\frac{1}{2}$], with a higher incidence among those born in the ... [South].[13]

One trouble with believing that such facts disconfirm a "cultural" approach is that it leads to the vain hope of expecting *causes* to emerge from mixing apples and horses, then counting them. It is hardly a discovery to "discover" that *cause* is not assessed in that way. Welfare, census, and clinical data are simply not predictors of cohesive behavior patterns. Unwed mothers fall into a series of superficially definable but amorphous categories. Contextual detail is needed, which is precisely why an insider like Frazier or McKissick rejects Moynihanish conclusions, much as a native speaker knows when a foreigner has made an error. It is method, of course, not identity that counts. The community study approach enables outsiders to achieve similar insights. Molière's *bourgeois gentilhomme* was an insider prose-speaker who did not know he spoke prose.

I do not wish to stereotype clinicians. Therefore, I shall begin by citing Rose Bernstein's article, "Are We Still Stereotyping the Unwed Mother?" This is an excellent exception to the tendency for welfare workers to entertain foregone conclusions that all unwed mothers are pathological.[14] And whether proportionately more of them are black is still another question. The putative "health" goal is the mother's resumption of a conventional single status as quickly as possible after delivering the illegitimate child. It is achieved by hiding the traces of "delinquent" (if not outright psychotic) behavior.[15] Leontine R. Young, for example, found that "All of these girls [100 agency cases], unhappy and driven by unconscious needs, had blindly sought a way out of their emotional dilemma by having an out-of-wedlock child ... Less than a quarter had even known the lover as a person ..."[16] Clark E. Vincent found high degrees of illegitimacy among middle-class whites by questioning obstetricians,[17] and Kinsey estimated that 90 percent of these women get abortions.[18] Christensen shows that illegitimacy is low in some communities because of "shotgun" marriages.[19]

Even confining the sample to ADC mothers, a patterned difference appears between Negroes and others if the researcher knows what to look for. Jones et al. found "subcultural elements" when they noticed that 62 percent of their Negro clients (as opposed to 21 percent of the whites) opted for keeping their babies.[20] Deficiencies in ego strength were found among those who did not willingly give up their children for adoption.[21]

Bernstein, on the other hand, concludes that "What we interpret as pathology may be the girl's valid use of a healthy mechanism to protect herself in crisis from a threatening reality."[22] She is aware that there are differences among middle-class whites who ignore abortions and the lower-class girls who have no information. To some, a baby is disturbing per se, whereas to others it is its illegitimacy. Furthermore, she says, the treatment of unwed mothers may itself cause trauma. I suggest that by using community studies (based on participant observation) as a bridge between rural and urban, and between the islands and the mainland, we will increasingly find reinforcement of the theory of variance rather than deviance.

ADAPTATION

Among anthropologists who emphasize variance is González (see above), who expresses this view, as I said in the introduction. She sees matrifocality as *adaptive* in lower-class segments of modern industrial societies. It is adaptive not only by virtue of the male's inability to provide, which she believes Raymond T. Smith to exaggerate, but primarily because it offers more choices to insecure people. "The consanguine household," she says, "offers financial and psychological security to the female and to the male . . ." When he angers his wife, his mother takes him in. "Conversely, a woman can ill afford to cleave only unto one man, cutting herself off from other . . . unions or from male kinsmen, for in such systems the chances that any one man may fail are high . . . By dispersing her loyalties and by clinging . . . to the unbreakable sibling ties with her brothers, a woman increases her chances of maintaining her children and household . . ."[23]

"Just so," I answer, as Kipling might. I, too, see this system as adaptive, but more fortuitously so than this model that is based on games theory. In my opinion, the interpretation implies too much intent and assumes too much information on the part of actors. Moreover, the Caribbean family would seem to be *pre*adapted to certain modern developments, since this was also the family form during preindustrial slavery. Finally, one wonders if the game is really won; for if a woman turns to three failures, on each of whom three others depend, is she not getting from any one man one-sixth of nothing?

The notion of Darwinian adaptation is ambiguous in the social sciences. González is one of many who extends her metaphors as far as games theory. For example, she speaks of the Negro family's "enhancing the survival chances of the sub-society . . . and the existing relationship between this and the whole."[24]

It would seem that extinction of the matrifocal subsociety would occur only if it became rich, just as religious sects often disappear by merging with denominations. In the absence of such an event, it is difficult to imagine how any mating institution would *disappear* short of becoming, perhaps, a wolf pack, that is, evolving into a new species. By definition, whatever *is*, is adaptive. More empirically, my criticism of such maximization notions of adaptation can be illustrated by considering the Hindus of Martinique. They are as poor as the blacks, more excluded than ex-slaves. Would they not benefit from "flexibility"? Yet they are not matrifocal by any definition, and they rigorously maintain a rule of legitimacy. The games model of adaptation thus fails to explain the Hindu divergence from matrifocality. Similarly, it cannot explain why the

Javanese studied by Hildred and Clifford Geertz developed matri-focal families.[25]

In short, although the Caribbean family, or matrifocality, is not deviant or pathological, and is therefore adaptive in many ways, this does not justify Just-So-ism. My alternative approach sought to analyze a species confined to the nonelite subcultures found in Afro-America, not a genus including all areas possessing matrifocality and/or illegitimacy.

NORMS AND RULES

My interpretation has been challenged, as I pointed out in the introduction, by William J. Goode. Is there an absence of the rule of legitimacy, as I suggest, or is there a lower "degree of . . . commit-ment" to a "norm" of legitimacy, as he maintains? To the extent that this difference in approach is definitional, a compromise "variance" model proposed by Hyman Rodman (as opposed to Goode's "deviation" model) might clarify the matter. But I believe the difference is substantive as well, and its essence lies beneath the threshold of perception unless the problem is restated.

Both Rodman and Goode construe the situation in such a way, I contend, as to distort patterns of social organization, personality, role behavior, and cognitive mazeways. A resolution can be opera-tionalized, I shall attempt to show, by revisiting my own material to look for something I did not have in mind when I collected the data. This is the kind of fishing I referred to in the introduction, whereby crucial facts can be retrieved because of the wide net cast in making an anthropological community study.

Goode argues, it may be recalled, that the Caribbean material merely qualified Malinowski's generalization about legitimacy, that the facts do not constitute an exception to the generalization. The function of marriage, says Goode, may now be seen as "status placement"[26] rather than Malinowski's paternal protection, but marriage still legitimates parenthood.[27]

The source for Goode's orientation here can be found in a standard text by Kingsley Davis.[28] Both draw on the Malinowski passage found in Calverton's 1930 reader[29] to emphasize the func-tion of a *pater* even when a *genitor* is not recognized, as among the matrilineal Trobrianders. The "principle of legitimacy," says Davis, is

> the universal social rule that "no child should be brought into the world without a man . . . assuming the role of . . . guardian and protector." Without this general rule, there would be no family; hence it is as universal and fundamental as the familial institution itself . . . [The principle] prevails no matter what other conditions prevail . . . [and] marriage is a *conditio sine qua non* [essential condition] of legitimate children.[30]

Goode reduces my multifaceted model to that aspect which claims illegitimacy to be no less prestigious than its opposite. He then cites other Caribbeanists who labor under the same alleged misapprehension that illegitimacy represents a cultural alternative.[31] Sweeping the ethnographies as if they were mined fields, Goode next attempts to show how we anthropologists contradict ourselves by unwittingly providing implicit evidence contrary to our misjudgments. Finally, he adduces explicit assertions by the actors that marriage is deemed better than nonlegal unions. These assertions are mostly based on responses elicited by questionnaires, although participant observers have occasionally made such reports, as I said when quoting Virginia Young on Georgia (see introduction, pages 7–8).

If the anthropologists were correct, Goode contends, you would not find that "those who violate the rule do suffer penalties."[32] Moreover, you would discover counternorms to legitimacy.[33] Since no counternorms are conspicuous, he concludes that the rule of legitimacy is therefore present.

Is Goode saving Malinowski's hypothesis in order to contribute to theory concerning the universal functions of marriage? If so, such questions of function are not necessarily dependent on whether a *rule* is *absent* or a low-commitment *norm* is *present.* Nor does the anthropological distinction rest on the contention that illegitimacy is not stigmatized—chimerical or not.

To convey my meaning of *rule*, the linguist's concept of structure must be understood as it is used in phonemic theory, which is to say an item is not a structural regularity unless it appears in contrastive distribution, that is, unless it makes a meaning difference to the speaker. For example, the sound in the middle of the English word *matter* may be *t* or *d* in most contexts without altering the significance of the utterance (*t* and *d* are allophones of the same phoneme). Similarly, by "rule" I mean an operant component crucial in making choices: Legitimacy is either phonemic or it is not. I claim that legitimacy is merely allophonic variation in the actual behavior in question. That is, when people disagree on whether *t* or *d* is present and/or required, the sound is not phonemic, and there is no "rule." In societies where the rule of legitimacy is operant it unambiguously differentiates between one state and another, as do the separate phonemes *t* and *d* in such words as *tie* and *die*.

Goode uses the terms *rule, law, principle,* and *norm* interchangeably, equating them solely with *ideal* in the sense of desired goal, or the actor's notion of what people "ought" to do. Moreover, it is anachronistic to consider this ideational aspect—as opposed to realized behavior—to be the only locus of culture, a position indicated in Goode's emphasis that "Malinowski was stating a proposition about a cultural element: he asserted that the norm would always be found, not that the members of the society would obey it under specified conditions." [34]

Malinowski's precise intention is beside the point, since I borrowed his phrase for analytic, not exegetic, purposes. However, Malinowski did say he knew of no "instance" where illegitimate children "enjoy the same treatment" as others. Following is the full quotation from *Sex and Repression in Savage Society*:

> In all human societies ... there is universally found what might be called the rule of legitimacy. By this I mean that in all human societies a girl is bidden to be married before she becomes pregnant. Pregnancy and childbirth on the part of an unmarried young woman are invariably regarded as a disgrace ... I know of no single instance in anthropological literature of a community where illegitimate children, that is children of unmarried girls, would enjoy the same special treatment and have the same social status as legitimate ones. [35]

Clearly, Goode's predecessors did not have Caribbean material in mind in formulating theory. When a "principle of legitimacy" is identified with "family structure," they refer to realized as well as idealized behavior, since the two tend to coincide in elite or traditional society in all but deviant cases, that is, incidents of rule breaking. On the other hand, where high *de facto* illegitimacy prevails, structure must explicitly refer to what men do as well as to what they think they do, or should do. In such societies, pre-Caribbean sociological expectations are not met. Structure should never refer to what a nonparticipant thinks actors think *they* ought to do.

This problem is related to the anachronistic notion of culture which some sociologists continue to use "in a sense far more restricted than the anthropological usage," say Kroeber and Kluckhohn.[36] Merton, they point out, once said in 1936 that "Culture comprises configurations of values of normative principles and ideals, which are historically unique."[37] Howard Odum still employed the concept *culture* in this sense in 1947, and it is still used by Talcott Parsons. Most others have adopted the anthropological usage, which pertains to all learned, patterned behaviors, as Harris points out in my discussion of this matter in the introduction.

VALIDATION

How can I validate an absence of a rule in my sense?—by the accuracy with which I can predict the circumstances under which various kinds of liaisons occur: consensual, extraresidential, Western marital, and native marital (e.g., the *fête* complex). To disagree with me in these terms, Goode would have to show, for example, that there is no expectation of a nonresidential union when a woman inherits a house; that legal marriage is not infra dig without a *fête*; that the latter does not covary with status equality, and the like. But he ignores the grammaticality of these existential values; he does not disconfirm them. I suggest that Goode will find the evidence of counternorms he requires and finds lacking if he examines these values.

ANOMIE

When Goode speaks of *rule* and *ideal*, he properly seeks their referent in motivation. But he does not examine the actors, preferring to extrapolate from elite data. Caribbean ideal and practice, he assumes without proof, are merely less congruent than elsewhere. I suggest, to the contrary, that their whole structure is different, motivations and all. Thus, we reach the distortion of personality patterns that are correctly intuited by insiders and participant observers. And this is precisely my source for attempting to retrieve data from the community study to restate the problem in the light of Goode's criticism.

High rates of illegitimacy in Goode's view are always an index of individual deviations—dropping out, so to speak—writ large (anomie). On the level of motivation, it follows, one would therefore expect demoralization, alienation, and the like. Rodman's hypostatized reality is essentially the same anomie, and calling it variance merely implies a lesser degree of self-recrimination or sense of failure. Both views, I contend, are inaccurate notions of what actually happened in history, and accordingly, of the present reflection of this past. As depictions of a cultural design for living, they are ungrammatical.

I shall try to demonstrate this charge by discussing four somewhat overlapping fallacies implicit in Goode's position, which is representative of all social scientists who take subculture for granted. (I include Rodman's position where pertinent.) The fallacies are:

1. Ethnocentrism
2. Monolithic views of a pluralistic set of societies
3. The reduction to a two-point scale (legality and nonlegality) of a multivalent field (i.e., numerous types of liaisons)
4. A pervasive fallacy of misplaced concreteness

ETHNOCENTRIC FALLACIES

Let us refer back to the community context to see how Goode strips elementary facts of their idiomatic qualities. First, his strategy begs the question of whether family norms must revolve around legitimacy. This can be seen by his a priori limitation of "respectability" to legitimacy. In one reference to Capesterre, for example, he quotes me as reporting what I have now called a phonemic distinction between the legitimate and illegitimate: "When talking about the consensual relationships of others the term '*concubine*' is used."

In fact, I report that *mari* and *femme* are interchangeable with it, and that its meaning is as neutral as the masculine equivalent, *concubin,* whose very existence forms an opposition which robs the condition of pejorative connotations. Respect for the *concubine* (chapter eight) was generated in a colonial situation when a planter's mate outranked a married slave. We have seen how rich *concubines* might have spawned "my son the mulatto," a man of distinction during many periods, including the present.

These attitudes have been retained by any black mother today who prefers her daughter to be a white's mistress to being the bride of a peer. That the mother might prefer her daughter to be the white man's wife is not the relevant contrast; that would be like saying that she might prefer her to *be* white. After all, in India the desire to be a Brahmin is hardly the norm among the Untouchables. Unrealities of this sort can be generated by questionnaires, but the facts of ascriptive status must be taken into account in a study of norms and their origins.

In another example where I seem in Goode's view to provide evidence that contradicts my explicit statements, he says: "In a few reported cases of girls having babies, the parents pretended that the children were their own."[38] This mother was disgraced because it is shocking for children to have sexual experience, not because of the legality or illegality of the sexual experience per se.

Similarly, when parental anger is expressed at a girl's first pregnancy, as many Caribbeanists report, Goode assumes a single focus for the displeasure or anxiety. On the other hand, as Raymond Smith says, stress may be caused by the threat that a second mother presents to the household head. Motherhood is a symbol of adult status, as so often in a folk society. Moreover, the anger in Martinique is mild if the lover plans a *ménage.* In Barbados, for another example, Constance Sutton says that the emotion itself is often token anger to goad the boy into entering a consensual union, not a marriage.[39] In short, there is simply no ethnonotion, or actor's mazeway, that splits arrangements into the legal and nonlegal.

Of course, many societies provide parallels of contradictory reactions when status change provokes anxiety, such as tears at a European wedding. But these conventions may be far removed from any emotional base, and structurally speaking, aspects of the seeming ambivalence to the status of the unwed mother might point to *ménage* as the alternative ideal, part of which (see chapter seven) may include late marriage, so that illegitimacy is a temporary anomaly. But anomalies per se may cause anxiety.[40]

Late Marriage A conspicuous tendency to late marriage would reveal the marital status of elderly individuals at the time of their death. While working in Guadeloupe, Jean Goossen examined the civil records in the community where I worked, recording the available data on all deaths occurring between 1954 and 1969. Among the total number of deaths, which ranged between three and fifteen a year, let us take as our index the 147 who were 60 years old or more; for if ever people intended marriage, they would have brought it about by then, and a sufficiently large number of men as well as women live their threescore years. Below is a table showing the marital status of this group by sex.

	Single	*Married*
Male	13	52
Female	24	59
Total	37	111

As we see, the married individuals (including the widowed) outnumber the singles three to one. But there is no simple alternative ideal that would justify setting up a variant form of legal marriage as a functional equivalent of elite and/or traditional rules of legitimacy.

As for Goode's use of raw legitimacy statistics, however, we see that late marriage is sufficiently frequent to make the figures more ambiguous than ethnocentric projection suggests.

THE MONOLITHIC FALLACY

Why does Goode grasp at such straws as the above, when the problem seems to him as simple as this: "As against the assertion that illegitimacy is not stigmatized, we note the opposing facts. Both upper and middle class opinion is set against 'concubinage.' The priests may shame the couple about the matter . . ."[41]

Thus Goode lumps different subcultures—the elite and the nonelite—together, treating the society as a monolithic whole. This is more than the semantic quibble that a norm of legitimacy exists because some people do marry. But similarly, I contend, we must exclude the negative sanctions of the elite as evidence for an operant norm for the nonelite. We must also exclude evidence of a nonelite norm based on the practice of placing poorer members of the elite in the wrong category, as if redheaded persons formed an interacting group.

Obviously the elite stigmatize illegitimacy for their own women, but little is gained by stating that polygynous societies have the norm of monogamy because the missions try to change them. Then too, the extent to which middle-class members of society concern themselves with the behavior of others is a variable, as is the form of proselytizing and the power to communicate or coerce. Moreover, in Martinique, as we saw, white French priests consider "living in sin" to be more venial than adultery, and they mistakenly consider promiscuity to be endemic. Furthermore, the church has other weapons than "shame."

Social scientists must distinguish among the following: acquaintance with the norms of another group; lip service paid to such standards; emulation of them; and internalization of the norms. Otherwise, the very facts of culture that are in dispute are ignored. Each of the processes is an empirical variable in Caribbean societies.

A more understandable claim made by Goode is the following: Quoting Edith Clarke, he describes a Jamaican community where the native observer states that the actors are aware of the shameful nature of their customary behavior.[42] Goode fails to mention, however, that churches in Jamaica sometimes distribute land only to the legally married. In one such situation Cumper has shown that the next generation, no longer pressed to bargain for land, resumed the consensual union.[43] "Shame" was fleeting, and in Capesterre, as we have seen, couples were ashamed of having been part of a mass marriage imposed by the missions. They described it, you may recall, as lacking in dignity, as mending torn cloth.

Thus, far from a singular form performing the function of status placement, as the sociology of the middle class suggests, marriage involves at least a distinction between the process of getting married and the state of being married. One is tempted to talk of conspicuous *consummation*. We have seen that only an outsider provided the sole example of an unadorned civil marriage. The in-group makes use of weddings to express community solidarity. This interpretation seems confirmed by the frequent attitude that couples have fulfilled their hospitality obligations by means of a baptismal *fête*. There may, of course, be low commitment to these native norms in rare deviant cases (as opposed to rare structural cases), and this state may or may not be accompanied by high commitment to the elite norm. A bad or reluctant thief is not necessarily an honest citizen.

Let us consider Goode's argument that those who violate the rule of legitimacy do suffer penalties. It seems that this view loses sight of the realities of nonelite status in a stagnant economy. First, as Goode himself points out, "Given a system in which consensual unions are common, it follows that the punishments for entering them cannot be severe, and the rewards for marrying cannot be great . . ."[44] The lower status of the nonelite (although there is a hierarchy) cannot be taken as prima facie evidence of penalties imposed on illegitimacy. To say there is no less prestige in illegitimate status is not to say there is no disadvantage in being nonelite—in being what Michael G. Smith calls "behaviorally black." But this status is seldom a matter of achievement in Caribbean societies. Since many factors determine nonelite status in a relatively closed society, intervening variables would rule out the consensual union as causal.

By treating society as an undifferentiated whole except for lower and upper strata, Goode measures its members in terms of conformity to another monolith—a putative single omnipresent norm. This view, reinforced by his confusion of ideal and real, leads directly to his conviction of deviance:

> Not only do some individuals reject particular norms, but the members of some strata are less concerned . . . Thus, one can find individuals who . . . reject marriage for one reason or another in all these societies . . . [The] empirical question is: what percentage of the society or stratum? In our society, too, . . . [a] poll will locate a few such individuals.[45]

If societies are distinguished only in terms of whether *some* or *many* of their homogeneous members are unwed mothers, analysis requires no more than consulting census tracts, as Goode does in a later paper on the subject.[46] Willy-nilly, a French mayor's daughter and a plantation grandmother are both crowded into the same pigeonhole—deviance by fiat. Not only does this strategy create a society of redheads, so to speak, it leads to some of the possibly false diagnoses of pathology.

This problem is related to the methodological bias against a "cultural" approach that I discussed in the introduction. To contrast the cultural with the "pathological" does not mean that is all there is to say about it by way of explanation. Nor does the appearance of a pattern within a given culture (or subculture) preclude its appearance elsewhere. The extent to which we may fruitfully extrapolate from rural to urban, island to mainland, depends largely on whether a common denominator is discovered.

One insight that pertains to the urban case, I repeat, is the notion that rather than departing from an ideal many Afro-Americans are acculturating to it, while some operate in a frame of interim or recurrent social arrangements that generate values in the absence of the ideal. Once the norm has been adopted, individuals may begin deviating from it for the same reasons that elite members occasionally do. Until then, the low incidence of legitimacy in the nonelite sectors of the Caribbean—not necessarily elsewhere—indicates, if anything, the emergence of elite legitimacy as a value, not its evanescence.

In addition to the Jamaican case, Goode offers two examples of explicit awareness of feeling shame vis-à-vis a nonelite reference group.[47] Braithwaite reports for Trinidad that "when working-class women quarrel, one may point out that the other is not properly married,"[48] and Bastien in Haiti ranks certain unions higher than others.[49] At the same time, these authors claim that illegitimate children are not disadvantaged. There are, then, communities where the subjects punish one another to a small degree, as Goode expects, for customary behavior. But one cannot put the head of one beast on the body of another. There is no reason to think that the Braithwaite situation applies, for example, in the American South, where Frazier says the residents are "completely unconscious of any violation of the mores in having children outside of marriage."[50]

What we have, obviously, is a range. Not only are various communities differentially located on the continuum of acculturation to elite values, but various individuals within a community are differentially located. In Capesterre today the values happen to be comparatively well integrated with nonelite social arrangements, which are associated with the practice of distributing children to kin. As in some of Frazier's communities, the actors approve of their customs. This community is closer to its plantation base than many others. At the same time, it allows the *petite bourgeoisie* to remain as marginal to elite norms as the cane cutters. This situation suggests that subcultural factors like community cohesion are more determinative than poverty per se in maintaining a separate, relatively isolated subculture (Michael G. Smith's "pluralism"). In most industrial societies it is not possible to make enough money to be bourgeois without becoming associationally and then behaviorally involved with the elite, but not in Capesterre.

By ignoring the direction of social change and assuming the static nature of a Malinowskian norm, Goode vitiates a tenable position about degrees of internalization of elite norms. In summarizing this problem in Capesterre, I described (pages 214–215) how

> Marriage today is many different things to different people, and sometimes several things to one person at the same time. . . . At one pole in the subsystem marriage is the vehicle for acting out solidarity expectations by means of a *fête*. At the opposite pole marriage is . . . independent of the *fête*. The latter shows independence from the . . . [conservative majority], a freedom which can be the result of deviation in an antisocial direction . . . or acculturation in the direction of the elite.

THE TWO-POINT SCALE

Goode[51] uncritically accepts questionnaire data presented by Hatt[52] and Blake.[53] Since criticisms of these approaches are numerous,[54] I shall consider them to be subsumed in my comments on Rodman's attempts to resolve some of the problems.

Rodman recognizes a necessity to restrict his sample to the lower class, although it is not clear whether his 176 respondents from Trinidad include poorer members of the elite. Six questions were "deliberately worded differently [from those of Blake et al.] in order to get some idea of the conditions under which a favorable reply [to accepting the nonlegal union] is more likely to be given."[55] Although many tended to prefer marriage, men were more likely than women to accept the nonlegal union, and the lower their class the more "environmental circumstances" would influence them to do so.

The sociologists, Rodman says, fail to distinguish between "preferential and normative structure" and commit the "fallacy of translating the former into the latter."[56] "Marriage," he maintains, "may very well be the ideal pattern, or the preferential pattern: but to say that the non-legal union is deviant because marriage is preferred is clearly fallacious."[57] He concludes that the "lower class ... stretch their values to accept both legal marriage and the non-legal marital union."[58]

In saying that "Both marriage and the non-legal union are normative,"[59] Rodman no less than Goode and Blake conceptualizes a simple duality—the legal and the nonlegal—thus narrowing a plurality to a two-point scale. The native semantic hierarchy, I submit, bypasses questionnaires designed around these categories. No matter how they are worded, such questionnaires will generate answers irrelevant to the cognitive reality. The actors' "mazeways" can be mapped only by an at least implicit use of a technique called "componential analysis."[60] The method is a way of getting at native semantics, called "emic" categories. It must be based on numerous and repeated observations *in situ*, when the patterns are not formalized by respondents. Rodman's technique is equivalent to asking an Eskimo to classify the environment as snow and nonsnow, whereas in the native world view there are some dozen categories discriminated by *components* which omit entirely the discrete discontinuities of Indo-European snow and nonsnow.

The Grammar of Values   Let me briefly recapitulate the grammar of values in this semantic domain from Capesterre. The actors conceptualize marriage in many ways: (a) as solely an expression of group solidarity with regard to hospitality obligations symbolized by a *fête*; (b) as a magical exorcism to remit sins, as in a deathbed ritual, and sometimes in a mass mission marriage; (c) as a symptom of mass hysteria, which a mission marriage may also represent; (d) as a stage in secular acculturation to the elite without religious considerations; (e) as a sacrament in a conventional Catholic attitude; (f) as social acceptance by the church as a recreational group; (g) as a means to a practical end, for example, a schoolteacher's job.

This grammar, of course, belongs to a particular dialect. Its "statements" are meaningful in a given context. For example, the rule that an *entrepreneuse* will not cohabit with a man is certainly of limited distribution. But the existence of some such principles which work in the absence of a regnant rule of legitimacy belongs to a family of languages, a family characterized by substitute principles.

Let us consider the following modification of componential analysis. An inappropriate marriage in Capesterre is a Western legalism of some sort, but in native thought it may share the component of shame together with promiscuity. Since promiscuity can occur within or outside of marriage, this pattern may or may not conform to Western legal norms. Both a wrong marriage and promiscuity are opposed, in turn, not to an entity, but to a series that does not distinguish the legality of the arrangement: permanent nonresidential union; developmental nonresidential union with serious intentions (not marriage); and stable cohabitation with or without marriage.

As to approved marriage, ethnomorality does not lump the various types, but separates them on the basis, for example, of whether a *fête* occurred or was excused on the grounds that the couple had had enough baptisms. When Rodman shows that individuals "prefer" it, do they have in mind late marriage, deathbed marriage, marriage before pregnancy, or some other variation? Certain forms of legal marriage or legitimacy are as foreign as the consensual union is to Malinowski's concept of legitimacy. They should not, therefore, be classified as congruent with an elite norm. Only what the French call *jeune fille* marriage (occurring before cohabitation or obvious pregnancy) coincides with the Western elite ideal. When parents invite their own children to celebrate the wedding *fête*, this form does not approximate the elite norm— which includes timing—any more closely than does the *ménage*. Moreover, alternate marriage choices, which either do or do not legitimate children, reveal no preference for any one of the forms.

Conversely, a high commitment to nonelite responsibilities and community roles is hardly indicated by a label of low commitment to a generalized "legitimacy." Furthermore, a two-point preferential scale omits such desiderata as these: At what age is it preferable to turn a *ménage* into a marriage, and with or without a *fête*? Holding age constant, is it better for a black or a mulatto to marry a man less or more educated than she? And in any of these cases, with what do the actions contrast a preferred marriage—promiscuity, being a white man's *concubine*? And if marriage is preferred to a specified alternative, is it better than being alone or with a mother, and the like? For a female cane cutter or a servant? And if the respondent has how many children?

Clearly, there is little isomorphism among the interviewer's elite notion of elite marriage, his notion of native marriage, the polymorphous ethnoconceptualizations of native marriage, and the numerous native conceptualizations of elite marriage.

MISPLACED CONCRETENESS

The subcultural nature of these patterns is evidenced by the very fact that they are beneath the threshold of awareness built into a priori procedures. The closest approximation to the existence of another grammar is Rodman's notion that members of the "lower strata" accept "alternative values . . . without abandoning the general values of the society . . ."[61] This feat is allegedly accomplished by means of an elasticized entity Rodman calls a "value stretch."[62]

Despite the logical sense of the notion, one wonders about the locus of these "general values" which may either be abandoned or cherished. Are there any behaviors that give them form besides answering a questionnaire designed without native categories in mind? Goode's monolithic elite norm is still hovering somewhere in Rodman's interpretation, and although it lives more comfortably with the status quo, it still seems to be disembodied.

In family organization, to live one life and prefer another conjures up the picture of a person who speaks Italian and Latin at the same time, someone who somehow married and did not marry. Goode's model seems to have been culled from the sociology of individual delinquency, whereas Rodman's schizoid actor, split into an existential and a preferential self, might be an appropriate image for the sociology of career choice. However, a mother raising children is not comparable to someone who would have preferred being a lawyer but settled for selling apples. If there is no real choice, what does preference mean? And if preference is indeed meaningful, why is there no choice?

Both "low norm commitment" and "value stretch" conceptualize people (especially women) who hankered after marriage but found it somehow beyond their grasp, regardless of whether we call the situation deviance or variance. Whether the concrete choices are localized in some demoralized corner of their mazeways, as Goode deduces, or in some rubberized limbo, as Rodman imagines, the actors in both views are portrayed as compromisers *vis-à-vis* an elite institution.

If this image is accurate, what are the manifest causes? According to Goode, the obstacle to marriage is lack of female bargaining power; according to Rodman, poverty. To use games as a metaphor, as Goode does implicitly, both theorists imply that the lower strata are playing (let us say) bridge without paying much attention to the rules, either because the stakes are too low (Goode) or because the game requires capital (Rodman). But bridge is what they are allegedly playing—for this is the sole elite or monolithic game. And since this is assumed, they of course seem to be playing badly.

"All courtship systems," says Goode, "are market systems, in which role bargains are struck"[63] on the basis of commodities like beauty, family, wealth, on whose value the group agrees. But, he continues, because of the clandestine courtship patterns, the girl must strike a bargain in "anonymity and isolation."[64] Unless she risks a nonlegal union, she has no chance of marriage. The American middle-class girl, he concludes, does not have to pay so high a price, for "she would be giving more than need be under the operating market system."[65]

Rodman thinks the people are playing bridge badly because "the lower-class male . . . finds it difficult to fulfill his economic obligations."[66] The expectation that the man must be the "breadwinner,"[67] and the assumption that these roles change upon legal marriage are stated as facts. They are not listed among Rodman's eight assumptions pertaining to mobility, poverty, promulgation of elite standards, and so on. If these indeed be facts in Trinidad and in some other places, I claim that they are not distributed widely enough to explain the Caribbean family in all the communities in which it appears. Like the other functional interrelationships described (for example by Raymond T. Smith, Solien, and others), this "explanation" is too geographically limited and ultimately deceptive.

To take a few examples, poverty is not a justification for an elite person to bear illegitimate children, for priests will marry couples without charge. In Capesterre, people of all categories from priest to cane cutter state that marriage is eschewed because no one can afford it, but this is folk sociology. The most cursory documentation shows that *within the nonelite community* there is no direct correspondence between marriage and income. Recall the old lady who stated that if you want a *fête* and "you don't have cake and champagne, you have drums and rum." If the hospitality obligations require a large outlay, this is hardly the same kind of economic pressure that Rodman is talking about, for it does not prevent marriage, only a *fête*, and not a drums-and-rum *fête*. In Carriacou, to take another instance, income has nothing to do with which women marry and which are *concubines*.[68] In other communities paternal responsibility is not altered with marriage. This is an element that does not universally covary with the Caribbean system.

In short, no open-ended interviews or anthropological reports support the purely deductive strategies of Rodman and Goode. Their view is cohesive only if one assumes that people are indeed playing bridge in the first place. Instead, anthropologists claim that the people are playing poker, so to speak, although certainly not always the Capesterre type. But so long as high rates of illegitimacy accompany what I call morphological triality (Lévi-Strauss's conjugal, subconjugal, and supraconjugal family), the game is not bridge; that is to say, the bid is not a *jeune fille* ideal.

Operationally, only participant observation permits insight into whether people are playing poker or bad bridge. Verification of one view or the other will lie, I suggest, in examining degrees of internalization, motives for making choices, and other subtler aspects of role behavior.

A DEMONSTRATION

I suggest the following hypothesis for documenting whether the Caribbean nonelite game is bridge or poker. If there is low commitment to norms that genuinely exist within the nonelite subculture, then

1. the actors will rank low in general conformism to expectations of their peers;
2. and/or the personality will rank low in sensitivity to opinions of the relevant reference group;
3. and/or the self-image will be low.

On the other hand, if the actor has not internalized the ideal to which he has low comitment, the reverse of the above will be detectable. We shall not prejudge whether the norms—commitment to which we are exploring—include elite legitimacy.

Of the three cases I shall recall from the community study, two informants are representative and show a highly conformist orientation, sensitivity to the neighbors, and an almost smug self-image. My judgment is that these unmarried mothers are not displaying a low commitment to elite legitimacy. They are poker players. They are not demoralized. Nor do they suffer penalties. Counternorms to elite standards are visible. The married man M. Malin (chapter seven), on the other hand, who is an object of considerable disapproval, is a deviant in Capesterre. Through a strong sense of religion, highly abnormal for men, he entered a *jeune fille* marriage. Whether he thus internalized an elite norm in addition to feeling alienated from rural standards of group interaction, I could not determine. This was the way this deviant entered my notes.

In one *quartier*, as I have recounted in chapter seven, I came across a married couple of social equals whose wedding was scorned, a seeming exception to the grammatical rules I was hypothesizing. M. Clément not only omitted a *fête*, but married on Christmas, an unforgivable form of *gaucherie*. He did it to save the expense of serving his family anything but the cheap traditional dish of pork, it was said.

"People who make a *totoblo* [a *faux pas*] like this," a neighboring *concubin* pointed out, "have to go to another village to marry. They wouldn't do it here! If one of *us* did that, no one would ever pass us the wine again . . . He's too unsociable to bother about. It's like wearing a borrowed suit to your own wedding." The implication clearly is that if one does not throw a proper party, it is indecent to marry (see page 183).

As in the case of M. Clément, each time I thought I found exceptions to the hypotheses which I built up as I went along, I would consult neighbors whom I got to know. "People make such *totosblos*," said a cane cutter's *concubine*, "because their relatives don't bring them up properly. When people beat their children, you should beat your children. When everyone is sleeping, you should sleep. The others grow up to be *mals élevées* like M. Clément . . . and people make up songs at *Carnaval* about you." This is hardly a woman who would miss committing herself to any norm available. Her words are a primer on conformity, yet she is a woman with six children born out of wedlock.

As a final example, I shall return to the case of Mlle. Narcisse (chapter seven), who is a light-skinned, forty-year-old mother of four children, all recognized by her *concubin*, a plantation executive who lives in a good cement house nearby. At this point in my study, may I repeat, I thought that marriage was primarily a *fête* for convivial equals, and these two had the qualifications. Moreover, they were popular and well-off. I wondered why they had not married, or whether they would have a wedding some day after the children had grown. I was on the verge of uncovering still another principle.

"I keep house for my *mari* [husband], but we couldn't live together [let alone marry]." I asked why. "Naturally, I am not married because I live *here*," she said, indicating her small wooden house with pride. I looked blank.

"But this is the *maison paternelle*," she finally explained, as if any idiot would know that. This was an inherited house, I later learned, and "The whites never abandon *la maison paternelle*." There were some very important norms, indeed.

"But why can't your *concubin* move into it with you?"

"Because he is a big man with a good job," she answered. It turned out that no man with self-respect would move into such a house because it gave the woman too much authority. The problem rarely arises, for in most cases a son inherits a house, for the women have usually moved off to go into *ménage*.

"But there are no problems," she said. "Isn't it simple to live so close together?"

Mlle. Narcisse clearly showed that the norm of legitimacy is not

within her cognitive mazeway. Paternal houses and male independence are certainly potent "counternorms" of the kind Goode seeks.
Counternorms are, of course, expressed idiomatically. The fact that
this informant left so many things unexplained until prodded is
indicative of her exclusive concern with her reference group, not my
elite notions. Mlle. Narcisse had been badgered by my queries a
long time before (I presume) she suddenly identified my logic with
that of the church and decided to pay token respect to my presumed
piety. "We must marry some day because I want to take Communion. But marriage is slavery," she hastily added, not on the defen-
sive, but as if she had made enough of a concession to foreign
values. This phrase is a formalized counternorm of a more direct
type.

Then she continued on her own initiative: "It isn't because I
want my liberty [to be unfaithful] that I don't marry. *Mon Dieu*, no!
Only tarts want that!" Mlle. Narcisse strode up and down, tossing
her head in the air, saying, "*Bonjour*" very curtly. She was playacting
to show me the way she snubs promiscuous women when they pass
her on the road, women with low commitment to the important
norm of fidelity. She pursed her lips in a mask of distaste. "These
mals élevées make me furious, and *I* will have nothing to do with
them." She outranked many others because of her white grandfather, her house, her lover's occupation, her phenotype. These are
the "emic" status-defining criteria that outsiders miss if they use
ethnocentric measurements.

This woman, like most, was certainly not making folkways of
mores. Her norm commitments are intense, and the range of norms
to which she is committed span the gamut of the subculture.
Furthermore, they do not include marriage as a mark of respectability. To characterize her as having low commitment to a norm of elite
legitimacy would be like saying that English workers have low
commitment to a norm of paying a visit at court. The norm is not
theirs, and for those who know about it, acting it out is pretentious.

The articulation of marriage with the family begins to fall into
place when one stops asking why most people most of the time are
unmarried, and starts asking why some ever do marry. The latter is
the more meaningful question because the society, I claim, is
actually structured without a rule of legitimacy.

CONCLUSION

It is gratifying to discover, since I first proposed my interpretation of the Caribbean family, that Michael G. Smith independently arrived at a similar definition of a core within the protean forms.[69] The problem, he says, is to "examine alternative domestic, mating and parental forms," rather than household composition alone.[70] The domestic forms reveal what he calls the "structural morphology." The mating and parental forms determine the "internal order and regularity" that constitute the "principles of family structure." This view is like my claim that the system contains a multiplicity of family arrangements whose very polymorphism (Michael G. Smith's "alternative forms") is crucial. Following is a parsimonious statement of this idea: Morphological triality (the simultaneous expectation of the conjugal, subconjugal, and supraconjugal) is the organizational expression of an absence of the rule of legitimacy.

This negative formulation—the *absence* of a single rule—is required largely in the interests of generalization. A positive formulation involves abstracting attitudes revealed in making choices relating to the production and rearing of children. What I have been calling a grammar of values emerges when this decision making covaries with predictable factors in organization. The two together constitute a model of the structure of the family system.

In the Caribbean grammar, certain kinds of marriage, such as a ceremony after the children mature, are only superficially analogous to the elite Western ideal. Conversely, young women who enter various types of consensual union, with or without cohabitation, have little in common with delinquent "unwed mothers." Simply because certain multifarious patterns variously recombine and converge on the interviewer's ethnocentric concept of marriage and nonmarriage is little reason to conclude that the Caribbean patterns surrounding legitimacy have any exclusive function. They are often aspects of the *fête* complex, and late marriage does not always legitimate offspring.

Although I have argued that Goode often falsely identifies indexes of shame regarding illegitimacy, shame also occurs. In some Caribbean communities, moreover, one finds Rodman's preferential attitude or Goode's low commitment to an ideal of marriage. But when such patterns are accurately identified without doing violence to a native or "emic" view of the semantic domain, the phenomenon still does not indicate deviation from a previously internalized norm. Rather, it reveals an acculturative situation potentially transitional to establishing an ideal of legitimacy. At what points the elite pattern becomes a goal to the actors or a measuring stick to the observers are contingent variables, for there are ever-changing ecologies of the contact situation.

Each community as well as the individuals within it may be placed along a continuum of differential accommodation to an elite complex. But they all began at the extreme where the individuals are not aware that in bearing illegitimate children they are violating an organizational principle in another group. I encountered the same situation in Africa when people stepped out of unilineal structures.[71] Some think they are honoring this exotic norm by means that the elite do not recognize—for example, late marriage. Close to this end of the continuum is the grammar I have presented for a community of Martinique, where people have not traveled far from the plantation base once shared by most Afro-Americans.

NOTES

[1] Nancie L. Solien, *"The Consanguineal Household Among the Black Carib of Central America"* (Ph.D. dissertation, University of Michigan, 1959).

[2] Peter Kunstadter, "A Survey of the Consanguine or Matrifocal Family," *American Anthropologist*, 65, No. 1 (1963).

[3] Daniel P. Moynihan, "Employment, Income, and the Ordeal of the Negro Family," *Daedalus*, 94, No. 4 (1965).

[4] Hyman Rodman, "Illegitimacy in the Caribbean Social Structure: A Reconsideration," *American Sociological Review*, 31, No. 5 (1966).

[5] Chandra Jayawardena, "Marital Stability in Two Guianese Sugar Estate Communities," *Social and Economic Studies*, 9, No. 5 (March 1960), 76–100; and "Family Organization in Plantations in British Guiana," *International Journal of Comparative Sociology*, 3, No. 1 (September 1962), 43–64.

[6] See my criticism of this point in Mariam K. Slater, "Review of R. T. Smith, *The Negro Family in British Guiana*," *American Anthropologist*, 59, No. 5 (1957), 972–973.

[7] Michael G. Smith, *West Indian Family Structure* (A Monograph from the Research Institute for the Study of Man [Seattle: University of Washington Press, 1962]).

[8] Nancie Solien González, "Toward a Definition of Matrifocality," in N. E. Whitten and J. F. Szwed, eds., *Afro-American Anthropology* (New York: Free Press, 1970), p. 236.

[9] Ibid., p. 237.

[10]Ibid., p. 238.

[11]Clellan Ford and Frank Beach, *Patterns of Sexual Behavior* (New York: Harper & Bros., 1951), p. 183.

[12]C. W. M. Hart and A. R. Pilling, *The Tiwi of North Australia* (New York: Holt, Rinehart & Winston, 1960).

[13]Jane Collier Kronick, "An Assessment of Research Knowledge Concerning the Unmarried Mother," in Robert W. Roberts, ed., *The Unwed Mother* (New York: Harper & Row, 1966).

[14]Bernstein's essay is in Roberts, *The Unwed Mother*.

[15]Wyatt C. Jones, Henry J. Meyer, and Edgar F. Borgatta, "Social and Psychological Factors in Status Decisions of Unmarried Mothers," in Roberts, *The Unwed Mother*.

[16]Leontine R. Young, "Personality Patterns in Unmarried Mothers," in Roberts, *The Unwed Mother*.

[17]Clark E. Vincent, "The Unwed Mother and Sampling Bias," in Roberts, *The Unwed Mother*.

[18]Alfred C. Kinsey, "Illegal Abortion in the United States," in Roberts, *The Unwed Mother*.

[19]Harold T. Christensen, "Cultural Relativism in Premarital Sex Norms," in Roberts, *The Unwed Mother*.

[20]Jones et al., "Social and Psychological Factors," p. 207.

[21]Ibid., p. 210.

[22]Bernstein, "Are We Still Stereotyping?" p. 114.

[23]González, "Toward a Definition of Matrifocality," p. 242.

[24]Ibid.

[25]Hildred Geertz, *The Javanese Family: A Study of Kinship and Socialization* (New York: Free Press, 1961), cited by Gonzáles.

[26]William J. Goode, "Illegitimacy in the Caribbean Social Structure," *American Sociological Review*, 25, No. 1 (February 1960), 30.

[27]Ibid., p. 22.

[28]Kingsley Davis, *Human Society* (New York: Macmillan, 1958).

[29]V. F. Calverton and S. D. Schmalhausen, *The New Generation* (New York: Macauley, 1930).

[30]Davis, *Human Society*, pp. 400–401.

[31]Goode, "Illegitimacy in the Caribbean," cites Herskovits (1947), p. 17; Henriques (1953), pp. 87, 90; Murra (1957b), p. 76; Mintz (1956), p. 377; Manners (1956), p. 144; Braithwaite (1953), p. 125; Simey (1946), pp. 15, 88. See references at end of text for full citations.

[32]Ibid., p. 24.

[33]Ibid., p. 27.

[34]Ibid., p. 23.

[35]Bronislaw Malinowski, *Sex and Repression in Savage Society* (New York: Meridian, 1927; 1955 reprint), p. 187.

[36]Alfred L. Kroeber and Clyde Kluckhohn, *Culture: A Critical Review of Concepts and Definitions* (Cambridge, Mass.: Harvard University Papers of the Peabody Museum, Vol. 47, No. 1, 1952).

[37]Robert K. Merton, "Civilization and Culture," *Sociology and Social Research*, 21 (1936), 103–113.

[38]Goode, "Illegitimacy in the Caribbean," p. 25.

[39]Constance Sutton, *Protest and Change in Barbados: The Study of a Sugar*

Community, (Rio Piedras: University of Puerto Rico, Institute of Caribbean Studies [forthcoming]).

[40] Mary Douglas, *Purity and Danger* (New York: Praeger, 1966).

[41] Goode, "Illegitimacy in the Caribbean," p. 24.

[42] Ibid., citing Edith Clarke, *My Mother Who Fathered Me* (London: Allen & Unwin, 1957), pp. 77–78.

[43] G. E. Cumper, "Labour Demand and Supply in the Jamaican Sugar Industry 1830–1950," *Social and Economic Studies*, 2, No. 4 (1954).

[44] Goode, "Illegitimacy in the Caribbean," p. 27.

[45] Ibid., p. 27.

[46] William J. Goode, "Illegitimacy, Anomie, and Cultural Penetration," *American Sociological Review*, 26, No. 6 (December 1961).

[47] Ibid., p. 25.

[48] Lloyd Braithwaite, "Social Stratification in Trinidad," *Social and Economic Studies*, 2, Nos. 2 and 3 (October 1953), 125–126.

[49] Cited in Goode, "Illegitimacy, Anomie, and Cultural Penetration."

[50] E. Franklin Frazier, *The Negro Family in the United States* (New York: Dryden Press, 1948), p. 94.

[51] William J. Goode, "Note on Problems in Theory and Method: The New World" (Commentary on Otterbein 1965), *American Anthropologist*, 68, No. 2 (1966).

[52] Paul K. Hatt, *Backgrounds of Human Fertility in Puerto Rico* (Princeton, N.J.: Princeton University Press, 1952).

[53] Judith Blake, "Family Instability and Reproductive Behavior in Jamaica," in *Current Research in Human Fertility* (New York: Milbank Memorial Fund, 1955); and *Family Structure in Jamaica* (New York: Free Press, 1961).

[54] See Raymond T. Smith, "Culture and Social Structure in the Caribbean: Some Recent Work on Family and Kinship," *Comparative Studies in Society and History*, 6 (1963); and "Review of Judith Blake: *Family Structure in Jamaica*," *American Anthropologist*, 65, No. 1 (1963).

[55] Rodman, "Illegitimacy in the Caribbean," p. 676.

[56] Ibid., p. 675.

[57] Ibid.

[58] Ibid., p. 679.

[59] Ibid., p. 674.

[60] See B. N. Colby, "Ethnographic Semantics: A Preliminary Survey," *Current Anthropology*, 7, No. 1 (1966).

[61] Rodman, "Illegitimacy in the Caribbean," p. 678.

[62] Ibid.

[63] Goode, "Problems in Theory and Method," p. 28.

[64] Ibid., p. 29.

[65] Ibid.

[66] Rodman, "Illegitimacy in the Caribbean," p. 679.

[67] Ibid., p. 687.

[68] Michael G. Smith, *West Indian Family Structure.*

[69] Ibid.

[70] Ibid., pp. 20, 23.

[71] Mariam K. Slater, *African Odyssey: An Anthropological Adventure* (New York: Doubleday Anchor, 1976).

References

American Geographical Society. *The European Possessions in the Caribbean.* New York: American Geographical Society, 1941.

Annuaire de la Vie Martiniquaise. 2 vols. Fort-de-France, Martinique: Imprimerie Officielle, 1947.

Arensberg, Conrad M. "The Community Study Method." *American Journal of Sociology,* 60, No. 2 (September 1954).

———. "Anthropology as History." In Karl Polanyi, Conrad M. Arensberg, and Harry W. Pearson (eds.), *Trade and Market in the Early Empires.* Glencoe, Ill.: Free Press, 1957.

Becker, Howard, and Reuben Hill. *Marriage and Parenthood.* Boston: D. C. Heath, 1955.

Bernstein, Rose. "Are We Still Stereotyping the Unwed Mother?" In Robert W. Roberts (ed.), *The Unwed Mother.* New York: Harper & Row, 1966.

Bidney, David. *Theoretical Anthropology.* New York: Columbia University Press, 1953.

Billingsley, Andrew. *Black Families in White America.* Englewood Cliffs, N.J.: Prentice-Hall, 1968.

Blake, Judith. "Family Instability and Reproductive Behavior in Jamaica." In *Current Research in Human Fertility.* New York: Milbank Memorial Fund, 1955.

———. *Family Structure in Jamaica.* New York: Free Press, 1961.

Braithwaite, Lloyd. "Social Stratification in Trinidad." *Social and Economic Studies* (Jamaica: University College of the West Indies), 2, Nos. 2 and 3 (October 1953).

Calverton, V. F., and S. D. Schmalhausen. *The New Generation.* New York: Macauley, 1930.

Christensen, Harold T. "Cultural Relativism and Premarital Sex Norms." In

Robert W. Roberts (ed.), *The Unwed Mother*. New York: Harper & Row, 1966.

Clarke, Edith. *My Mother Who Fathered Me*. London: Allen & Unwin, 1957.

Cohen, Yehudi. "The Social Organization of a Selected Community in Jamaica." *Social and Economic Studies* (Jamaica: University College of the West Indies), 2, No. 4 (1954).

Colby, B. N. "Ethnographic Semantics: A Preliminary Survey." *Current Anthropology*, 7, No. 1 (1966).

Cumper, G. E. "Labour Demand and Supply in the Jamaican Sugar Industry 1830–1950." *Social and Economic Studies* (Jamaica: University College of the West Indies), 2, No. 4 (1954).

Davis, Kingsley. *Human Society*. New York: Macmillan, 1958.

Delawarde, R. P. *La Vie Paysanne à la Martinique*. Fort-de-France, Martinique, 1937.

Dollard, John. *Caste and Clan in a Southern Town*. New York: Harper & Row, 1937.

Douglas, Mary. *Purity and Danger*. New York: Praeger, 1966.

Du Tertre, Père (pseudonym). *Histoire Générale des Antilles Habitées par les Françaises*. 4 vols. Paris: 1667–1671.

Edjam, Gaby. *La Martinique: La Population et Ses Diverses Activités Économiques*. Fort-de-France, Martinique: École Normale, n.d. (1950s).

Firth, Raymond. *Elements of Social Organization*. New York: Philosophical Library, 1951.

Ford, Clellan, and Frank Beach. *Patterns of Sexual Behavior*. New York: Harper & Bros., 1951.

Frazier, E. Franklin. *The Negro Family in the United States*. New York: Dryden Press, 1948.

Gallagher, Buell G. "American Caste and the Negro." In A. A. Locke and B. J. Stern (eds.), *When Peoples Meet*. New York: Hinds, Hayden & Eldridge, 1946.

Gillin, John Philip. *Moche, a Peruvian Coastal Community*. Washington, D.C.: Government Printing Office, 1947.

González, Nancie Solien. "Toward a Definition of Matrifocality." In N. E. Whitten and J. F. Szwed (eds.), *Afro-American Anthropology*. New York: Free Press, 1970.

Goode, William J. "Illegitimacy in the Caribbean Social Structure." *American Sociological Review*, 25, No. 1 (February 1960).

———. "Illegitimacy, Anomie, and Cultural Penetration." *American Sociological Review*, 26, No. 6 (December 1961).

———. "Note on Problems in Theory and Method: The New World" (Commentary on Otterbein, 1965). *American Anthropologist*, 68, No. 2 (1966).

Goodman, Morris F. *A Comparative Study of Creole French Dialects*. The Hague: Mouton, 1964.

Goossen, Jean Griffin. "Kin to Each Other: Integration in Guadeloupe." Unpublished Ph.D. dissertation, Columbia University, 1970.

Goyheneche, Eugène. "Causerie Radio Diffusée." Unpublished broadcast, Fort-de-France, Martinique, July 11, 1955.

Hannerz, Ulf. *Soulside: Inquiries into Ghetto Culture and Community*. New York: Columbia University Press, 1969.

Harris, Marvin. *The Rise of Anthropological Theory*. New York: Crowell, 1968.

———. *Culture, Man and Nature: An Introduction to General Anthropology*. New York: Crowell, 1971.

———. "Review of *Culture and Poverty: Critique and Counter-Proposals*." *American Anthropologist*, 73, No. 2 (1971), 330.

Hart, C. W. M., and A. R. Pilling. *The Tiwi of North Australia*. New York: Holt, Rinehart & Winston, 1960.

Hatt, Paul K. *Backgrounds of Human Fertility in Puerto Rico*. Princeton, N.J.: Princeton University Press, 1952.

Hearn, Lafcadio. *Two Years in the French West Indies*. New York: Harper & Bros., 1890.

Henriques, Fernando. *Family and Colour in Jamaica*. London: Eyre & Spottiswoode, 1953.

Herskovits, Frances S. (ed.). *The New World Negro*. Bloomington, Ind.: Indiana University Press, 1966.

Herskovits, M. J. "The Negro in the New World." *American Anthropologist*, 32, No. 1 (1930).

———. *The Myth of the Negro Past*. New York: Harper & Bros., 1941.

———, and F. S. Herskovits. *Trinidad Village*. New York: Knopf, 1947.

Homans, George C. *The Human Group*. New York: Harcourt, Brace & World, 1950.

———, and David M. Schneider. *Marriage, Authority, and Final Causes*. Glencoe, Ill.: Free Press, 1955.

Horowitz, Michael M. "Morne-Paysan: Peasant Community in Martinique: An Approach to a Typology of Rural Community Forms in the Caribbean." Unpublished Ph.D. dissertation, Columbia University, 1959. Ann Arbor microfilm.

———. *Morne-Paysan: Peasant Village in Martinique*. New York: Holt, Rinehart & Winston, 1967.

Jayawardena, Chandra. "Marital Stability in Two Guianese Sugar Estate Communities." *Social and Economic Studies* (Jamaica: University College of the West Indies), 9, No. 5 (March 1960), 76–100.

———. "Family Organization in Plantations in British Guiana." *International Journal of Comparative Sociology*, 3 (September 1962), 43–64.

Jones, Wyatt C., Henry J. Meyer, and Edgar F. Borgatta. "Social and Psychological Factors in Status Decisions of Unmarried Mothers." In Robert W. Roberts (ed.), *The Unwed Mother*. New York: Harper & Row, 1966.

Keur, John Y., and Dorothy L. Keur. *Windward Children: A Study in Human Ecology of the Three Dutch Windward Islands in the Caribbean*. Assen, Netherlands: Van Gorcum, 1960.

Kinsey, Alfred C. "Illegal Abortion in the United States." In Robert W. Roberts (ed.), *The Unwed Mother*. New York: Harper & Row, 1966.

Kluckhohn, Clyde. *Mirror for Man*. New York: McGraw-Hill, 1949.

Kreiselman, Mariam J. "The Caribbean Family: A Case Study in Martinique." Ph.D. dissertation, Columbia University, 1958.

Kroeber, Alfred L., and Clyde Kluckhohn. *Culture: A Critical Review of Concepts and Definitions*. Harvard University Papers of the Peabody Museum. Cambridge, Mass.: Peabody Museum, 1952, Vol. 47, No. 1.

Kronick, Jane Collier. "An Assessment of Research Knowledge Concerning the Unmarried Mother." In Robert W. Roberts (ed.), *The Unwed Mother*. New York: Harper & Row, 1966.

Kunstadter, Peter. "A Survey of the Consanguine or Matrifocal Family." *American Anthropologist*, 65, No. 1 (1962).

Labat, Père Jean Baptiste. *Nouveau Voyage aux Îles de l'Amérique*. 1722. Paris: Duchartre, 1931.

Labrousse, Paul. *Deux Vieilles Terres Françaises*. Colombes: 1935.

Leacock, Eleanor Burke (ed.). *The Culture of Poverty: A Critique*. New York: Simon and Schuster, 1971.

Leiris, Michel. *Contacts des Civilisations en Martinique et en Guadeloupe*. Paris: UNESCO, 1955.

Leridon, Henri. "Fertility in Martinique." *Natural History*, 79, No. 1 (January 1970).

Lévi-Strauss, Claude. "The Family." In Harry L. Shapiro (ed.), *Man, Culture and Society*. Oxford: Oxford University Press, 1956.

Lewis, Oscar. *Children of Sanchez: Autobiography of a Mexican Family*. New York: Random House, 1961.

Leyburn, James G. *The Haitian People*. New Haven: Yale University Press, 1941.

Malinowski, Bronislaw. *Sex and Repression in Savage Society*. New York:

Meridian, 1927; 1955 reprint.

Manners, Robert A. "Tabara." In Julian H. Steward (ed.), *The People of Puerto Rico.* Urbana: University of Illinois Press, 1956.

————, and Julian H. Steward. "The Cultural Study of Contemporary Societies: Puerto Rico." *American Journal of Sociology,* 59, No. 2 (September 1953).

Matthews, Dom Basil. *The Crisis in the West Indian Family.* Jamaica: University College of the West Indies, 1953.

Meehan, Thomas. "Moynihan of the Moynihan Report." *New York Times Magazine,* July 31, 1966.

Merton, Robert K. "Civilization and Culture." *Sociology and Social Research,* 21 (1936).

Métraux, Rhoda. "Some Aspects of Hierarchical Structure in Haiti." In Sol Tax (ed.), *Acculturation in the Americas.* Chicago: University of Chicago Press, 1952.

Mintz, Sidney W. "The Folk-Elite Continuum and the Rural Proletarian Community." *American Journal of Sociology,* 59, No. 2 (September 1953).

————. "Cañamelar." In Julian H. Steward (ed.), *The People of Puerto Rico.* Urbana: University of Illinois Press, 1956.

Moynihan, Daniel P. "Employment, Income, and the Ordeal of the Negro Family." *Daedalus,* 94, No. 4 (1965).

————. *The Negro Family: The Case for National Action.* Washington, D.C.: Government Printing Office, 1965.

Murch, Arvin. *Black Frenchmen: The Political Integration of the French Antilles.* Cambridge, Mass.: Schenkman, 1971.

Murdock, George P. *Social Structure.* New York: Macmillan, 1949.

Murra, John V. "Discussion." In Vera Rubin (ed.), *Caribbean Studies: A Symposium.* Seattle: University of Washington Press, 1957; 2nd ed. 1960.

————. "Studies in Family Organization in the French Caribbean." *Transactions of the New York Academy of Sciences,* 19 (1957).

Newton, Esther. "Men, Women and Status in the Negro Family." Unpublished Master's thesis, University of Chicago, 1964.

Padilla, Elena. "Nocorá." In Julian H. Steward (ed.), *The People of Puerto Rico.* Urbana: University of Illinois Press, 1956.

Peytard, Lucien. *L'Esclavage aux Antilles Françaises Avant 1789.* Paris: Librairie Hachettes, 1897.

Powdermaker, Hortense. *After Freedom.* New York: Viking, 1939.

Redfield, Robert. *The Little Community.* Chicago: University of Chicago Press, 1955.

Registres de l'État Civil à Basse-Pointe, Martinique.

Revert, Eugène. *La Martinique: Étude Géographique*. Paris: Nouvelles Éditions Latines, 1949.

Roberts, Robert W. (ed.). *The Unwed Mother*. New York: Harper & Row, 1966.

Rodman, Hyman. "Illegitimacy in the Caribbean Social Structure: A Reconsideration." *American Sociological Review*, 31, No. 5, 1966.

Rohrer, John H., Munro S. Edmonson, Harold Lief, Daniel Thompson, and William Thompson. *The Eighth Generation: Cultures and Personalities of New Orleans Negroes*. New York: Harper & Row, 1960.

Schoelcher, Victor. *Esclavage et Colonisation*. Paris: Presses Universitaires de France, 1948.

Sengher, Leopold S. *Anthologie de la Nouvelle Poésie Nègre et Malagache de la Langue Française, Précédée de "Orphée Noir," par Jean-Paul Sartre*. Paris: Presses Universitaires de France, 1948.

Simey, T. S. *Welfare and Planning in the West Indies*. Oxford: Clarendon Press, 1946.

Simpson, George F. "Haiti's Social Structure." *American Sociological Review*, 6, No. 5 (1941).

———. "Sexual and Familial Institutions in Northern Haiti." *American Anthropologist*, 44, No. 4 (1942).

———. "Discussion." In Sol Tax (ed.), *Acculturation in the Americas*. Chicago: University of Chicago Press, 1952.

Slater, Mariam K. "Review of R. T. Smith, *The Negro Family in British Guiana*." *American Anthropologist*, 59, No. 5 (1957), 912–913.

———. "The Caribbean Family: A Case Study in Martinique." Ph.D. dissertation, Columbia University, 1958.

———. *African Odyssey: An Anthropological Adventure*. New York: Doubleday Anchor, 1976.

———. "The Rule of Legitimacy and the Caribbean Family: A Case Study in Martinique." *Ethnic Groups*, 1 (1976).

Smith, Michael G. *West Indian Family Structure*. A Monograph from the Research Institute for the Study of Man. Seattle: University of Washington Press, 1962.

———. *A Framework for Caribbean Studies*. Jamaica: University College of the West Indies, n. d. This pamphlet is reprinted in a collection of Smith's work entitled *The Plural Society in the British West Indies*. Berkeley: University of California Press, 1965.

Smith, Raymond T. *The Negro Family in British Guiana*. London: Routledge & Kegan Paul, 1956.

———. "Culture and Social Structure in the Caribbean: Some Recent Work on Family and Kinship Studies." *Comparative Studies in Society and History*, 6 (1963).

———. "Review of Judith Blake: *Family Structure in Jamaica*." *American Anthropologist*, 65, No. 1 (1963).

Solien, Nancie L. "The Consanguineal Household Among the Black Carib of Central America." Unpublished Ph.D. dissertation, University of Michigan, 1959.

Steward, Julian H. (ed.). *The People of Puerto Rico*. Urbana: University of Illinois Press, 1956.

Sudia, Cecilia E. "An Updating and Comment on the United States Scene." *Family Coordinator*, 22, No. 3 (July 1973), 309–311.

Sutton, Constance. "Social and Cultural Factors Affecting Family Size Motivation in Barbados." Unpublished paper, 1960.

———. *Protest and Change in Barbados: The Study of a Sugar Community*. Rio Piedras: University of Puerto Rico, Institute of Caribbean Studies (forthcoming).

United Nations Yearbook, 1957.

Valentine, Charles A. *Culture and Poverty: Critique and Counter-Proposals*. Chicago: University of Chicago Press, 1968.

Vincent, Clark E. "The Unwed Mother and Sampling Bias." In Robert W. Roberts (ed.), *The Unwed Mother*. New York: Harper & Row, 1966.

Westoff, Leslie Aldridge. "Kids with Kids." *The New York Times Magazine*, February 22, 1976, p. 14.

White, Leslie A. *The Science of Culture*. New York: Farrar, Straus, 1949.

Williams, Eric. *The Negro in the Caribbean*. Washington, D.C.: Association in Negro Folk Education, 1942.

Wolf, Eric R. "San José." In Julian H. Steward (ed.), *The People of Puerto Rico*. Urbana: University of Illinois Press, 1956.

Young, Leontine R. "Personality Patterns in Unmarried Mothers." In Robert W. Roberts (ed.), *The Unwed Mother*. New York: Harper & Row, 1966.

Young, Virginia Heyer. "Family and Childhood in a Southern Negro Community." *American Anthropologist*, 72, No. 2, 1970.

INDEX

Acculturation, 174, 238–239
  folk-elite continuum and, 191
  norms and, 39
Adaptation
  culture and, 4–5
  matrifocality and, 7, 227–229
  subcultural family pattern and, 1
Adolescent girls, 94–95
Adultery, inheritance and, 164
Age
  mating patterns and, 140–143
  of population, 47–48, 76
  reproductive, 146
Aisés (rich), 99–104
  amount of money spent by, on *fêtes*,
    170–171
  expressions of status differences by,
    101–104
  *See also specific members of aisés;
    for example: Commerçants; Fonc-
    tionnaires*
Allocation familiale (family allotment),
    88, 97–98, 112, 158, 160, 161
Annamite population, 47
Arable land, division of (1936), 54–55
Artisans, 118–119
Association, stratification and, 91–105
Associational color, defined, 57–58
Au lit de mort marriages (on-the-death-
    bed marriages), 156

Baptismal *fêtes*, 170–171, 184
Békés (*blancs*; whites), 58–63, 77
  hostility to, 83
  interactions of, with *mulâtres*, 62–63
  mulâtres compared with, 61
  race relations and, 66, 68
  sexual behavior of blacks as viewed
    by, 151–152
Békés goyaves (indigent *Békés*), 49, 60
Béni' péché marriage (remission-of-sin
    marriage), 136, 142, 143
  described, 156
  status equality and, 176
  in Voltaire, 144
Birth rates, 12
Bourgs (small towns), 17, 53, 56, 73–74,
    77–78

Caribbean area, general characteristics
    of, 42–44
Chef-lieu (administrative division), 53
Childrearing, 129–131; *see also specific
    types of households*
Children
  father-child relations, 140
  mother-child relations, 130–131
  See also Illegitimacy; *and specific
    types of households*
Chinese population, 46–47
Christian families, 28, 29

259

Chromatic color scale, socioeconomic status and, 60
Civil marriages, 157
Color
  chromatic color scale, 57–58
  race relations, 65–68
  stratification and, 57–58
Commerçants (blancs noirs; business-men), 99
  capital investments of, 97
  income of, 106–107
  as investors in fishing industry, 117
Communes, 53, 55
  folk traits present in, 63–65
Communities, approach used in study of, 13–22, 38–39
Companionate families, 28
Concubins (feminine *concubines*)
  defined, 136
  slave women as, 200–201
  uses of term, 158
Congos, les (African members of pop-ulation), 47
Conjugal households, 133–135, 155, 222
  characteristics of, 216
  defined, 13
  as ideal, 220
  land ownership and, 33
  matrifocality in, 126; *see also* Matri-focality
  stability of, 126–127, 143, 159, 205, 211
Conjugal unions, types of, 157–158; *see also* Marriage; *Ménage*
Consanguine households, 225, 228
Contraception, 11, 147, 152
Conviviality-hospitality pattern, 103, 177–180, 215
Counternorms, 246–247; *see also: Mai-son paternelle* inheritance
Courtship system, 243
Cross-sex roles, matrifocality and, 1, 8–9
Cultural color (behavioral color), 58
Cultural focus, theory of, 30–31
Cultural phenomena, social vs., 3–5
Cultural-historical approach to family typology, 30–31
Culture, as learned behavior, 4–5
Culture of poverty, 3

cross-sex relations and, 9
matrifocality as precipitate of, 1

Dances (ballroom dancing), 94–95
Diet, 120–121
  serving of family meals, 87
Disintegrate families, 28
Division of labor, sexual, 127, 177, 220
Divorces, 152
Domestic work, 119

East Indian population, 46–47, 77
Ecological approach to family typol-ogy, 32–33
Economic activities. *See* Occupations
Economic approach to family typol-ogy, 33
Economic factors
  family type and, 33
  of marriage, 161–162
  in matrifocality, 5–6, 29–30
  as obstacles to marriage, 243–244
  See also specific economic factors; for example: Land ownership; Oc-cupations
Educational system, 53, 107–108
Engagés (poor whites), 49
Entrepreneurs. *See: Commerçants*

Family organization, 35–37
  characteristics of, 206–207
  central feature of, 27; *see also* Matri-focality
  demonstration of model of, 244–247
  model of, 204–223
Family typology, 27–35
Father-child relations, 128–130
Father-husband role, marginality of, 30, 32; *see also* Males; Matrifo-cality
Females
  fertility rates, 11, 145
  as *fonctionnaires,* 127
  as *marchandes,* 92, 118–120
  mother-child relations, 130–131
  prostitutes, 11, 151
  role of, in households, 128–29; *see also specific types of households*
  social life of, 95

See also: *Maison paternelle* inheritance; Matrifocality
Fertility rates, 11, 145
Fêtes (festivities), 94, 96
  basis of participation in, 100
  hospitality and, 180
  legitimacy and, 248
  marriages followed by, 156, 166-171, 182-187, 212, 213
Field work of study, described, 18-22
Films, 96-97
Financial stratification, 99-100
Fishermen, 115-118
Folk-elite continuum, 62-65, 191
Fonctionnaires (civil servants), 99
  as fathers, 129-130
  as investors in fishing industry, 117
  male and female, 127
  parental role among, 129
  status differences as expressed by, 102-104
  See also: *Instituteurs*
Fond d'Espoir (*quartier*), 81, 84-85
  household composition in, 132-140
  mating patterns in, 140-143, 145
  single households in, 146
  status and residence in, 174
  types of conjugal unions in, 158
Functional approach to family typology, 32-33

Genealogical color (genotypic color), 57
Gens casés (plantation workers housed on plantations), 61, 84, 99, 100, 208
  economic activities of, 113-114
  land ownership by, 84-85
  life rhythms of, 92, 93
  matrifocality among, 208
  settlements of, 79
  status differences and, 102, 104
Godparents, 131
Grandmother households (maternal households), 29, 37, 133-139
  matrifocality and, 126, 208, 210

Habitations (plantations), 78-79
  work on, described, 114-115
Hauteur Pelée (*quartier*), 81, 83-84, 174

Historical approach to family typology, 33-34
Historical-cultural approach to family typology, 30-31
Hospitality-conviviality pattern, 103, 177-180, 215
Households, 125-153
  composition of, 132-140
  financial needs of, 128
  individual as functioning family units, 12
  mating patterns and, 140-143
  nonmodal, 144-145
  parental roles within, 127-132
  sex, reproduction and, 145-153
  See also specific kinds of households
Housing (dwellings), 79, 81, 85-89, 127-128, 132
Husbands, see Males

Illegitimacy, 15-16
  inheritance and, 160-161
  matrifocality and, 7-8
  rates of, 159-160
  recognition of illegitimate child, 159
  social disadvantages of, 163
  among unwed mothers, 225-227
  See also Legitimacy, rule of
Income
  of *commerçants*, 106-107
  of *instituteurs*, 107-109
  of plantation workers, 114-115
Individual households, as functioning family units, 12
Inheritance, 160-161
  adultery and, 164
  household formation and, 145
  legal aspects of, 80, 160-161
  in *ménages*, 158
  See also: *Maison paternelle* inheritance
Instituteurs (schoolteachers)
  economic aspects of marriage and, 161-162
  expression of status differences by, 102
  income of, 107-109
  life rhythms of, 93
Institutions, values and, 37-38
Internal family system, 220-221

Jeune fille marriage (marriage to a virgin), 136, 143
  described, 156
  fête following, 166–170
  incidence of, 158
Journaliers (landless day laborers), 99, 100, 104

Keeper families, 29
Kinship, marriage and, 188–189

Land, division of arable (1936), 54–55
Land acquisition, 56
Land ownership, 74, 84–85
  marriage and, 33
  matrifocality and, 208
Late marriage, 235
Legitimacy, rule of, 5, 9–11, 154–156, 216, 218–221, 229–242
  absence of, 14–15
  anomie and absence of, 232–233
  counterpart to, 155
  ethnocentric fallacies on, 233–235
  grammar of values and, 240–242
  monolithic fallacy about, 235–239
  norms and, 229–232
  significance of, 10–11
  supraconjugal families and, 14
  two-point scale and, 239–240
  See also Illegitimacy; Marriage
Life rhythms, 91–97
Literature, family typology in, 27–33

Machismo, 8
Magic, 178–182, 192–193
Maison paternelle inheritance (inheritance of family home), 36, 136
  conjugality and, 220
  formation of subconjugal households and, 145
  marriage and, 246
  matrifocality and, 205
Males
  father-child relationship, 140
  machismo, 8
  male role in households, 128–129; *see also specific types of households*
  marginality of father-husband role, 30, 32; *see also* Matrifocality
  marital relations, 95, 129
  social life of, 95

Marchandes (market women), 92, 118–120
Marital relations, 95, 129
Marriage, 37, 154–189, 210–215
  common-law, *see: Ménage*
  defined, 14
  economic factors as obstacles to, 243–244
  land ownership and, 33
  late, 235
  legal aspects of, 160–161; *see also* Inheritance
  mobility and, 214
  of slaves, 198–201
  status and, 129, 171–177, 213, 214, 229
  See also Legitimacy, rule of; *specific types of marriages*
Mating patterns, 140–144
Matrifocality, 2, 5–8, 30, 32, 205–211
  adaptation and, 7, 227–229
  in Afro-American families, 1–2
  in consanguine families, 225
  defined, 1, 126
  effects of stability in conjugal unions on, 126–127, 143, 159, 205, 211
  elements characterizing, 126–127, 131, 211
  machismo and, 8
  nonimmediate relatives living in households and, 139
  socioeconomic bases of, 5–6, 29–30
  status differentiation and, 209–210
  vagueness of term, 6–7
  variables of, 208–209
Men. *See* Males
Ménage (common-law marriage), 33, 37, 140–143
  as accepted form, 187
  conviviality and setting up, 177
  defined, 136, 158
  fête following, 182
  incidence of, 158
  parental roles in, 128–129
  status inequality and, 172–174, 176
Methodology of study, 13–22
Miscegenation, 48–53, 59; *see also: Mulâtres*
Monogamy in conjugal households, 138
Morne Liberté (*quartier*), 81, 83
Mothers, *see* Females

Mulâtres (mulattoes)
  associational color and, 58
  attitudes of, toward race relations, 66–68
  East Indians as, 47
  phenotypic color and, 57
  socioeconomic status of, 60–62
  status inequality and marriage of, 173, 174
Multiracial stratification, 43

Nègres a culture (fieldhands), 52, 174
Nègres piece d'Inde (recent arrivals from Africa), 52, 174
Nègres a talent (skilled workers), 174
Nègritude, 67–68
Negro population, 45–46; *see also* Slavery
Nonelite, defined, 17–18
Nonmodal households, mating patterns in, 144–145
Norms
  acculturation, 39
  counternorms, 246–247; *see also*: *Maison paternelle* inheritance
  establishment of, 35
  rules and, 229–232

Occupational stratification, 99–100
Occupations (economic activities), 106–121, 174–176

Parental roles, 127–132
Patrifocality
  economic aspects of, 29
  elements characterizing, 126–127
  See also Western family
Petits blancs, mulâtres opposed by, 49, 52
Petits propriétaires (*petits cultivateurs*; small landowners), 99–100, 102
  economic activities of, 109–113
  life rhythm of, 91
  sexual division of labor among, 127
  status differences as expressed by, 102, 103
Phenotypic color, defined, 57
Plantation workers, *see*: *Gens casés*; *Journaliers*
Political climate, 12–13
Political status, 43, 44

Political structures, 53
Polygyny, 201
Population, 44–48, 74–76, 82
  age of, 47–48, 76
  composition of, 17–18
  concentration of, 55
  rural-urban character of, 62–65
  semiurban character of, 55–56
Population growth, 11–12, 47–48, 76
Poor, the, *fêtes* following marriage as prohibitive for, 170, 171, 182–186; *see also* Culture of poverty; *specific groups of poor*
Power distribution, matrifocality and bilateral, 205, 208, 210
Prestige attached to marriage, 162–163
Promiscuity, 142–143, 149–152
Property ownership, 128; *see also* Inheritance; Land ownership
Prostitution, 11, 151

Quartiers, 80–85
  marriage and residence in, 174
  See also specific quartiers
Quimboiseurs (medicine men), 47, 178–182, 192–193

Race relations, 65–68; *see also* Color
Racial composition of population, 45–48, 74, 82
Religion, 43
  of East Indians, 47
  marriage and, 163–166, 214
  slave marriages and, 191–202
Reproduction, sex and, 145–153
Residence, status and, 174
Rites de passage, 182, 192, 213
Rules, norms and, 229–232; *see also* Legitimacy, rule of

Settlement patterns, 53–57, 82, 83
Sex
  distribution of population by, 48, 76
  double standards in matters of, 148–150
  miscegenation, 48–53, 59
  promiscuous, 142–143, 149–152
  reproduction and, 145–153
  between stepdaughters and stepfathers, 188–189

Single households, 2, 133–135, 139, 146, 201–202
Slavery
    economic basis of, 45–46
    miscegenation and, 48–53
    religion and slave marriages, 191–202
Slavery school approach to family typology, 31–32
Social life, 94–97
Social organization, 34–37
    defined, 221
Social phenomena
    cultural vs., 3–5
    family patterns and, 7–9
Socioeconomic factors. *See* Economic factors
Solidarity in marriage, 182–188
Status
    of *Békés*, 59–60, 62
    in marriage, 129, 171–177, 213, 214, 229
    expressions of differences in, 100–104
    housing and, 85, 86
    matrifocality and, 209–210
Stratification, 127
    association and, 91–105
    color and, 57–58
    matrifocality and, 211
    multiracial, 43
Structural approach to family typology, 34–35
Subconjugal households, 13–14, 133, 134, 136, 145

Supraconjugal households, 13–14, 155, 216–217, 222

Three-generation households, 126, 133, 137
Two-point scale, 239–242

Unwed mothers, illegitimacy and, 225–227
Usine workers (sugar refinery workers), 98, 111
Usines (sugar refineries), 71, 79

Value stretch concept, 242–243
Values
    grammar of, 240–242
    institutions and, 37–38
Veillée (wake), 95, 96
Voltaire (*quartier*), 81, 82
    mating patterns in, 140
    nonmodal households in, 144
    sex and reproduction in, 147
    single households in, 146
    status based on residence in, 174
    types of conjugal unions in, 158

Western family
    changing, 2
    legitimacy in, 15
    as restricted family, 216
White population, 45–46; *see also*: *Békés*
Women. *See* Females